SOCIAL JUSTICE

ISSUES IN BIOMEDICAL ETHICS

General Editors
John Harris and Søren Holm

Consulting Editors
Raanan Gillon and Bonnie Steinbock

The late twentieth century witnessed dramatic technological developments in biomedical science and in the delivery of health care, and these developments have brought with them important social changes. All too often ethical analysis has lagged behind these changes. The purpose of this series is to provide lively, up-to-date, and authoritative studies for the increasingly large and diverse readership concerned with issues in biomedical ethics—not just health care trainees and professionals, but also philosophers, social scientists, lawyers, social workers, and legislators. The series will feature both single-author and multi-author books, short and accessible enough to be widely read, each of them focused on an issue of outstanding current importance and interest. Philosophers, doctors, and lawyers from a number of countries feature among the authors lined up for the series.

Social Justice

*The Moral Foundations of
Public Health and Health Policy*

Madison Powers and Ruth Faden

OXFORD
UNIVERSITY PRESS

OXFORD

UNIVERSITY PRESS

Oxford University Press, Inc., publishes works that further
Oxford University's objective of excellence
in research, scholarship, and education.

Oxford   New York
Auckland   Cape Town   Dar es Salaam   Hong Kong   Karachi
Kuala Lumpur   Madrid   Melbourne   Mexico City   Nairobi
New Delhi   Shanghai   Taipei   Toronto

With offices in
Argentina   Austria   Brazil   Chile   Czech Republic   France   Greece
Guatemala   Hungary   Italy   Japan   Poland   Portugal   Singapore
South Korea   Switzerland   Thailand   Turkey   Ukraine   Vietnam

Copyright © 2006 by Oxford University Press, Inc.

Published by Oxford University Press, Inc.
198 Madison Avenue, New York, New York 10016

www.oup.com

First issued as an Oxford University Press Paperback, 2008

Oxford is a registered trademark of Oxford University Press

Library of Congress Cataloging-in-Publication-Data
Powers, Madison.
Social justice: the moral foundations of public health and health policy / Madison Powers
and Ruth Faden.
p. cm.—(Issues in biomedical ethics)
Includes bibliographical references and index.
ISBN 978-0-19-518926-1; 978-0-19-537513-8 (pbk.)
1. Public health—Moral and ethical aspects.   2. Medical policy—Moral and ethical
aspects.   3. Social justice.   4. Equality—Health aspects.   5. Discrimination in
medical care.   I. Faden, Ruth R.   II. Title.   III. Series
RA427.25.P69 2006
174.2—dc22   2005050856

Printed in the United States of America

To Tom, with more gratitude than
I can ever express.

(R. F.)

To my teachers.

(M. P.)

PREFACE

Issues of justice in public health and health policy have been animating concerns for us both, independently and as research collaborators, over many years. We first worked together on *AIDS, Women and the Next Generation* (Faden, Geller, and Powers 1991). In the late 1980s, HIV/AIDS was emerging as a growing public health problem among women and children. There was no way at that time to interrupt transmission of the virus from mother to baby, and no way even to verify which newborns had acquired the infection. It was possible, however, to improve outcomes for babies if at-risk infants were identified early. We found ourselves puzzling over whether or under what conditions pregnant women or newborns should be screened for HIV. One familiar tenet of traditional public health doctrine recommends that we should seek the greatest health benefit achievable from the limited public health resources available. In line with that tenet, many argued for a policy in which only pregnant women at highest risk of HIV would be screened, which turned out to be disproportionately poor women of color. We were troubled by this position, however. We framed the question as follows: "Whether only high-risk pregnant women, in contrast to all pregnant women or all individuals, may be the target of HIV antibody screening programs is a classic example of a justice-based problem" (Faden, Kass, and Powers 1991, 19).

Even if such a program were voluntary, and even if the public welfare would be enhanced, we worried that it might not be warranted because of the "disproportionate burden that would result from targeted screening" (Faden, Kass, and Powers 1991, 19). Our underlying assumption, perhaps better appreciated by us now than then, was that matters of justice are at stake beyond the usual questions of the proper distribution of scarce resources. Our conclusion was that a variety of aspects of well-being other than health were relevant to judging whether this public health policy was just.

That more than health was at stake in crafting a just public health program offered no easy path to resolution of the question we had set for ourselves, however. On the one hand, it might seem that a targeted program is exactly what justice demanded. After all, the children who would benefit, in addition to being at risk of a grave disease and of inadequate health care, also experienced multiple disadvantages that even then we believed were relevant to determinations about justice and health policy. They and their mothers were poor, subject to social stigma and discrimination, and frequently lacked both strong social support structures and opportunities to lead minimally self-directing lives. Yet, the very list of considerations that suggested to us that a targeted policy might be appropriate also revealed reasons for caution. Our biggest concern was that a targeted program would exacerbate the stigma and disrespect these women disproportionately experienced by reinforcing invidious social views about which communities, and which women, get HIV. In the end, after almost two years of struggle and study, we and our colleagues concluded that these nondistributional considerations of justice were sufficient to reject a targeted program. We advocated, instead, for a public policy of voluntary screening of all pregnant women. Our quest to identify the right public policy for women and children during those dark days of the AIDS epidemic left both of us with a deep conviction that the nondistributive aspects of well-being are essential to evaluating the justice of health policy.

Indeed, each of us, in differing ways, had longstanding commitments to social justice in health policy, understood in the broadest sense of that term. Our path to collaboration was by chance, but in the spring of 1989, Madison took over for a term a seminar on justice and health policy that had been taught by Ruth for many years at the Johns Hopkins School of Public Health. In subsequent years, each took a turn at revising a syllabus for some successor to that original course, with Ruth continuing with the course at Johns Hopkins and Madison doing the same within the philosophy department curriculum from his position at the Kennedy Institute of Ethics at Georgetown University. The revisions made by one of us during one academic year would be incorporated into the syllabus of the other in the following year.

This pattern of collaboration continued (and continues), and by 1994 we decided to apply for a grant from the Robert Wood Johnson Health Policy Investigator Award Program. We were fortunate to receive a generous award that gave us some relief time with which to do research without the full weight of other university responsibilities bearing down upon us. More importantly, the program allowed us to become a part of an extraordinary community of scholars working out of numerous disciplinary backgrounds on a wide range of matters in health policy. In addition, we received a book publication award from the National Library of Medicine that allowed us to extend both the release time and the scope of our project. Without question, these two grants gave us the opportunity to think more expansively about our work, and for that we are immensely grateful. What began as a project to look rather narrowly at questions of justice in the use of formal, economic methods of appraisal such as cost-benefit and cost-effectiveness analysis (now chapter 6) led us to take several steps back and focus on bigger questions.

Our interest in cost-effectiveness analysis evolved in ways that forced us to think about what justice requires of social institutions and practices in the here and now, that is, in the real world as we find it. The policies that we set out to examine needed to be sorted in a time and place in which significant inequalities in power, privilege, and health are commonplace and where dependence and disadvantage are inescapable. Increasingly we came to see that questions of justice in health policy could not at their foundation be tackled without an understanding of the relation of health to other dimensions of well-being and of the historical and social factors in which actual opportunity for well-being is situated. Inevitably, we came to think especially about those contexts where multiple dimensions of well-being are affected by multiple social determinants in ways that systematically disadvantage some socially situated groups. The account of the job of justice that emerged for us highlights the remedial aims of justice and the corresponding need to be vigilant for opportunities to prevent or blunt the force of persistent social injustices.

Our central focus, only vividly appreciated in hindsight, was in a notion of social justice that went beyond issues of distributive justice, micro-allocational questions of priority setting in medical care, or any number of questions centered on how one individual fares relative to some other individual. Beginning, as we did, with moral questions in public health and health policy, it is perhaps not surprising that our focus in social justice is largely directed at the well-being of people in social communities or groups. Unlike medicine, which is concerned with the health of individual patients, public health and health policy are concerned with the health of populations. When questions are raised about the justness of a particular health policy, the issue is almost always about whether the "groups" or "populations" affected by the policy are being treated fairly. As we discuss in chapter 4, there is often an implicit reliance on intuitions about justice, if not an explicit eye on justice, in judgments about which groups or populations to consider. This focus on socially situated groups is, we believe, essential to any account of social justice that is concerned with addressing real world conditions, not just in health but in any realm of social policy central to human well-being.

Our interest lies in the design of basic social institutions, including but not limited to government and the market, and the impact of those institutions on these socially situated groups. What makes any group of special interest within a theory of justice is contingent upon the totality of social arrangements that, in the aggregate, contribute to the combined adverse effect of various inequalities. And so our theory of justice is a nonideal theory, in the sense that we start from a consideration of the concrete circumstances of socially situated groups and ask the question: Under conditions in which various socially situated groups interact with one another under conditions of inequality, what inequalities matter the most?

The aim of this book is to broaden the debate about justice and health policy in other ways as well. Although the limited role of medical care in

explaining inequalities in health status and life expectancy is widely recognized, this profound finding has received inadequate commentary in the
bioethics literature. Insofar as bioethics has concerned itself with justice
and health policy, the focus has been almost exclusively on access to
medical care and the allocation of medical services. It is here that we depart
from the norm of most scholarship in bioethics. We contend that it is impossible to make progress in our understanding of the demands of justice
within medical care without looking *outside* of medical care to public health
and to the other determinants of inequalities in health and indeed without
situating an analysis of justice and health policy in the wider social and
political context. We also care about how medical care is distributed, but
not in the same way as others who are primarily concerned with questions
about how organs should be distributed or how some program such as
Medicare or Medicaid should evaluate bariatric surgery versus heart
transplants. We think our theory bears upon such issues, but only indirectly
as an articulation of an enlarged inventory of justice-based considerations
that constrain morally eligible public policy options. More centrally, our
concerns, operating at the level of institutional design, examine the means
rather than the principles for allocation of health care. For example, we look
at the requirements of justice in markets for health insurance, how public
health ought to think about the claims of children in their crucial developmental stages, how justice constrains the use of cost-effectiveness analysis in priority setting, and why the desperate circumstances of the world's
poorest represent the most urgent inequalities in need of redress.

Unlike other books on justice and health policy, our aim is not the defense of some specific proposal for allocating resources based in a specific
theory of justice, such as libertarianism, utilitarianism, or one of the many
versions of egalitarianism. Indeed, we doubt the prospect for success of
such projects, and along the way we offer a variety of reasons for rejecting
these familiar approaches to the subject. We do not think that the key to
understanding what we call the "job of justice" lies in the service of any
synoptic value, such as freedom of choice or efficiency, or the task of
maximizing or equalizing anything. Nor do we argue for some specific algorithm for allocation, such as age-based rationing, maximizing quality-
adjusted life years (QALYs), or giving special priority to some type of good
such as life-saving, life-preserving, or the restoration of functional capacity
to members of society through their most productive years. We do address,
however, the conditions under which many of these algorithms may be
morally unacceptable, morally acceptable, or even morally obligatory.

In place of some single theory of justice drawn from one of the leading
contenders for being the "right" account of justice, we argue instead that
most of these other contenders have it wrong. Indeed, we use the term
'theory' somewhat cautiously. We are mindful of the lively debates over
whether any approach within normative philosophical theory should be
described as a theory. There are those who would prefer to reserve the term
for disciplines that more closely resemble the natural sciences (Williams

1985). Others discuss whether we need anything like a theory in moral and political philosophy (Baier 1985). Some also question whether even the most systematic work in bioethics reflects a significant debt to moral theory (Beauchamp 2004).

We choose to steer a middle course on the question, and we agree with Thomas Nagel's conclusion that whatever we are likely to attach the label of 'theory' to in the realm of normative inquiry will reflect an aspiration to develop some systematic but noncomprehensive account of some part of the moral landscape (Nagel 1979). Nagel reasonably claims that we should not conclude, from our lack of a general theory of what we ought to do, that we must retreat from all efforts to systematize some insights about which we have some confidence and rely on unsystematic intuitive judgment.

Indeed, we intend by the name 'theory' no more than what Nagel calls a "loose framework for deliberation," but it is a framework nonetheless that aims to capture more of what is fundamentally at stake in assessing issues of justice in concrete, real-world settings. The job of justice, as we see it, is to specify those background social and economic conditions that determine whether certain inequalities, that may themselves result from the promotion of other indispensable moral aims, should be seen as unfair. Ours is an account of justice that denies that there are separate spheres of justice, within health policy or within social policy more generally. We reject treatment of questions about what justice requires as a matter of finding the right principle of distribution within a discrete sphere of social policy such as health care. We repudiate the widespread view that any proposed distributive principle for health policy can be plausible in isolation from larger issues of social justice. At the same time, however, we do not maintain that productive philosophical work requires the resolution of every problem of justice at once.

More cautiously, we reject simple formulaic claims, such as the claim that any system of priority setting that takes account of quality and length of life is unacceptable, or the claim that no justifiable health care system can make substantial use of the market as a means of allocating health care. We argue that the justification of any of the major approaches to resource allocation will be a function of its context and the nature and extent of inequalities in the determinants of health as well as in society generally. Markets, for example, might be defended if supplemented and regulated so as to eliminate predictable unfair inequalities, although no such reforms will eliminate all elements of unfairness. Rationing of care using formal methods of economic comparison like QALYs can be morally acceptable as well, but only under particular social and economic arrangements.

Our book is meant to serve dual purposes. On the one hand, this book is intended as a contribution to the public debate about public health and health policy, one that is sufficiently free of disciplinary jargon that those not steeped in moral philosophy or the philosophical foundations of disciplines such as welfare economics or decision theory will want to read. On the other hand, this book is meant to reflect our exploration in some depth of numerous ethical issues that philosophy has wrestled with extensively, especially over the last three decades.

Since we embarked on this journey, our basic approach to social justice has appeared, in varying degrees of development, in numerous incarnations. We have taken up the problems of systematic disadvantage in medical care markets (Faden and Powers 1999; Powers 1992; Powers 1997). We have worried about race and ethnicity in medical care and the question of how health disparities are relevant to the organization of medical care delivery and the education of physicians (Powers and Faden 2002). We have studied how medical research priorities are set, and we have written about the injustice of failing to attend adequately to the health needs of women in medical research (Faden, Mastroianni, and Federman 1994; Powers 1998). We have examined similar questions about whether groups have been treated justly in the context of smallpox vaccine (Faden, Taylor, and Seiler 2003), stem cell research (Faden et al. 2003; Bok, Schill, and Faden 2004), and the conduct of biomedical research in the global south (Isjsselmuiden and Faden 1992; Faden and Kass 1998). We have examined the extent to which core issues of genetic privacy are fundamentally questions of justice (Powers 1997; 2000), and we have looked hard at a variety of questions of justice raised by age, gender, and ethnicity (Powers and Faden 2000; Faden and Kass 1996; Faden, Kass, and McGraw 1996; Powers 2002).

Many people have helped us along the way, either through timely intervention that saved us from more errors and confusions than presently persist, or by reminding us of the many things left undone or untouched by this book. Colleagues at Johns Hopkins, Georgetown, and the NIH Clinical Bioethics Center have been willing and provocative audiences for various iterations of the manuscript. Successive cohorts of Greenwall Fellows and graduate students in both public health and philosophy have endured similar fates. We are deeply indebted to our students and fellows from whom we have learned so much over the years. We are indebted as well to many audiences in universities and other venues too numerous to mention or remember who were subjected to earlier and evolving versions of our thinking. Maggie Little, Hilary Bok, Alisa Carse, Sarah Flynn, Nancy Sherman, Allen Buchanan, and Jacqueline Fox deserve special mention for their close and careful reading of various chapters in the book, sometimes more than once. We have tried to learn as much as possible from each of these dear colleagues and friends.

We have been on this road for many years. We could not have predicted at the outset where we would end up. After throwing out far more pages than we retained, we hope that our reflections will prove useful to others, including those who, by occupational hazard, are not routinely exposed to the mix of policy and philosophy that is the essence of this book.

CONTENTS

SOCIAL JUSTICE

1

The Job of Justice

1.1 Which Inequalities Matter Most?

Inequalities come in many forms. Some people are poorer, less well educated, and live shorter and less healthy lives than others. Some have fewer rewarding life experiences, satisfy fewer of their personal preferences, have a limited array of valuable life options from which to choose, exercise little power and authority within political and economic arenas, and in numerous other possible ways can be counted as less fortunate than others. Some who fare worse than others, often in multiple respects, are members of groups who are socially situated within densely woven patterns of disadvantage. Are all of these inequalities injustices? Is the primary job of justice to prevent or redress all of these inequalities, only some, or perhaps none?

Discussions of justice within bioethics have concentrated on inequalities in health and access to health care, and on questions about how priorities should be set when resources are scarce. Are all inequalities in health and access to health care morally problematic? How important are moral concerns about setting priorities in health care and public health compared to inequalities in health and quality of life? How much inequality in health, if any, can a decent society tolerate? How, if at all, should the existence of other inequalities matter to our judgments about health care and public health?

The central question we pose in this book is, Which inequalities matter most? The aim of this book is to develop a theory of social justice suitable for answering questions of this kind in a variety of concrete circumstances. Although our specific aim is to elaborate the theory in the specific context of health policy, its application is not strictly limited to the health policy arena. Indeed, the theory we develop rejects the prevailing idea that justice with respect to health, education, or employment opportunities, for example, can be understood as "separate spheres," each with its own unique set of morally relevant concerns or distributive principles.

3

Why is another theory of justice needed? Arguably, the answers to our questions might be sought using the available, rich theoretical framework developed by John Rawls and elaborated upon by others in the context of specific matters of public policy such as health care or education. There are important differences, however, between our project and the Rawlsian one.

The Rawlsian approach is one that Rawls labels an "ideal theory of justice." In Rawls's terminology, such a theory is meant to be a complete set of fully ranked distributive principles governing what he calls the "primary social goods." These goods include liberties, opportunities, income, and wealth. The Principle of Equal Liberties, the Principle of Fair Equality of Opportunity, and the Difference Principle, taken together, are constitutive of a just society. They form an ideal set of distributive principles by which existing social orders might be judged.

Rawls's ideal theory is not meant to address a range of more specific issues of justice arising in concrete social conditions. In particular, Rawls notes that many questions arise from noncompliance or partial compliance with one or more of the governing principles and that questions of justice in the workings of actual social institutions are among the most urgent that a complete theory of social justice must address. Indeed, many Rawlsians have developed illuminating and imaginative extensions of the ideal theory designed to address practical problems of justice under less than ideal conditions or problems arising in more concretely described circumstances. Should the implications of various attempts to extend the Rawlsian theory converge with those of our account, this would be both welcome news for the plausibility of our own view and further evidence of the enormity of the contribution Rawls's theory has made. However, we have chosen a quite different theoretical path for three primary reasons.

The first difference is that we do not start with an ideal set of distributive principles that are presumed reasonable for all persons to accept or agree to as the basis for governing their mutual association. In this respect, ours is not an ideal theory of justice as Rawlsian social contract theorists might understand the concept. We start with the assumption that the best justified set of distributive principles are not readily ascertainable apart from a more detailed account of the ends of human action underlying them. We do not suppose that we can answer in the abstract whether a particular distribution of wealth and income is just from the perspective of hypothetical deliberators charged with reaching agreement on the terms of a social contract. For us, the adequacy of any distributive share of income and wealth, for example, depends on some more detailed account of what ends or purposes the distributive principles are meant to achieve. Our own answers to questions of this sort fall within the tradition of theories that start with some conception of human well-being as a basis for evaluating proposed distributive principles. Aristotelian theories, some natural law theories, and, more recently, capability theories such as those of Amartya Sen and Martha Nussbaum are examples. As Sen correctly notes, a theory of justice of this sort begins with some underlying account of what persons "can do and be"

(Sen 1993). Theories in this tradition start with ideals, to be sure, but they are ideals of a very different kind from those that form the starting points of Rawlsian ideal theory. The relevant ideals are ones about the specific ends of human activity informing an account of justice, not an account of the principles that govern the distribution of the various means to their achievement. Our own account takes the job of justice to be the achievement of a sufficiency of six essential dimensions of human well-being. Questions about the appropriate distributive principles or other means to the achievement of these six dimensions of well-being are therefore theoretically secondary.

A second difference between ideal theory as it is understood in the Rawlsian tradition and our approach is that, given the primacy we place on the ends to be achieved, we assume that empirical judgments of how various inequalities affect one another in concrete circumstances are ineliminable moral data. In a nonideal world, questions of justice emerge from the operation of the totality of social institutions, practices, and policies that both independently and in combination have the potential for profound and pervasive impact on human well-being in all of its essential aspects. In our account, questions about which inequalities matter most are comprehensible only by examining all of the social determinants having cumulative and interactive effects on human well-being. "Which inequalities matter most?" is thus a question appropriate to a concrete empirical context. We need to know how inequalities of one kind beget inequalities of another kind. We also assume that inequalities of all kinds work, not in isolation, but often in ways detrimental to the aim of achieving a sufficiency of well-being in all of its essential dimensions. Inequalities are interactive. They can combine to make the adverse effects of one greater than they might have been alone. Taken in tandem, they can reinforce and perpetuate clusters of disadvantage, and in the worst of possible scenarios, the cumulative disadvantages that emerge become nearly impossible to escape or avoid without heroic effort or extraordinary good luck.

In short, our assumption is not simply that we face instances of noncompliance with the ideal set of distributive principles. Ours is a nonideal theory in a much more fundamental sense. We reject the theoretical completeness of any set of distributive principles developed in abstraction from an account of the job of justice, or the ends that any chosen set of distributive principles serve. Accordingly, we assume that unjust inequalities will continue to provide the real world context in which questions of justice will arise—not as a consequence of noncompliance with ideal principles, but for the more basic reason that achieving justice is an inherently remedial task, constantly shifting in its specific requirements as social circumstances themselves change. Justice, then, is not a matter of conforming society to an antecedently identifiable set of distributive principles, but rather it is a task requiring vigilance and attentiveness to changing impediments to the achievement of enduring dimensions of well-being that are essential guides to the aspirations of justice.

A third difference also explains why we have chosen to take a different theoretical path from the most well-established one. A familiar criticism, which we echo in part, is that justice is concerned with more than distributive principles. In addition, much of what justice comprehends lies beyond an assessment of each person's distributive shares and includes equally concerns about the nature of the relations among persons. For example, worries about social subordination and stigma, lack of respect, lack of institutions, and social practices that adequately support capacities for attachment and self-determination also are matters of justice—for both individuals and groups.

The need for a better integration of the distributive and nondistributive aspects of justice became apparent to us years ago when we were writing on issues of justice in the design of HIV/AIDS screening policies targeting minority women and newborns (Faden, Kass, and Powers 1991). While the initial impetus for our critique of such proposals was directed at the folly of a simple-minded health benefit maximization approach to health policy, we came to see such a proposal as a failure to appreciate that issues of respect and other nondistributive matters of justice were at stake as well. Among the essential dimensions of well-being, for which it is the job of justice to secure a sufficient level for all, in addition to health, are dimensions we include under the headings of reasoning, self-determination, attachment, personal security, and respect.

1.2. Justice and Well-Being

Chapter 2 provides the basics of our account of justice as concerned with human well-being. In our view, well-being is best understood as involving plural, irreducible dimensions, each of which represents something of independent moral significance We maintain further that justice is concerned with six essential dimensions of well-being, and these are described in some detail in roughly the first half of chapter 2. We contend that each of these dimensions is an essential feature of well-being such that a life substantially lacking in any one is a life seriously deficient in what it is reasonable for anyone to want, whatever else they want. Each is thus a separate indicator of a decent life which it is the job of justice to facilitate.

The remainder of chapter 2 is devoted to a discussion of the main alternatives to our view, some of the principal objections that our view is likely to encounter, and the relation of our theory to the increasing interest many in the field of health policy have shown toward human rights approaches. Among the main alternatives are welfarist accounts of how well-being is best understood, as well as various Rawlsian approaches that rely on far fewer assumptions about the constituents of human well-being that underlie justice. We examine also the capabilities approaches, with which our own view has many affinities, and we articulate our reasons for preferring a different way of formulating our theory. We also address three potential objections to our theory: first, that it endorses a form of moral relativism, second, that it embodies elements of moral imperialism, and, third, that it violates any reasonable principle of political neutrality. Finally, we show how our theory might be used as a basis for further development of a theory of basic human rights as applied to public health and health policy, and we show why we think that a theory of the sort we defend, rather than a theory of human rights itself, is the most plausible starting point for linking social justice concerns to health policy.

1.3. Justice, Sufficiency, and Systematic Disadvantage

Chapter 3 articulates the broadly egalitarian commitments of our theory. We discuss strict egalitarian theories in light of the powerful criticisms and appealing alternatives suggested by prioritarian and sufficiency theorists, and we provide reasons for favoring a version of a sufficiency approach. Sufficiency theories and prioritarian theories reject strict equality as the proper distributive ideal of justice, preferring instead some priority for the worst off or a policy of ensuring that those who are the least well off have enough. While many of the well-developed prioritarian and sufficiency theories focus their attention on ensuring that the worst off have some priority or have enough income and wealth, our theory reflects a very different aim and different distributive implications as well. Sufficiency will depend on more than the distribution of income and wealth. A variety of other social determinants of well-being will be relevant in assessing each dimension, and the totality of those determinants often will have significant impact on more than one dimension simultaneously. Moreover, a sufficiency for each of the essential dimensions of well-being will differ in what is required. For some dimensions, substantial departures from equality will never be acceptable, while in others, inequalities will trigger a need for special moral scrutiny but may not in the end be unjust.

A sufficiency in health, for example, may not be possible to specify fully in the abstract, but in several chapters we develop a number of arguments meant to give practical guidance in specific contexts. A few key points at the outset suggest the kinds of arguments we pursue. Judgments about sufficiency begin with an empirical assessment of what is technologically feasible with regard to both length and health-related quality of life (chapter 3). A crucial point also is that the theoretical usefulness of the notion of health sufficiency primarily arises in the comparison between populations or subpopulations, not in the comparison between two individual candidates for a public health or medical intervention (chapter 4). While there are borderline (and hence morally less urgent) cases, it is feasible to offer some indicators of the clear instances in which populations or population subgroups fall below a level of sufficiency in health (chapter 4). An important claim that our theory emphasizes is that the aim of ensuring health sufficiency can be dependent on life-stage. For some aspects of health, the requirements of human development necessitate interventions and protections at critical junctures early in the life course (chapters 3 and 4). In addition, our account of sufficiency distinguishes the crucial life-stage-dependent requirements from those cases in which a sufficiency in health encompasses domains of health that matter equally throughout all life stages (chapter 6).

Sufficiency in each of the essential dimensions, including health, represents the positive aim of our theory. However, the basis for answering questions about which inequalities matter most from the perspective of justice involves another step in the analysis. We also need to know how all of the dimensions of well-being are interrelated in order to realize the theory's permanent, remedial aims of preventing and mitigating densely woven patterns of systematic disadvantage. Such patterns of systematic disadvantage represent additional reasons for judging that threats to sufficiency of one or more essential dimensions of well-being are of increased moral urgency.

Our theory starts with the assumption that inequalities beget inequalities, and existing inequalities—in the social determinants of well-being and ultimately in the essential dimensions of well-being themselves—can compound, sustain, and reproduce a multitude of deprivations in well-being, bringing some persons below the level of sufficiency for more than one dimension. The disadvantages associated with inequalities in the social basis of well-being in all of its dimensions are various, they often travel in tandem, and they can mutually reinforce and perpetuate one another. In turn, they can and often do affect a whole range of dimensions of well-being. Taken in their totality, the interactive effects of multiple sources of disadvantage add up to markedly unequal well-being, leaving some with greatly decreased prospects in every major aspect of their lives.

Some familiar forms of oppression and subordination, including racism and sexism, are paradigm cases of the multicausal and multifaceted social structural barriers to achieving a level of sufficiency for all of the dimensions. In addition, our theory identifies other kinds of systematic disadvantage that are not based on animus toward persons because of group membership. In particular, our theory accounts for systematic patterns that involve especially powerful effects on self-determination, as well as densely woven webs of constraint on the development of well-being in all of its dimensions where neither group animus nor impediments to self-determination are centrally at issue. Most notably, many of the social structural constraints our theory takes into account affect *children and their futures*, but not initially or even primarily through constraints on their choices. Systematic constraints that typically lock in the life prospects of some at an early age virtually guarantee diminished futures for reasons that are more foundational than a lack of suitable choices in their adult lives. For us, the real diagnostic test of all three of these patterns is whether the totality of social relations imposes systemic constraints on the development of the essential dimensions of well-being and do so in ways that guarantee profound and pervasive adverse effects on all aspects of their well-being.

Our nonideal theory, then, defines a positive aim of justice in terms of a sufficiency of each of the dimensions of well-being, and the vigilance against systematic patterns of disadvantage define its remedial aims. Only when we consider what sufficiency requires in real-world, concrete social circumstances can we say which inequalities are most urgent from the point of view of justice.

1.4. Foundations of Public Health

In chapter 4 we argue, contrary to much of what has been written about the ethics of public health, that the foundational moral justification for the social institution of public health is social justice. In particular, we put forward multiple related reasons why social justice as explicated in our theory provides a fine, if not perfect, fit with the commitments and practice of public health. The positive point of justice for public health is to secure a sufficiency of the dimension of health for everyone. The negative point of justice, which in our view requires a commitment to policing patterns of systematic disadvantage that profoundly and pervasively undermine prospects for well-being, shines the spotlight of moral urgency on the health needs of oppressed and subordinated groups, on people whose prospects for well-being, including for health, are so limited that their life choices are not even remotely like those of others, and on children, whose prospects for well-being, not only in childhood but throughout life, are at risk because of the locking in of systematic constraints at an early age. This is not the standard way in which the ethics of public health is understood. Commentary on ethics and public health is, at best, thin, but insofar as a standard view about the moral justification or moral point of public health has emerged, it formulates its positive aims as the promotion of human welfare by bringing about a certain kind of human good, the good of health. The moral foundation for public health thus rests on general obligations in beneficence to promote good health. Depending on the interpretation, public health is further understood as having utilitarian commitments to bring about as much health as possible. Concerns about justice are commonly understood as ethical considerations external to the moral purpose of public health. Such concerns serve to balance public health's single-minded function to produce the good of health with other concerns such as individual liberty or respect.

Our account of the positive aims of public health accommodates the standard view's central concerns, but it is broader than those usually articulated. Justice in our view requires ensuring for everyone a sufficient amount of each of the essential dimensions of well-being, of which health is one. Our account thus rejects the separate-spheres view of justice in which it is possible to speak about justice in public health and health policy without reference either to how other public policies and social environments are structured or to how people are faring with regard to the rest of their lives. So does much of what is written and argued for in public health circles, notwithstanding the narrower moral justification often ascribed to it. Public health historically, and public health today, recognizes that there are multiple causes of ill and good health, that policies and practices that affect health also affect other valued dimensions of life, and that health itself is sometimes a causal factor with regard to other important human goods. Moreover, what the standard view about public health also gets wrong is that it frames public health as if the enterprise were solely concerned with health outcomes and not matters of distribution. Public health in theory and practice has exhibited a special focus upon those most disadvantaged and has therefore reflected concerns far more encompassing than the standard view can accommodate. Accordingly, our view of the negative as well as the positive aims of justice captures what we believe are the twin moral impulses that animate public health: to improve human well-being by improving health and related dimensions of well-being and to do so in particular by focusing on the needs of those who are the most disadvantaged.

Our account also provides a moral framework for what is sometimes referred to as the "boundary problem" in public health. While the broad scope of public health is often interpreted, we think rightly, as the correct perspective, public health is sometimes viewed as being so expansive in its compass as to have no real core, no institutional, disciplinary, or social boundaries. Everything from war, terrorism, and crime to genetic predisposition to disease; from environmental and occupational hazards to income inequality; and from personal behavior to natural disasters has been claimed as a public health problem. The World Health Organization's definition of health as a state of physical, mental, and social well-being takes this broad-brush approach to public health and wrongly conflates a distinction that is precisely what our theory emphasizes. Our theory thus accounts for the sense in which many of the ills of diverse things such as war, natural disasters, and environmental hazards affect adversely many dimensions, while acknowledging that justice in this or any other area of public policy requires more than an attention to effects on a single dimension of well-being.

In chapter 4, we also develop in greater detail the significance for the practice of public health of the discussions of systematic disadvantage and oppression begun in chapter 3. In particular, we discuss the special moral urgency our theory assigns to groups affected by multiple disadvantages in the global context as well as those who are affected adversely within affluent nations. We address some of the main implications of our theory for children, for persons whose disadvantages occur within poorer or despotic nations unwilling or unable to provide their citizens with the conditions necessary for health, and for our understanding of influential discussions of international human rights and public health.

1.5 Medical Care and Insurance Markets

In chapter 5 we discuss the implications of our theory for how medical care and health insurance ought to be financed. This chapter, unlike the rest of the book, focuses primarily on the American experience, although the arguments we make have relevance for other countries contemplating market-based approaches. We discuss the familiar moral and theoretical underpinnings for markets in general, markets for medical care and health insurance, and what many economists at least since Kenneth Arrow have claimed make them different from most markets for goods and services. As Arrow predicted, and as a large body of empirical literature has confirmed, some of their inherent features explain the tendency toward market failure, or to produce results that differ from the efficient outcomes expected by neoclassical economic theory. Our ultimate concern, however, is not simply the prospect that utilitarian and efficiency-based arguments for reliance on health care and health insurance markets might not succeed on their own terms, but rather how predictable responses to those market failures tend to produce consequences that, from the perspective of our own theory, are unjust. In particular, we examine the roots of moral hazard and adverse selection and their implications for access to health care.

In addition, we consider how particular forms of social organization can compound and exacerbate the potential for systematic disadvantage associated with these twin threats of market failure. We examine the moral significance of the employment-insurance nexus for health and other dimensions of well-being, especially for the most vulnerable or already most disadvantaged members of society. We also consider some moral challenges posed by the combined effects of mixed systems of private insurance and public safety nets for health care, with particular focus on the non-distributive aspects of human well-being, including respect for self and others, self-determination, and attachment.

We reach four conclusions in this chapter. First, because of the *inherent* tendencies of markets to have a systematically disadvantaging impact on well-being (especially on those experiencing multiple disadvantages), the justice of a market system of health care financing depends on the existence of appropriate background political and economic conditions that can mitigate, rather than compound, its potential ill effects. Second, market-based health care finance under some specific social and economic conditions, especially employer-based insurance arrangements, add to the problems inherent in health care markets and thus pose additional challenges to any efforts to make markets conform to the minimum requirements of justice. Third, whatever role markets might permissibly play in securing access to health care, justice requires a system of universal, continuous access to a reasonably comprehensive level of medical care. Fourth, many currently accepted ways of combining private markets and public safety nets are unjust. The reasons on which we rely in reaching all four conclusions take into consideration the potential negative effects of market mechanisms on all of the dimensions of well-being, not on health alone.

1.6 Setting Priorities

In chapter 6 we examine a number of issues associated with the problem of setting priorities either in health care or in public health contexts when resources are not adequate to produce or provide all of the health benefits that are technically feasible to achieve. We first trace the origins of the most popular of the formal methods used in health policy analysis and examine their conceptual roots in welfare economics. We distinguish the normative implications of cost-benefit analysis, cost-effectiveness analysis, and a variant of cost-effectiveness analysis known as cost-utility analysis.

An important theme we press in this chapter is the claim that our theory counts as unjust the use of any priority-setting algorithm that adversely affects a sufficiency of health or other essential dimensions of well-being for some groups by creating, compounding, or perpetuating a range of disadvantages experienced by those segments of society such that the adverse effects are made harder to avoid or escape. Many of the existing critiques of formal methods either fail to take systematic disadvantage into account entirely or do not offer an extensively developed view of the sort of considerations that are relevant in this analysis.

Another considerable portion of this chapter defends a particular view of the relevance of age in priority setting. Our view is built out of the life course model discussed in chapters 3 and 4, and we examine the differences in theoretical rationale for and implications of this approach in contrast to both CUA (cost utility analysis) and pure age-based approaches such as the "fair-innings" principle. While we defend a strong priority for children in a large range of allocation decision contexts, within this section also we distinguish those domains of health that matter equally in any life stage.

Although our theory operates at the level of social design, we argue that it nonetheless has important implications for how priority decisions should be made at the macro level and sometimes at the micro level as well. In particular, we argue that much that is morally relevant in resolving issues involved in trade-offs within health include considerations of the proposed trade-off's implications for other dimensions of well-being. Similar to arguments made in chapter 5 regarding the evaluation of markets and other mechanisms for access to medical care, our view of the priority-setting process rejects several prominent versions of the "separate spheres doctrine"— namely, that only health benefits or health-related concerns should count in health priority decisions. Our arguments are developed in the context of a family of related but distinguishable objections. The objections include (a) the claim that life saving is unique among health benefits and is thus strongly resistant to trade-offs; (b) the broader claim that numerous small benefits should not be permitted to outweigh some larger benefits (other than life saving) to fewer persons; (c) the claim that what has been called the "rule of rescue" demands greater priority in meeting the significant health needs of identifiable persons; and (d) the claim that cost-utility analysis runs afoul of a reasonable commitment to giving priority to the worst off.

1.7 Justice, Democracy, and Social Values

In chapter 7 we examine some recent lines of argument emphasizing both the limitations of theories of justice to resolve priority-setting issues and the need to incorporate the public's values into such decisions in ways that formal methods such as CUA do not. In particular, the proponents seek to make more room for considerations of justice.

We examine a methodological variation of cost-effectiveness analysis, known as cost-value analysis (CVA), and some claims made on behalf of procedural solutions to the priorities problem, including the application of some prominent theories of deliberative democracy to the priority setting process using quality adjusted life years or disability adjusted life years (DALYs). Contributions from democratic theory offer a general approach to any deliberation about allocation priorities that emphasize the need for an "accountability for reasonableness" in decision processes affecting the public, while the aim of some procedural theorists is a "filtered consensus" that provides a firmer moral rationale for the value choices incorporated in DALY calculations.

While we acknowledge the importance of better understanding the public's (or some community representative's) values or ensuring that decisions fall within a range of reasonableness, the community's values and judgments of reasonableness, no less than the underlying commitments of philosophical theories, are often objects of deep disagreement. Resolution of such disagreements, in the end, will require recourse to underlying theories of justice, and that will necessitate an evaluation of which theories offer the most compelling arguments. We argue also that the reach of philosophical theories of justice is not as readily exhausted as some of the alternative empirical or procedural solutions suggest, and we claim that the arguments developed from within our theory set significant constraints on the permissible range of choices produced by the various democratic or procedural justice approaches. In particular, we argue that many of the often-overlooked questions of justice with regard to socially situated groups can be addressed by our theory in ways that public opinion surveys or procedural constraints on deliberation alone may not address.

In the end, for a variety of reasons we conclude that an appeal to theory is inescapable. Moreover, the distributive concerns sought to be accommodated do not exhaust the justice-based concerns that are relevant to priority setting. As is the case in all other areas of health policy, an important consideration to bear in mind is that there are no separate spheres of justice such that other equally relevant dimensions of well-being in addition to health are outside its purview. Even as we denominate the proper aim of health policy as its central focus on health, all of the essential dimensions of well-being function as inherent constraints on the very way we understand what the just pursuit of public health involves.

Justice and Well-Being

2.1 Introduction

Social justice is concerned with human well-being. In our view, well-being is best understood as involving plural, irreducible dimensions, each of which represents something of independent moral significance. Although an exhaustive, mutually exclusive list of the discrete elements of well-being is not our aim (and may not be possible), we build our account around six distinct dimensions of well-being, each of which merits separate attention within a theory of justice. These different dimensions offer different lenses through which the justice of political structures, social practices, and institutions can be assessed. Without attention to each dimension, something of salience goes unnoticed.

Not all dimensions of human well-being are centrally important within a theory of social justice. Some aspects of human well-being are matters of great importance to particular individuals because they are central to their specific goals and personal aspirations. Social justice, by contrast, is concerned with only those dimensions of well-being that are of special moral urgency because they matter centrally to everyone, whatever the particular life plans and aims each has.

Our theory does not require or suppose that a threshold level of each dimension of well-being identified by our theory of social justice is a *necessary* condition for a decent life. Indeed, for many of us, even this is not the case. However, we do claim that to the extent that a human life is seriously deficient in one or more of these dimensions, it is likely that an individual is not experiencing a sufficient level of well-being. Our theory, then, embraces a moderate essentialist claim. While a threshold level of well-being across each dimension may not be present (or even possible) for everyone, our list of essential dimensions of well-being is offered as an account of those things *characteristically* present within a decent life, whatever a person's particular life plans and personal commitments. Moreover, each dimension is important enough to be an independent concern of justice. The job of justice, positively stated, is the task of securing a sufficient level of each dimension for each individual, insofar as possible.

Our theory is open to a number of challenges. After we present the basic features of our positive account of well-being, we discuss these challenges in varying degrees of detail. One line of argument reflecting the trajectory of our own journey toward the theory we propound involves a comparison with other theories of justice that either depend less heavily on any particular account of well-being or offer their own alternative accounts of well-being. Other challenges include objections by the moral relativist against even a moderate essentialism, raising doubts about the plausibility of articulating universally applicable standards for evaluating well-being. Some will charge that the construction of such a list is inevitably ethnocentric, while others may conclude that any recommendation of the use of such a list across cultures is a form of moral imperialism. In addition, holding governments accountable for the dimensions of well-being on our list may be said to violate reasonable principles of political neutrality.

Finally, since ours is a theory of social justice, we need also to give an account of why we start with the dimensions of well-being, rather than with an account of basic human rights and the duties they impose on governments, nonstate entities, and other nations within a global community.

2.2 Essential Dimensions of Well-Being

Unless we can characterize the dimensions of well-being in a way that reveals their moral distinctiveness, we will miss part of what an adequate theory of justice should take into account. This oversight can have the theoretically undesirable consequence that a specific, but crucially important, rationale for viewing a pattern of social organization as unjust will be absent from a moral analysis. For these reasons, we offer our own list, even as we acknowledge that no final and complete list is to be expected. Our list contains six core dimensions: health, personal security, reasoning, respect, attachment, and self-determination. While we do not doubt that there are other theoretically appealing ways to specify the contents of the list, we think that the one we propose represents a useful set of criteria for illuminating the requirements of justice within public health and health policy and beyond. The discussion under each heading below elaborates our rationale for the inclusion of each as a separate category.

Health

There are perhaps as many accounts of the concept of health as there are cultural traditions and healing professions. The account of health with which we work has been constructed for a particular moral purpose and from a particular point of view. Specifically, we work with what is essentially an ordinary-language understanding of physical and mental health that is intended to capture the dimension of human flourishing that is frequently expressed through the biological or organic functioning of the body. While health is a state or condition that in many respects can be described in organic or functional terms, it is important for our account to note that the absence of health refers to more than biological malfunctioning or impairments to some functional ability such as mobility, sight, or hearing. Being in pain, even if that pain does not impede proper biological functioning, is also incompatible with health. So, too, are sexual dysfunction and infertility. Health, so understood, thus reflects a moral concern with the rich and diverse set of considerations characteristic of public health and clinical medicine, including premature mortality and preventable morbidity, malnutrition, pain, loss of mobility, mental health, the biological basis of behavior, reproduction (and its control), and sexual functioning. All of these matter crucially in sustaining a human existence across the whole life span. Moreover, health is of independent (although not exclusive) moral concern when threatened by war, violence, environmental hazards, consumer products, and natural disasters, all of which have been claimed, to one degree or another, as public health problems as well.

Our approach to health differs from some other accounts in ways that illuminate the salient moral issues captured by our particular focus. For example, it is quite different from the World Health Organization definition, which views health as a state of physical, mental, and social well-being (World Health Organization 1946). The problem with this otherwise noble aspiration is that it conflates virtually all elements of human development under a single rubric and thereby makes almost any deficit of well-being into a health deficit. Were we to adopt the World Health Organization definition, we would lose the capacity to maintain any distinctive interest in dimensions of human well-being such as respect, affiliation, and reasoning that we believe have independent moral significance as matters of social justice, however intertwined with health they may be.

Although health as a dimension of well-being is offered as the primary moral foundation for public health and health policy, there is no reason to suppose that every policy decision that bears on public health or medical care rests on the single moral foundation of health any more than any other intellectual discipline, profession, or social institution necessarily rests on a single moral foundation. For example, policies against female genital mutilation rest on concerns for health, the physical and psychological inviolability encompassed by the dimension we label as personal security, and self-determination. In this case, the moral foundation in justice for the policies draws upon three dimensions of well-being, none of which is reducible to the others. Each signals a separate kind of injustice produced through the mutilation.

The moral justification for health policies involving the distribution of medical services may depend as much on dimensions of well-being other than health as on health itself. For example, we argue in chapter 5 that society's obligation to ensure universal access to medical care rests not only on the effects of access on health but also on what justice requires with regard to what is necessary for being respected as a moral equal. Thus, each dimension offers a lens intended to highlight a different, particular kind of moral saliency, any one of which, or any combination thereof, may be used to illuminate the requirements of justice in a specific policy context. Accordingly, we argue that the concerns of any plausible theory of justice are multiple, and this plurality of concerns informs answers to questions about what justice in health policy requires.

In addition, the six general dimensions, which we put forward as a way of capturing and classifying the moral territory of social justice, are no substitute for more finely grained accounting of the many moral aspects *within* each dimension. This is perhaps particularly true of health, our primary concern, since policy makers often need to evaluate the justice of trade-offs among the various aspects of health. For example, potential reductions of morbidity, or health-related quality of life, can be traded off against mortality or length of life. Health-related quality of life can be decomposed further into a variety of aspects ranging from the functioning of specific organ systems such as the heart or lungs to task-oriented physical functional measures such as mobility or the functioning of complex sensory apparatus such as taste to psychological functioning. Our approach does not entail that one description lays claim to being the one most appropriate for all theoretical or public policy purposes. Indeed, within health policy, many have sought to develop all-inclusive health status measures as well as measures specific to particular diseases for a variety of purposes, including comparative judgments of cost-effectiveness analysis of alternative treatments and the setting of public health priorities. As we argue in chapter 6, our approach is a useful reminder that aggregate health measures are not value-neutral. The selection of such measures carries implications for justice that are in need of evaluation.

Our account of health, viewed as a morally independent dimension of overall well-being, and thus of social justice, provides an analytic framework whereby one can see the full range of health-related, moral saliencies of a public policy question. A result of this account is that it does not conflate all of the numerous and diverse concerns relevant to human well-being with concerns that are distinctively about health. At the same time, it avoids the arbitrary exclusion of some deficits in health from what counts as a concern of justice on the grounds that those deficits are not produced through the vectors of disease, injury, or illness.

Personal Security

Many injustices involve harms to one's health, but they also involve so much more that is not reducible to the effect on health alone. Some injustices that involve harms to health involve different, additionally salient harms to other dimensions of well-being. For example, an arm broken in an unsafe workplace differs from an arm broken while being tortured. Criminal acts such as rape or battery do more than harm the body. Assault (placing another in fear of imminent bodily harm) and intimidation are invasions of personal security, even when they do not eventuate in bodily injury or pain. It is arguably extremely difficult if not impossible to live a decent life if one is in constant fear of physical or psychological abuse. Experiencing such abuse is surely a setback to well-being, regardless of who we are or what values we might otherwise have. Violations such as rape, assault, and torture are of concern to the public health community because of their impact on health, but even more so they are the objects of concern for those persons and institutions having a special focus on human rights abuses, domestic violence, crime, war, and terrorism.

Injustices involving assault, enslavement, degradation, and rape also violate any minimal notion of respect for persons as moral equals. However, these injustices are not reducible to a simple failure to treat someone as a moral equal; they treat persons as having no morally significant standing and violate human interests everyone has in maintaining physical and bodily integrity and psychological inviolability.

Reasoning

Reasoning is the name given to a broad set of diverse skills and abilities, including those classified within philosophical discussions since Aristotle under the headings of practical and theoretical reason. As the Aristotelian point is sometimes put, theoretical reasoning skills aid us in answering empirical questions and forming our understanding of what there *is*, while the skills of practical deliberation aid us in deciding what we *ought* to do or how we *ought* to live. Within the psychology literature, both practical and theoretical reasoning are often subsumed under the more general heading of cognition or cognitive reasoning. The broad account of cognitive reasoning abilities includes a "combination of skills, including attention, learning, memory, praxis (skilled motor behaviors), and the so-called executive functions, such as decision making, goal setting, and judgment" (Whitehouse et al. 1997).

Theoretical reasoning abilities include the basic intellectual skills and habits of mind necessary for persons to understand the natural world. Such skills include analytical ability, imagination, the ability to form beliefs based on evidence, the ability to reflect on what counts as relevant evidence for those beliefs, and the ability to weigh the probative value of each. Theoretical reasoning abilities also include certain habits of mind, or intellectual virtues, necessary for successful application of human intelligence to understanding and grasping truths about the world. They include a willingness to take seriously evidence contrary to settled belief and being open to revision of current beliefs.

The nature and degree of theoretical reasoning skills and abilities needed, of course, vary in historical contexts. Literacy and numeracy are vital in complex industrial and postindustrial societies and perhaps less so in primitive agrarian or hunter-gatherer societies. Nonetheless, humans need some level of ability to reason deductively and inductively. They need the ability to make logical connections and detect logical errors; to measure, count, and perform other mathematical computations; to communicate effectively with others in a culture; and to make causal inferences. Like the other categories of well-being on our list, without them, whatever other dimensions of well-being we may have, we lack something crucial to our ability to function.

The abilities we associate with practical reason include the ability to form and revise a conception of how we each wish to live, to conform behavior to ideals and ends that are a part of that conception, and to deliberate among alternative means to the achievement of those ends. Practical reason is valuable for more than just the development of individual life plans or the setting of one's own personal goals and ends. It is necessary for the very possibility of other-regarding morality. In order to function as a member of a moral community, we need to be able to deliberate with others about the reasonableness of our actions and choices and to reflect on those actions and choices from the perspectives of others affected by them.

Practical reasoning abilities also involve the capacity to take up a critical, self-reflective stance toward our own desires, preferences, values, and ideals so that we are able to revise them if they are found wanting (Frankfurt 1971). We need the ability to subject our current or immediate desires and preferences to scrutiny so that we may better harmonize them with our longer-term goals and aspirations (Griffin 1986). In addition, the skills of practical reasoning allow our judgments of value to be examined in light of how well they cohere with our more global personal ideals for our own character (Taylor 1982). Practical reasoning abilities also include some capacity to examine the origins of our moral beliefs, value judgments, and personal ideals and to reflect upon the process by which those commitments were acquired (Christman 1991). As Mill observed, the skills of reflective persons include the ability to step back from one's beliefs and opinions about how one should live and to "adopt" them as one's own, rather than simply "inheriting" them (Mill 1991).

Although theoretical reasoning is distinguishable from practical reasoning, judgments of what to do necessarily piggyback on basic theoretical abilities. The abilities that allow us to form beliefs about the natural and social world provide us with a reliable factual basis for forming practical conclusions. Theoretical reason and practical reason thus work together, allowing us to navigate both the natural and social world.

The development of reasoning abilities is obviously dependent on an adequate level of biological or organic brain functioning. Prenatally and during early childhood, assaults to brain development can have a profound effect on cognitive capacity. These abilities can also be set back in adults through any number of compromises to health, including trauma, stroke, and progressive dementias. These common causal pathways, however, do not reduce the moral significance of reasoning to health. Cognitive deficits are linked to multiple causal contributors including genetics, poverty, illness, and disease. But the existence of an overlap in the causal pathways to either ill health or low cognitive functioning is not a conceptual problem for our classificatory scheme. The only claim of distinctiveness for the dimensions of well-being on our list is whether each captures a morally salient aspect of human flourishing that is not reducible to the others. Moreover, reasoning abilities of both kinds are importantly related to other dimensions of well-being on our list. They are necessary for self-determination, for example. From the perspective of justice, however, deficits in reasoning abilities matter morally, apart from how they are caused and independent of what else they enable us to do.

Above and beyond the biological and physiological substrate of reasoning abilities, we can see that much more is required for their exercise than healthy brain structures and the nutrition, physical environments, and medical care needed to sustain them. Certain kinds of health states are necessary for reasoning, but they are not sufficient. What further distinguishes reasoning abilities from healthy functioning of the brain is that the former also require an understanding of the world that must be *learned*.

What is learned in the first few years of life has a profound affect on our abilities to reason across the life span. In part, the impact of learning in early childhood is mediated through the brain, whose continued development throughout childhood is influenced by environmental learning. Thus, reasoning abilities are affected not only by physical well-being during childhood but also by characteristics of the social world in which childhood is experienced. In modern societies, we often think of reasoning capabilities as promoted most directly by access to education. Schooling provides the skills of literacy and mathematics, skills that in many contexts are important, if not essential, for the exercise of reason in everyday life. Schooling also provides knowledge about the physical and social world which forms the basic data for cognition and which prepares us to assume responsibilities of democratic participation and to protect our interests in the marketplace. Without the knowledge gained through education, it is in many contexts difficult if not impossible to exercise the capabilities of reason.

However, as Allen Buchanan has described in some detail, schooling is but a part of the story (Buchanan 2002). Cognitive capacities are shaped by far more than formal educational institutions, an especially important point for a theory of the sort we defend. We are concerned about the full range of social determinants of each dimension of well-being. Buchanan's point is that social practices and other institutions produce culturally accepted "epistemic" authorities, or persons whose judgment is routinely respected and often deferred to within a culture. These epistemic authorities include religious leaders, educators, journalists, and a vast number of persons who routinely pronounce on important matters of public interest or controversy. Such epistemic authorities to whom much deference in judgment is shown include not only certain key figures who might be described as "public intellectuals" or members of the "learned professions" but also increasingly popular musicians, entertainers, sports celebrities, and others.

What all of these authorities have in common is the fact that they are among those who have a large role in transmitting moral beliefs, inculcating virtue, shaping patterns of sympathy, and providing the factual beliefs underlying the formation of social bonds. Such authorities may or may not be deserving of their trusted status, and their beliefs can be false, distorting, or self-serving, such as when they reinforce beliefs about ethnic or gender differences, undervalue the epistemic credibility of some groups, or exaggerate the epistemic credibility of those in dominant institutions and positions of cultural authority. In order to exercise abilities of practical reason so that our beliefs are adopted on due reflection and not just inherited, as Mill warned against, persons need to develop sufficient critical faculties and independence of judgment. In order to counter the risk of unjustified epistemic deference to persons in institutional and cultural roles of authority, we thus need both critical intellectual faculties and independent habits of mind.

Respect

John Rawls and many others of widely differing philosophical emphases argue that respect is an essential element of human flourishing and that it is a proper concern of justice (Rawls 1971; Sen 1992; Nussbaum 2000; J. Cohen 1989; Anderson 1999). There are many ways of putting the point, and not all highlight precisely the same set of considerations. At minimum, respect for others involves treatment of others as dignified moral beings deserving of equal moral concern. Respect for others requires an ability to see others as independent sources of moral worth and dignity and to view others as appropriate objects of sympathetic identification.

Respect for others is closely linked to self-respect as well. A capacity for self-respect involves an individual's capacity to see oneself as the moral equal of others and as an independent source of moral claims based on one's own dignity and worth.

Respect then matters to human well-being in two related ways. A life lacking in the respect of others is seriously deficient in something crucial to well-being. So, too, is a life lacking self-respect. It is entirely possible, however, that someone may not be respected by, and may not be shown respect by, others but may still be someone who retains her self-respect. That lack of respect by others tends to undermine self-respect is a contingent matter, but a morally significant one nonetheless. Similarly, those seriously deprived of the respect of others may have difficulty in developing their own capacities for respect for others, but this too is a contingent matter. Both lack of self-respect and not being respected by others are assaults upon the status of the person as a morally worthy agent, deserving of and entitled to treatment as an equal. In one case, the assault is mounted externally; in the other, the assault comes from within.

Lack of respect is a dimension of well-being characteristically under assault when an individual is the object of discrimination based on judgments of intrinsic inferior social status, often linked to properties of group membership, such as ethnicity, gender, or social class, or to ability or appearance. While it is possible for individual members of a socially disfavored group to retain their self-respect under discriminatory and oppressive social conditions, they are able to do so only with heroic efforts or good fortune. Being respected and retaining one's self-respect, however, are of much too great moral importance for human development and flourishing to be left to the vicissitudes of individual luck or heroism. That individuals can, with hard work and good luck, be self-respecting does nothing to vitiate the injustice of being disrespected by others. A lack of respect from others and an awareness of one's own exclusion from the reciprocal system of mutual respect that others in one's society enjoy are profound injustices in their own right.

Our account can be made more concrete by drawing upon a distinction Stephen Darwall makes between what he calls "appraisal respect" and "recognition respect." Appraisal respect involves the judgment by others that our conduct or projects are estimable or worthy of praise. Such judgments are matters of degree, and not all people are equally worthy of appraisal respect (Darwall 1992, 77, n. 18). Some deserve Nobel Prizes for what they have accomplished or praise and admiration for the obstacles they have overcome, but many are not so worthy. By contrast, recognition respect is what is owed to each of us as agents entitled to treatment worthy of members of the moral community on a par with all others. Recognition respect, then, is what our theory is concerned with. Respect in this sense is what is characteristically lacking in invidious judgments of persons on the basis of their group membership, as in the phenomena of racism or sexism. It is also what is lacking centrally in self-respect where individuals internalize the belief that they are worthless and not deserving of the treatment others are entitled to expect.

Respect as we understand it affects well-being not because our projects are judged estimable by ourselves or others, but because we are respected by ourselves and others as of equal moral worth, entitled to recognition of our moral claims on a par with other persons. Respect and therefore well-being is set back whenever we are perceived as being of lesser value because of membership in a particular race, gender, economic class, or other group about whom invidious judgments are made. Our account thus reflects the fact that the well-being of individuals is often tied to the well-being of groups. Respect for individuals is often a function of respect for the groups with which they are identified. Individual members of a group can be deprived of the respect necessary for individual well-being as a consequence of their group being deprived of respect.

Thus, there are many ways of suffering the indignity of not being respected by others, and there are many ways in which that failure of respect contingently undermines self-respect. Some failures of the social structure to provide for or respond to needs for preserving health through health care, or needs for developing capacities of reason through education, not only affect health or reason respectively, but can cause an additional injustice associated with the loss of respect. One can experience the humiliation of being disrespected with perfect awareness that one does not merit the insult or is not less worthy of respect. Disrespect is therefore an insult to one's dignity and is an injustice independent of any further harms that persons experience as a consequence of being disrespected.

Attachment

The formation of bonds of attachment is one of the most central dimensions of human well-being. Such bonds include both friendship and love in their most intimate expressions, as well as a sense of solidarity or fellow-feeling with others within one's community. As the philosopher Martha Nussbaum observes (with reference to what she labels "affiliation"), such bonds matter for reasons of both friendship and justice.

At the personal level of intimates, our account of attachment engages the capacities for love, friendship, emotional engagement, compassion, and sympathetic identification with others. As Nussbaum notes, the capacity to care for and to be cared for by others, to feel longing in their absence, and to grieve for their loss are matters that are essential to well-being, whatever else is valuable (Nussbaum, 2000, 79). Empirical evidence suggests there is a tight link between the ability to form bonds of attachment between children and parents and between children and others known as "authoritative communities" which are charged with the transmission of social values. When these attachments fail to take hold, the result is a lack of social connectedness that is exhibited in conduct disorders, lack of self-restraint, and antisocial levels of aggressiveness (Commission on Children at Risk 2003). Human capacities for attachment are not important solely for the bonds they sustain at a personal, intimate level. They also are prerequisites for the formation and perpetuation of a just society. They are not prerequisites simply because they make discriminatory failures of respect less likely or play a catalytic role in activating a sense of justice and fair treatment. Both are no doubt true. Although respect and attachment are dimensions of well-being that reinforce one another, they are distinct moral concerns, each mattering in their own right as a separate concern of justice. Inability to see others, or at least some others, as moral equals, deserving of respect, is one way in which others may suffer unjust treatment, but even among those persons accorded equal moral status, a failure of attachment may still result in their unjust treatment. Respect for others as independent sources of moral claims may counsel some degree of forbearance, perhaps even some sense of minimal duty to come to the assistance of others. However, respect alone is arguably lacking in the emotional depth that comes with a more robust attunement to the deepest needs and longings of others. Attachment is thus essential to justice in the same way that respect and reasoning ability are. The level of emotional engagement and sympathetic identification with others is what in our view distinguishes attachment as an essential, irreducible element of what is necessary for the processes of forging bonds of mutual forbearance and mutual aid and for participation in the responsibilities of caring for one another. A theory of justice that does not require that its basic social institutions conform to and reproduce capacities for human attachment leaves out something of crucial moral significance.

One way to illustrate the importance we attribute to attachment, not simply as a matter of well-being generally, but as a matter that deserves a central place within justice, is to contrast our account with some assumptions made within John Rawls's theory. Rawls starts from the assumption that the task of a theory of social justice is to formulate the terms of fair competition and rules of mutual advantage acceptable to a community of persons who are mutually disinterested and live lives characterized by freely chosen relations between moral equals. As the philosopher Annette Baier observes, the implementation of such theories, if not supplemented, "may *unfit* people to be anything other than what its justifying theories suppose them to be, ones who have no interest in each others' interests" (Baier 1994, 29). While rights and respect for rights may provide a "good minimal set" of moral categories for social appraisal, she continues, they "are quite compatible with very great misery" (Baier 1994, 23). She concludes that while Rawls claims that "justice is the first virtue of society," there is a "need for more than justice."

Perhaps the heart of Baier's objection lies in her observation that such theories, if implemented as conceived, are not sufficient to "form persons to be *capable* of conforming to an ethics of care and responsibility" (Baier 1994, 29). By that she means that traditional theories of justice condemn infringements of liberties or seek to curb material inequalities, but they do not speak to other social values and virtues. They do not address the importance of developing and cultivating capacities for attachment and for living lives characterized by dependency and interdependency, vulnerability, and the potential for exploitation.

Instead of a need for more than justice, we think that internal to a theory of social justice is the requirement that the totality of social institutions and social conventions should be such that it *does fit* people for lives in which the bonds of attachment and capacities for sympathetic identification with others are cultivated. In some instances, the injustice of a particular social arrangement consists not simply in the fact that a valuable social opportunity or good is unavailable to some members of society, but that those arrangements do not cultivate the kinds of relations among persons that justice demands. Justice in nonideal contexts, characterized by dependence, vulnerability and a potential for the interests and aspirations of some persons to be limited and thwarted by the cumulative impact of the various elements of the social structure, thus views the formation of bonds of attachment as an essential dimension of well-being.

Self-Determination

The value of self-determination, the linchpin of liberal political theory, is a broad and encompassing category of human good. It is widely endorsed in many moral and political systems, even among those who complain that in specific cultures or concrete cases too much concern is placed on individual choices. The value of self-determination underlies many accounts of the importance of political liberty, and as we shall claim, it is a foundation for other conclusions about what a just social structure requires.

From Locke to Rawls, a hallmark of liberal political thought has been a commitment to an extensive system of political liberties intended to guarantee individuals a degree of protection against interference by the state or one's fellow citizens in their choices and actions. Political liberties themselves, however, are not the constituents of well-being, but merely a means to some further good. As Rawls argues, liberties are like the "primary goods" of income and wealth. They are all-purpose means that have instrumental value to individuals, whatever their personal ideals, plans of life, or preferences (Rawls 1971). The ultimate values political liberties serve, therefore, depend on some deeper, often unarticulated moral justification.

Mill offers a plethora of arguments, some of which famously concentrate on the good consequences of leading a self-directed life—or a life that is guided and shaped by one's own choices and values. He variously argues that a self-directed life facilitates the advancement of truth, the achievement of civil peace, individual self-discovery, and the perfection of individual human faculties. All of these arguments point to the importance of self-determination, which, in turn, gets its value from its consequences. However, one of Mill's suggested justifications that is perhaps the most straightforward is that being self-directed, or living one's life from the inside, according to one's own inclinations and values, is itself a constituent of human well-being. In being self-directed "there is a greater fullness of life" (Mill, 1991, 76).

The force of Mill's insight regarding the direct value of leading a self-determining life can be explicated by a simple thought experiment. Imagine a life in which the other essential dimensions of well-being are present. A person is healthy, has strong bonds of attachment, is self-respecting and enjoys the respect of others, is secure in his person, and has developed capacities for reasoning. However, from his earliest years onward, this person has been told what his path in life will be. All the elements of his life have been determined for him, including how much and what kind of schooling he will have, how he will make a living, with whom he will be friends, where he will live, whether he will have children and how, and so on. Although his life in many ways goes well, he has been denied any opportunity to shape its contours through his own choices and thus has been denied the chance to make something of his life through his own efforts. Such a life would be rich in all other respects but seriously lacking in what is required for a decent life. Isaiah Berlin sums matters up this way:

"I wish to determine myself, and not be directed by others, no matter how wise or benevolent; my conduct derives an irreplaceable value from the sole fact that it is my own, and not imposed on me" (Berlin 1969, xliii).

Joseph Raz puts matters in similar fashion, claiming that an important, irreducible dimension of well-being consists in "people controlling, in some degree, their own destiny, fashioning it through successive decisions throughout their lives" (Raz 1986, 369). Jim Griffin offers a similar description of what he labels an essential element of well-being: "Choosing one's own course through life, making something out of it according to one's own lights, is at the heart of what it is to lead a human existence" (Griffin 1986, 67). Like Berlin, these accounts emphasize that, in addition to the reasoning abilities that are necessary to set and revise our own ends, and in addition to the political liberties that are necessary means to their pursuit, our well-being consists in being in a condition in which our ends contribute effectively to the shaping of the course of our lives. It is "controlling [our] own destinies," or "the making of something out of" our lives, that is the "irreplaceable value" that Berlin's account takes as the ultimate aim.

Berlin is clear that the ideal of human well-being underlying the defense of political liberty is the foundation for more than just an absence of interferences by others. To be self-determining in the sense Berlin envisions is to be in a condition characterized by an "absence of obstructions on roads along which a man can decide to walk" (Berlin 1969, xxxix). Berlin is quick to note that what is of value to us is not that we are "self-sufficient" or wholly independent of all obstacles created by nature or human social institutions (Berlin 1969, xxxix). What we do care about, however, is "how many doors are open, how far they are open, upon their relative importance in my life, even though it may be impossible literally to measure this in any quantitative fashion" (Berlin 1969, xxxix–xl). While those doors will not open without the development and exercise of the capacities for reason, reason and self-determination are not equivalent moral concerns. Reasoning allows for so much more that is valuable than the facilitation of self-determination. Reasoning also is not sufficient to our being self-determining. Self-determination is thus a separate dimension of well-being, even though it partially depends on reasoning capacities. Like all of the other dimensions of well-being examined thus far, each in some measure requires or is advanced by at least some of the others.

Moreover, doors will not open without political liberties. Some large area of noninterference is necessary as a means for leading self-determining lives, but political liberties too are not sufficient for leading a self-determining life (Berlin 1969, 124). Unless legal systems and cultural norms are structured in ways that provide social room for meaningful choices and their implementation, then leading a self-determining life is unlikely. More to the point, without the proper economic, legal, and social structures, one's chances for being self-determining are thwarted. Perhaps most foundationally, certain material conditions are essential to our being self-determining. People who live from meal to meal; who do not know if tomorrow there will be food for themselves or their children; who are dying of exposure, star-vation, or exhaustion are not positioned to be self-determining in any meaningful respect. As Rousseau noted, "necessitous men are not free men." People who are entirely beholden to others for their very survival cannot be said to play any substantial part in directing their own lives (Raz 1986, pp. 379–80).

Our defense of self-determination as an essential dimension of well-be-ing thus rests on simple and we believe widely shared views about having some control over who we are and who we will become. It does not depend on some controversial metaphysical claims about the nature of the self or the sources of all value. Unlike one of Mill's famous arguments for political liberty, we do not rest our claim on any argument that self-determination is important because it leads to self-discovery or a better understanding of one's true or authentic self. Indeed, our account of self-determination as an essential dimension of well-being makes no assumption about the existence of some authentic self. Nor does it claim that shaping our own lives through our own choices will get us closer to the truth (Gray 1996). What matters is that our lives be shaped at least in part by our choices, informed by our values and interests.

It is equally important to note that our account does not assume that the "source of value" or the "source of obligation" lies solely in one's choices or the exercise of one's rational capacities for choice (Korsgaard 1996, 91, 165). That the process of "self-creation through choice-making" involved in self-determination is one constituent of our well-being does not entail the controversial claim that our having made certain choices or our capacity to choose is the fount of all value and hence the basis of all dimensions of well-being (Raz 1986, 388–89; Gray 1996, 21; Richardson 2001).

Nor does our defense of the irreducible importance of self-determination entail any claim that it is the synoptic value or the single dimension of well-being to which all others are subordinate. In our view, all dimensions of well-being are independently important to guarantee. As we argue in greater detail in chapter 3, for example, we care about the health and other di-mensions of well-being for children, not simply for their instrumental contribution to children's becoming self-determining adults. We care about children being healthy, even if that does little or nothing to advance their being self-determining now or in the longer term.

Aristotle's account of the helmsman further illuminates our sense of self-determination (Aristotle, *Politics* 1279a 1–5, cited in May 1994, 139–42). The helmsman sets a course on an open sea, but does not command the winds nor decide the boundaries between land and sea. Her choices are therefore bounded. She cannot decide to sail upon the land, and she cannot will the wind to blow in the desired direction or at the desired velocity. She does not choose her course wholly without regard to necessity or need, and she does not proceed on any course without the help or hindrance of luck. And yet the helmsman charts her own course within the parameters of these external influences. Charting her course is not possible, however, when the seas are so rough and her vessel so damaged that the helmsman must work feverishly just to keep from drowning. Self-determination requires some material basis for its exercise—a sturdy boat, so to speak. The successful exercise of self-determination, like the successful navigation of the helmsman, will depend also on the favorable circumstances in which other dimensions of well-being, health, personal security, attachment, respect and the exercise of reason, are present in sufficient quantity. For joint enterprises, involving a common objective with others, the cooperation of other crew members is required. Many journeys are not conceivable on one's own. Like the image of the helmsman, our notion of self-determination is not some fixed state that can be asymptotically approached or a quantity that can be maximized. It is not something that depends on reasoning capacities alone, or that can be achieved outside of a web of interdependencies, or that needs only an absence of human interference. Rather, self-determination is a valuable state or condition for which enough is required for our well-being, and without which the prospects for a decent life are undermined in ways not reducible to deficits in the other valuable dimensions of well-being.

2.3 A Moderate Essentialism

Our view of justice rests on a form of essentialism about the nature of human well-being. Our claim, however, is a moral claim, not a metaphysical claim regarding the essential nature of human beings. We claim that each dimension of well-being is distinct. Each represents a matter of different moral salience, which, if not taken into account within a theory of justice, omits something of importance. We contend also that each dimension is an essential feature of well-being, not in the sense that without it a life is not a truly human life. The more moderate claim is that each dimension is such that a life substantially lacking in any one of these is a life seriously deficient in what it is reasonable for anyone to want, whatever else they want. Each is thus a separate indicator of a decent life which it is the job of justice to facilitate.

Moreover, it is important to emphasize that our moderate essentialist account is offered for a limited theoretical purpose. It offers only a basis for assessment of social institutions and practices, not a basis for judging whether a life is worth living or as a basis for determining whether a person is entitled to the same moral consideration as others for whom fewer dimensions of well-being are deficient.

Social justice, stated in its positive aim, aspires to sufficiently high levels of well-being in each of these dimensions for everyone. A society may fall short of that aspiration for any number of reasons, not all of which constitute an injustice. For some of us, achievement of a sufficient level of health, for example, may not be possible. However, the lack of sufficient levels of well-being in any of its essential dimensions is for us evidence suggesting the possibility of an injustice within a society. Each dimension therefore focuses our attention on separate matters of concern to justice.

The moderate essentialist view, then, serves as a basis of appraisal for how well social structures are carrying out the obligations of social justice, but it is not meant as a basis for making a number of other claims about individual lives. Our view does not claim that a life deficient in some important dimension of well-being on our list is not a valuable life, or one not entitled to the same moral concern as others. It does not claim that such a life cannot be a decent life. Indeed, lives full of pain, illness, and physical infirmity are familiar enough to all for us to know that lives lacking in good health can count as among the paradigms of decent lives.

While our theory is one that sets some limits to trade-offs among the separate dimensions of well-being, the limits on trade-offs are applicable only in certain contexts. We do not claim that individuals would be acting irrationally or unjustly if they themselves make trade-offs among the dimensions. An individual may well be rational and morally entitled to make a trade-off, for example, sacrificing physical health for the sake of pursuing refinement of reasoning abilities. However, it is not permissible in the design of social institutions and social structures to ignore one dimension of well-being on the grounds that, all things considered, the lives of most of us are going well enough on balance.

2.4 Well-Being and Nonideal Theory

Our moderate essentialism offers an ideal of human well-being with which justice should be concerned and against which social structures can be assessed. It is an ideal to which a just social order should aspire. However, in all other respects, our theory is a nonideal theory.

We do not follow the precedent of some leading theories of justice that offer distributive principles meant to govern the operation of just institutions, embedded within the background of a just social structure. By contrast, ours is a nonideal theory of justice, intended to offer practical guidance on questions of which inequalities matter most when just background conditions are *not* in place. We assume that unjust inequalities will continue to provide the real-world context in which questions of justice will arise. Our background assumption is that some persons are more vulnerable, less powerful, less advantaged than others, and that all live lives of dependency and interdependency. By contrast, the nature of Rawls's project allows him to put aside worries about gender, ethnic, and religious discrimination, which for us figure prominently (Rawls 2001, 66). This omission in Rawls is not because they do not matter morally for him; ideal theories set themselves the different task of working out distributive principles where unjust inequalities of these sorts are not a part of the background, and thus the agreed-upon principles that emerge from his theory are ones acceptable by parties in positions of equality.

For us, however, the answer to the question, "Which inequalities matter most?" will depend on how actual institutions and social practices are arranged and on their impact on differentially situated persons and groups. We view facts about inequality as essential contextual information, necessary to the task of understanding when inequalities of any sort merit heightened moral scrutiny. Real but socially contingent inequalities such as the existence of poverty, inequalities in power and social standing, and ethnic and gender discrimination therefore matter for our very different theoretical task. From the perspective of nonideal theory, only when such facts about the concrete human condition figure into the analysis is the task of saying which inequalities matter most comprehensible. This does not mean, however, that our theory is simply one aimed at making the most of a bad situation. It sets aspirations for achieving human well-being in all of its essential dimensions, but it concentrates our attention on those gaps in well-being that are most urgent.

One reason for our concern about those that are most urgent reflects the fact that inequalities in a nonideal world are interrelated. Inequalities of one kind beget and reinforce other inequalities, and their cumulative effect on human well-being will depend on their causal interaction. One implication of this interrelatedness is that, while each dimension of well-being marks something of distinct moral salience, the factors affecting them are rarely casually distinct and therefore their moral significance will in part depend on how they interact, potentially compounding and reinforcing disadvantage in more than one dimension of well-being.

Our theory does follow Rawls insofar as we agree that the primary subject of the principles of social justice is the "basic structure of society, the arrangement of major social institutions" (Rawls 1971, 54). How Rawls understands or should best conceive of what constitutes the basic structure is a matter of considerable disagreement (G. Cohen 1997; Murphy 1999; Pogge 2000). Rawls acknowledges that "the concept of the basic structure is somewhat vague" and that "it is not always clear which institutions or features should be included" (Rawls 1971, 9). Rawls concedes that the precise boundaries of the basic structure cannot be set in advance and that it is a contingent matter (Rawls 2001, 11). However the finer points of Rawlsian scholarship are resolved, we think that his stated rationale for concentrating on the basic structure has great significance for how we understand our nonideal theory of justice. Rawls notes that the case for taking the basic structure as the subject for a theory of justice lies in the fact that "its effects are so profound and present from the start" (Rawls 1971, 7). For us, this translates into a requirement that we attend to all those aspects of the social structure that exert a profound and pervasive effect on the *development of each of the essential dimensions of human well-being, separately and in combination under actual social conditions.*

While the importance of political, social, economic, and certainly legal institutions should not be understated, we do not take an *exclusively* institutional view of the basic social structure. Social conventions and customs have similarly profound and pervasive effects on human development. We view our account of justice as having strong affinities with an older, established tradition of social thought. In *On Liberty,* Mill notes that "[t]he despotism of custom is everywhere the standing hindrance to human advancement" (Mill 1991). Elsewhere, in *The Subjection of Women,* Mill makes the case that it is not only the legal [i.e., institutional] subordination of women that interferes with human development. The "mental chains" imposed by custom and convention also interfere with the many-sided development of human faculties and with the very possibility of fully developed human relationships. Mill concludes "that custom, however universal it may be, affords in this case no presumption, and ought not to create any prejudice, in favor of the arrangement which places women in social and political subjection to men" (Mill 1986, 22). The prevalent norms regarding gender roles, responsibilities, and aptitudes serve as structural barriers that limit what some will demand for themselves and understand as appropriate moral claims in relation to others. Social customs affect more than material well-being. They affect also the moral relationships between persons. The respect of others and the development of sympathetic identification with and attachment to others are necessary for forging intimate relationships and sustaining bonds of justice.

2.5 The Main Alternatives

Theories of justice, as well as theories of morality generally, can begin with different assumptions about human well-being. Some, including Rawls's well-known theory, attempt to work with minimal assumptions. Rawls largely leaves such matters to individual judgment, preferring to concentrate on the means by which individuals pursue their own ends, whatever they happen to be. Others offer a rich account of human well-being, including certain versions of traditional natural law theory that infer the existence of natural rights from detailed accounts of the proper ends of human activity (Finnis 1980). Welfarist theories, developed for application both within egalitarian theories of justice and utilitarian moral theory, reduce human well-being in all of its dimensions to a common denominator such as mental states or preference satisfaction. Our theory is one that is intended as an alternative to all of these approaches, and we owe a considerable debt to the capabilities approaches of Amartya Sen and Martha Nussbaum. However, we part company with both Sen and Nussbaum in both our choice of nomenclature and in our substantive judgments of what justice requires with regard to securing human well-being.

Well-Being as Welfare

The principal alternatives among welfarist theories include mental state and preference satisfaction accounts (Griffin 1986). On the mental state account, a person's welfare consists in her having the right mental states, namely the experience of pleasure and the absence of pain or happiness. While this is perhaps the oldest approach within utilitarian moral theory, it is less influential today. We consider it below only insofar as it demonstrates some of the reasons both it and other utilitarian attempts to reduce all dimensions of well-being to a single metric are implausible.

By contrast, many current utilitarians, including neoclassical economists, as well as some egalitarians who take as their object the equalization of welfare, adopt a preference-satisfaction account of welfare. All share the assumption that, because of the enormous diversity in the sources of well-being, what makes a life go well is explicable only insofar as it involves the satisfaction of the preferences of the individual whose life it is. Maximization (for utilitarians) or equalization (for egalitarians) of the satisfaction of preferences is solely determinative of what counts as moral or immoral (or just or unjust). There are no further moral constraints on what preferences count.

Critics of preference-satisfaction accounts are troubled by this conclusion. They argue that such theories make no room for the possibility that some preferences may be repugnant, such as those of the racist or the sadist, and hence ought not count (Powers 1994).

Others object to preference-satisfaction versions of welfarism because of what is called the social hijacking objection (Rawls 1982, 168–169; Dworkin 1981a). Theories that employ a conception of individual well-being that depends inherently upon differences in personal satisfaction means that those with expensive tastes, say, for fine foods and wine, count on a par with those whose preferences are for the satisfaction of basic or more urgent needs. The more important goal of morality, or of justice in particular, should be the narrower aim of helping those whose well-being is low, not the satisfaction of exotic tastes.

Some preferences do not deserve to count on a par with others because they are adaptive preferences, or ones shaped unduly by unjust social circumstances (Elster 1982). Through a process of socialization into inferiority, some acquire self-sacrificing preferences or preferences that are not in their genuine self-interest. When persons adapt their preferences to oppressive social conditions they may lose the ability to see that their own preferences are incompatible with their own interests or to see that they serve the interests of their oppressors.

Repugnant preferences, expensive preferences, and adaptive preferences are problems for both utilitarian and egalitarian theories that take preference satisfaction as the sole criterion of well-being (Griffin 1994). The kind of problem identified in each of these objections is that such theories allow morally irrelevant information to count in determining what is moral or immoral, just or unjust.

A further problem for welfarist theories of both sorts is that they also exclude morally relevant information. Robert Nozick asks us to imagine that we might be plugged into "an experience machine" whereby our brains would be stimulated in ways that give us the mental states of doing certain things without actually doing them. What is apparent on reflection is that we want also to do certain things and not be a passive receptor of pleasurable mental states. The preference-satisfaction account fares no better. We might suppose that instead of an experience machine we could plug into a preference-satisfaction machine and things we desire to have happen would simply happen. For example, we typically want our children to be taken care of, but our preference for such an outcome is not the whole story. We also value our role in caring for our children ourselves. The objection is similar to the one lodged against the mental-state accounts in that the central role of the agent is left out of the accounts. Just as we want more than the experience of having lived a life, we want not only the satisfaction of our preferences for certain outcomes, but also our own participation in bringing about some of those outcomes. In sum, both welfarist accounts leave out something very often of great importance to well-being. In many instances, what we want is to be a certain kind of person, one who not only has certain kinds of experiences or has certain preferences satisfied, but someone for whom one's good consists in what we *can do and be* (Nozick 1974, 42–45).

Primary Goods

In Rawls's theory, justice is not directly concerned with the realization of human well-being under any description. It is concerned with how the basic structure of society distributes certain primary goods, which he defines as including "rights, liberties and opportunities, income and wealth, and the social bases of self-respect" (Rawls 1971, 62). In themselves, they are said to be neutral among competing conceptions of the good. They are the goods everyone "is presumed to want," whatever one's conception of the good, because they are necessary requirements for the achievement of any end. The upshot is what Rawls labels a "thin theory of the good" which, unlike a full or comprehensive theory of the good, neither assesses the moral worth of final ends, nor establishes a "perfectionist ideal" of "human excellences" for which all are expected to strive, independent of social role, natural talents, and personal inclinations (Rawls 1971, 396–442).

Rawls's theory differs in its implications from the welfarist alternatives and from the emphasis our theory places on specific dimensions of well-being, each of which matters directly to justice. Rawls's Difference Principle, which governs the distribution of wealth and income in his scheme, permits inequalities only when such inequalities work to the greatest advantage of the least-well off persons in society. The principle, Rawls claims, is not harnessed to any concerns about the potential for inequality in welfare (measured either by preference satisfaction or desirable mental states achieved) or inequality of individual ability to convert resources into ultimate well-being. His is a conception that emphasizes the fact that people have both different views of the good and different capacities to achieve well-being. He concludes that each individual should be held responsible for his or her own ends and the adjustment of means to the realization of those ends each judges most important. As a consequence, for Rawls, justice ought not be concerned with the problem of unequal preference satisfaction or unequal happiness. Nor should it mark out specific goods for distributive priority over others or denominate any specific dimensions of well-being as more important than others for society to seek to advance for everyone (Rawls 1982).

Some of the earliest and most illuminating commentary on Rawls' theory came from economists, most notably Kenneth Arrow and Amartya Sen, whose practical test cases for evaluating the theory frequently came from reflection on health and health care inequalities (Arrow 1973; Sen 1979). The criticisms, however, pull in opposing directions. Arrow points to the potential "bottomless pit" problem. If the Difference Principle were applied on the basis of giving priority to the medically worst off (as opposed to the economically worst off, as Rawls's theory in fact requires), the needs of the medically worst off would be so severe and so expensive to meet that the devotion of social resources to this one dimension of well-being, perhaps without ever achieving great benefits, would leave too few resources left over for addressing other dimensions of well-being.

Sen's criticism is quite the opposite. He argues that "Rawls takes primary goods as the embodiment of advantage, rather than taking advantage to be a relationship between persons and goods" (Sen 1979, 158). Building on his own work in developmental economics, Sen's point is that what matters is what people can actually do with those goods. The ultimate concern of justice, then, according to Sen, is on the well-being or "quality of life to be assessed in terms of the capability to achieve valuable functionings" (Sen 1993, 31). Functionings represent "the various things that he or she can do or be in leading a life" (Sen 1993, 31). He includes a variety of separate metrics by which we can assess how well a life is going. They include such things as the ability to meet nutritional requirements, to be educated, to live without shame, to have self-respect, to be sheltered, and to escape avoidable disease (Sen 1983, 163).

Sen also drew upon health differentials as an example of his critique. Some persons have few medical care needs over a lifetime while others require expensive treatments merely to survive. Still others need constant care to overcome or ameliorate functional impediments. The costs of meeting those needs vary widely as well. The upshot is that, even if everyone were entitled to equal shares of wealth and income—and not merely some additional distributional priority provided by the Difference Principle—preventable and perhaps large differences in health status that seem intuitively unjust will persist under the application of Rawls's theory.

A Modified Rawlsian Theory

One influential strategy for preserving the basic Rawlsian scheme while meeting, in part, some of Sen's objections, at least in the realm of health-related well-being, is Norman Daniels's account of just health care. His strategy involves an elaboration of Rawls's account of the principle of Fair Equality of Opportunity by building upon its fairly robust distributive implications. Rawls notes that "[i]n pursuit of this principle greater resources might be spent on the education of the less rather than the more intelligent" (Rawls 1971, 101). The rationale for this conclusion is the assumption that education has special strategic value for ensuring equality of opportunity. Daniels adds health care to education as a distinct category of resources also having special strategic importance for equality of opportunity. His addition is facilitated by a shift in two assumptions. First, Daniels modifies Rawls's theory by dropping the assumption that we are all more or less comparably functioning mature adults. In Daniels's account, there are considerable differences in health and, accordingly, considerable differences in the level of resources needed to ensure comparable opportunities. Second, the kinds of opportunities that Fair Equality of Opportunity is meant to protect are broadened to encompass the fundamental interest we all have in forming and revising our life plans (Daniels 1985, 28). Health care thus joins education in occupying a privileged strategic role in ensuring equality of opportunity, even more broadly construed.

Daniels's account is an important improvement over other resource-based theories that leave one's share of health-affecting resources to the vagaries of the distribution of personal wealth and income. There are, however, significant limitations to his view. For Daniels, the value of health only becomes the focus of justice *indirectly*, insofar as it matters to Fair Equality of Opportunity. Arguably, however, a comprehensive theory of justice ought to value health *for its own sake*, as an important part of the conditions for human flourishing. Health may be adversely affected without seriously compromising one's opportunities to live out a reasonable range of life plans, yet these setbacks may raise considerations of justice in their own right. Consider, for example, relief of pain and suffering and palliative care. These health concerns would not be considered matters of justice under Daniels's account unless they occur during a stage of life in which major life plans are affected and the pain and suffering is great enough that it undermines those life plans (Buchanan 1984; Gutmann 1981). The absence of a direct commitment to a conception of health as an important dimension of well-being relevant to justice leaves Daniels's theory vulnerable to charges that it cannot adequately account for ordinary intuitions about what a just health policy would entail.

An important contribution of Daniels's approach, from our perspective, is the relaxation of the Rawlsian assumption that the subjects of justice are conceived of as mature, healthy adults. Our shift to a nonideal theory generalizes this understanding of differences among persons in real-world contexts. We are engaged in the task of spelling out the job of justice for persons who *do* vary greatly in their basic needs and vulnerabilities—who are children as well as adults, ill as well as healthy. Attention to the distribution of income and wealth, under the Difference Principle, a principle of fair opportunity, or some other algorithm for income distribution, by itself, is not plausible for our real-world task. One reason is the fact of human diversity. "We differ in age, sex, physical and mental health, bodily prowess, intellectual abilities, climatic circumstances, epidemiological vulnerability, social surroundings, and in many other respects" (Sen 1992, 28). We care not abstractly about the distributive shares each person would think fair, absent any awareness of his or own needs; we ask first what the needs are and work backward toward some account of the just distributive share of material resources.

2.6 Capabilities, Functioning, and Well-Being

Our theory of justice has many affinities with and owes a considerable intellectual debt to capabilities theories as developed by Amartya Sen and Martha Nussbaum. However, for a variety of reasons we prefer a somewhat different terminology and reach some considerably different conclusions about how best to characterize the central interests in human well-being. We find many of the insights about the importance of what persons can do and be compelling, but we find the language of capabilities and functioning confusing. We view the emphasis on capabilities rather than functioning as misplaced, and we find the emphasis on the capabilities that individuals may exercise if they so choose an inadequate way of accommodating the moral significance of choice and responsibility for well-being.

One of the most compelling insights of the capabilities approach is its shift of attention away from the means (e.g., resources) for achieving well-being to what persons "can do and be." Nozick's critique of the welfarist theories showed that, because they did not take into consideration what we could do and be, they rested on an implausible account of the outcomes about which we should be most concerned. Sen's critique of the primary-goods approach similarly showed that disavowing any commitment to the relevant outcomes we should strive for also fails to give adequate attention to the moral importance of what we can do and be.

There is a crucial ambiguity between functioning and capability that has led to some measure of confusion. For many of the dimensions of well-being on our list, a central concern is for certain desirable states—being secure in our person, being healthy, being respected, and being a self-determining person. It is a stretch of language to describe them all as functionings, for example, in the case of health. While some health states are readily describable in functionalist terms, being free from pain is better understood simply as a desirable state. So a part of what we can be—being healthy—is more clearly expressed in the language of desirable states of being rather than in the language of functionings.

We also value the things that we can do, not just the states of well-being—for example, exercising our reason and forming bonds of attachment. Many of these valuable dimensions of well-being can be expressed in terms of what we can do or in terms of what we can be, each revealing an important aspect of what may often matter morally in the realization of a certain kind of good. Take, for example, the differing ways John Finnis treats practical and theoretical reason. Finnis includes knowledge on his list of what he calls basic human goods. Knowledge is the fruit of a valuable human activity that we describe under the heading of theoretical reasoning. Knowledge is, in his own terms, an "achievement-word" (Finnis 1980, 59). Finnis prefers this to terms such as "understanding, pursuit, and the realization of truth" for the reason that they are accounts of the "pursuit of the value" and not "the value itself" (Finnis 1980, 82). The locus of value is thus said to lie in an outcome, not in the exercise of a capacity or capability. Compare, however, Finnis's account of another basic good on his list, "practical reasonableness." By that term he means to emphasize the fact that "there is a basic good in being able to bring one's own intelligence to bear effectively (in practical reasoning that issues in action)" (Finnis 1980, 88). In the first case, the active element or what we do as an integral element of realizing the good is downplayed while it is given emphasis in the second. In our view, theoretical reason matters not only because of the desirability of the outcomes or states of being (being knowledgeable), but also because a morally significant aspect of our well-being consists in our active role exercising our essential human capabilities, thereby bringing about those states.

Although the contrast between capability and functioning is meant to capture the dual importance of being and doing in assessing one's well-being, the language of functionings is not sufficiently illuminating. We think it is better to simply note that there are distinct dimensions of well-being and that, for each dimension, a part of its value lies in what states are achieved and another part often consists in our active role in bringing the states about.

The ambiguity in the capabilities and functioning language has the potential to be misleading in another respect. It can lead to some confusion in how we understand its practical implications. For example, Sen often says that the focus of egalitarian concern is equal capabilities to achieve certain functions, rather than equal levels of functioning. "Capability," he says, "is primarily the freedom to achieve valuable functionings" (Sen 1992, 49; see also Sen 1985, 200). However, as G. A. Cohen observes, the focus of the theory is not on the value of exercising some capability but the achievement of desirable states of well-being, that is, of functionings (G. Cohen 1993). He notes further that the fundamental focus of egalitarian concern is not always an individual's capabilities, such as being able to nourish oneself, but rather the value of being well-nourished. Babies, for example, do not feed themselves. Being "free from" hunger and disease often has little to do with any capability having been exercised by individuals.

Sen's reply is that he intends a conceptual priority of functionings and that, accordingly, valuable "capabilities are defined derivatively from functionings," but he argues that capabilities should occupy the central place in political and social analysis (Sen 1993, 38, 45; cf. Nussbaum 2000).

He observes that what makes us morally concerned about the hunger of a poor person who is starving, and not the hunger of a rich person who is fasting, is the difference in their capabilities. One lacks the capability to achieve a valuable functioning while the other has the capability but chooses not to exercise it (Sen 1993, 45).

While the emphasis on capabilities rather than functionings makes some sense for adults, there are instances of the sort that Cohen identifies in which the focus of justice will not be upon the functional capabilities, but upon actual functioning. In the case of many of the dimensions on our list, the development of the associated capabilities in adulthood will depend substantially on whether the social order secures adequate levels of *actual* functioning for children. For the young, then, we are necessarily concerned about health, reasoning abilities, and attachments, in part because they will develop properly, if at all, only if nurtured and secured in an appropriate developmental stage.

Moreover, securing well-being for children can only be done by the assistance of others and through the existence of social conditions favorable to their development. Dimensions such as security in their persons and being respected also require the actions of others; their value for children does not therefore depend centrally on what they can do. For a variety of reasons, for children, the priority is reversed. It is therefore misleading to assign central place in political and social analysis to the capabilities when, in all likelihood, much of what will matter most in terms of justice will turn out to be what we do for children. (We make this case in more detail in chapters 3 and 4.)

There are other reasons to doubt the plausibility of giving priority to capabilities over actual functionings, even for adults. For some capabilities such as Sen's capability to be well-nourished, he claims that at least "for adult citizens," the freedom to achieve well-being "may be more relevant to state policy ... than well-being achievement" (Sen 1993, 36). Similarly, Sen elsewhere notes that "the central feature of well-being is the ability to achieve valuable functionings" (Sen 1985, 200). Martha Nussbaum also endorses this general conclusion, noting that the state (the city-state in Aristotle's theory) "aims at enabling people to live well" and that the "goal is a certain sort of capability—the capability to function well if one so chooses" (Nussbaum 1988, 160).

We think that even for adults, these generalizations are unwarranted, at least for the dimensions of well-being we take to be central to justice. Even for adults, our active participation in bringing about our own well-being is not definitive of our well-being. Well-being consists of being in some state or condition, such as being healthy, being respected, or leading a self-determining life. Being healthy matters to our well-being whether or not that state is achieved by our action or by the action, say, of governmental bodies that secure for us potable water. Being respected requires that others exercise their capabilities for respect. Being self-determining is in part a consequence of what we do, what capacities of reason we develop, for example, but in large measure it also is a function of the social structure and the role others play in making possible the achievement of that aspect of our well-being.

Moreover, for most of the dimensions on our list, the focus on "capability of achieving it if one wishes" misunderstands the central aims of justice. While there is some truth in the notion that a part—but only a part—of what matters in being healthy is room to pursue our own health objectives if and to the extent that we wish, most of our dimensions are quite different. We want to be respected by ourselves and by others, not simply for us and others to have the capability to exercise respect if we, or they, so choose. We want to form attachments to others for our own sake and for reasons of sustaining just institutions and practices. What we want is the success of these attachments, not simply that some can form them if they so choose. Justice requires not just the capability for attachment if individuals wish to exercise it; rather it is essential for the capability to be developed and exercised for the success of other-regarding morality. We typically want to be secure in our person, not just to have that capability if we so choose. While to some degree both health and reason are matters for which the individual is largely the proper judge of how much achievement is worth pursuing, even here the emphasis on capabilities is misplaced. In some sufficient measure, the actual development and exercise of reason is essential to the functioning of society and the well-being of others, no less than respect. The same might be said of a certain level of good health. The moral importance of each of these dimensions, therefore, is inaccurately accounted for as centrally concerned with development of capabilities that individuals can exercise if they choose. The central concern of justice, then, is with achievement of well-being, not the freedom or capability to achieve well-being.

The real distinction that the capabilities emphasis seems meant to capture lies beyond that of deciding between capabilities and actual functionings. What is relevant for public policy and political theory is the difference in how well-being is brought about and how we ought to define the legitimate role of others, including the agents of the state, in bringing about valuable outcomes. We cannot achieve many things for others, but we can do things that support or enable others to achieve those outcomes themselves. For example, David Copp notes that "although the state can hardly provide people with self-respect, companionship, and social acceptance and recognition, it may design social institutions that enhance the ability of people to meet these psychological and social needs" (Copp 1992, 252). We can design institutions that enable persons to be more likely to have and exercise their capabilities for affiliation and respect, and this is the outcome that justice aims for. At bottom, we care centrally about well-being, but we recognize also that many societal duties related to bringing it about involve a supportive role.

It is important to note that our account of well-being itself, since it includes respect for persons and the value of self-determination, sets further limits on what others might justly do to bring about good outcomes. This, rather than the central importance of capabilities, is what must be kept in mind. The language of well-being is adequate to that political task, and additionally it allows us to see more clearly the senses in which both what we can do and what we can be might mean more concretely.

2.7 Relativism, Moral Imperialism, and Political Neutrality

Moral Relativism

The relativist claims that there are no universally applicable standards by which individual actions, social practices, and institutional arrangements can be evaluated. The challenge to the capabilities account is the claim that there are no universally applicable standards by which we can identify which functionings are the valuable ones. Similarly, the challenge to our view is the claim that there are no universally applicable standards by which the essential dimensions of well-being can be identified and by which social practices and institutional arrangements can be judged as just or unjust. That there are no *universally applicable* standards is a much stronger claim than the purportedly factual (which may or may not be true) claim that there are no *universally accepted* standards. The relativist challenge is meant not simply to deny that we can offer arguments that can convince those who disagree with us. It is meant to undermine our confidence in our own moral judgments. The relativist position is that once we concede that there are no universally applicable standards, then we must also concede that any social practice, institution, or social structure is as just as any other.

Nussbaum notes that an urgent moral question posed by the relativist is, "What are the functionings with which...[society] should be concerned, and how do we arrive at our list of functionings?" (Nussbaum 1988, 174). If this question cannot be answered satisfactorily, then the relativist has made some progress in undermining confidence in the basis of our own judgments and their universal applicability.

A part of Nussbaum's own answer is that her account is universally "objective in the sense that it is justified by reference to reasons that do not derive merely from local traditions and practices" (Nussbaum and Sen, 1993, 243). And it is essentialist in the sense that it aims to get at "features of humanness that lie beneath all local traditions and are there to be seen whether or not they are in fact recognized" (Nussbaum 1993, 243). Like the Rawlsian account of primary goods, Nussbaum's valuable functionings are said to be "such that it is always rational to want them whatever else one wants" (Nussbaum 2000, 88–89).

Nussbaum invokes also a style of moral reasoning known as reflective equilibrium (Rawls 1971). In this style, we start with some bedrock of shared experience within a culture and perhaps supplement that with experience accumulating across cultures as well. We revise and refine our considered judgments with the expectation that we can attain some degree of coherence and stability among them and that our confidence will increase as they reveal themselves to be mutually supporting. To this end, Nussbaum claims that some judgments are "more in keeping with the totality of our evidence and the totality of our wishes for flourishing life than others" (Nussbaum 1993, 261). As Sen similarly suggests, for some dimensions of human well-being, the burden of argument rests squarely on the relativist. The relativist must show, contrary to our considered judgments, that such things as good health, reasoning ability, and respect are not things that we all want whatever else we might want. The suggestion is that such judgments are so much within the core, and not the periphery, of our self-understandings as to be highly resistant to revision or reasonable doubt.

These arguments offer a good beginning, but the relativist and the proponent both have more to say in marking out their differences. The relativist can respond that reflective equilibrium is more likely to be a reliable guide to the moral landscape of one's own local tradition than any reliable guide to universally applicable standards. Bringing one's own judgments into coherence is certainly admirable, but the relativist will still object that such an exercise brings us no closer to showing that the standards reaffirmed on reflection are anything other than the artifact of allegiance to local custom.

A more detailed reply to the relativist, which we endorse, simply asserts that moral reflections, at any level of generality or particularity, necessarily start and end *in medias res.* That we are unable to convince the skeptic or the person who demands of us a defense of standards of judgment that could win the support of those who do not share our reasoning tradition is not the problem for some views of moral epistemology as it is for others. An older tradition since Descartes was easily impressed by the relativist's challenge. Absent some foundation or bedrock of shared starting points that could compel agreement across cultures, then none of one's own firmest commitments and beliefs were thought secure. The relativist gets a foothold of doubt only within a framework of justification that shares the relativist's premise, namely, that confidence in one's judgments can be attained only by appeal to standards that lie outside of one's epistemic tradition.

An alternative account of moral epistemology, which we endorse, does not share that premise. There is simply no plausible way of understanding what standards of justification external to our own epistemic practices might look like. The only standards to which we have access are our standards. To think otherwise is simply an artifact of an intellectually discredited foundationalist approach to moral epistemology that falsely assumes that the relativist challenge can be met on its own terms (Rorty 1991). Social practices and institutional arrangements can be assessed only from within one's own tradition, enlarged perhaps by critical and reflective dialogue with other traditions. At bottom, however, argument never reaches some terminus point at which the relativist will be convinced, or where we can expect the ultimate foundations of our commitments to be laid bare in such as way as to compel universal agreement in judgment.

The residue of the relativist objection is the charge of "ethnocentrism," as Rorty reminds us, or the risk of moral imperialism when our view is applied to other cultures. This is a problem in itself, but it does not show that our conclusions are not reasonable to apply to other cultures, or that we must conclude with the relativist that the limitations of our reasoning means that any standard is as good as any other (Rorty 1989). It is therefore important to distinguish what kind of judgments our view does and does not license.

Our view is not as prescriptive in its recommendations to an individual for how to live a good life as, for example, Aristotle's political theory. We do not answer the question of what the best life for individuals and political associations is with an account of the *summum bonum*, or single, best-integrated conception of the intellectual and practical virtues rendered in fine detail. Whether the best kind of life is one of detached contemplation or engaged political participation (claims for which one alternately finds arguments in different parts of Aristotle's work) may retain a measure of residual philosophical interest, but not for our theory of justice or for what it implies about the responsibility of the state or bodies charged with implementing international law or human rights accords.

Nor is our theory especially prescriptive about matters that fall squarely within the domain of personal morality, domains that liberals are reluctant to enter. It does not tell us whom to love, whether to marry, or whether and how to reproduce. Much of personal morality is therefore left open and beyond the reach of what our theory is intended to assess. It does tell us, for example, that social institutions and conventions are to be judged just or unjust in light of how well they contribute to generating and sustaining capacities for attachment, sympathetic identification with others, and respect for self and others. Such a view does effectively rule out a number of possible ways of life that other cultures take as valuable. Consider the female genital mutilation example. Suppose that, contrary to fact, such practices were performed only on mature adult women, not upon girls. Suppose further that the weight of social pressure is not so great, or that the economic options for those not conforming to such customs are not so severe as to negate any prospect that women in this culture are self-determining. One might then judge that a culture in which some women participate in such practices is not thereby unjust, even if one judges those individual decisions as repugnant and incompatible with important dimensions of human well-being. However, such practices, when imposed on children, within an oppressive patriarchal society in which women's options are constrained in ways that men's options are not, are unjust. They are incompatible with women's chances for an important aspect of sexual health and functioning, inconsistent with any minimal degree of self-determination that a society should afford to all of its citizens, and, when forcibly performed, a gross violation of personal security.

The Principle of Political Neutrality

When applied within our own culture, our theory is subject to the further charge that it violates a principle of political neutrality that many have claimed central to the liberal political tradition (Dworkin 1985, 237–92). The doctrine of political neutrality itself is open to a number of divergent interpretations, but one of the least controversial versions supposes that government policy should not intentionally favor one way of life over others. A variety of arguments have been put forth for this view (Larmore 1987). The relativist will argue for neutrality of intention on skeptical grounds that, because there are no independent standards for adjudicating between competing ideals, government should not take sides on controversial issues. Others argue on pragmatic grounds, claiming that, as an empirical matter, the depth of disagreement and the likely bad consequences of taking sides will undermine civil peace. Libertarians argue that respect for individual autonomy dictates that government policy should leave as much room as possible for individual choice about how best to pursue the good life. A Millian argument for minimal governmental intervention in the lives of its citizens claims that the best way to discover the good is to allow citizens to conduct their own experiments in living, such that the cumulative effect will be firmer knowledge of what does and what does not produce well-being.

The arguments based on skepticism, the pragmatic requirements for civil peace, the libertarian's deference to individual choice, and the experimentalist approach to knowledge of the good are all directed at worries about the lack of neutrality of a certain kind. Each is aimed primarily at comprehensive conceptions of the good and thus articulates reasons that the state should not take sides on large questions about which there is great controversy and which divide us.

Ours is not a comprehensive conception of the good, however, and it does not impose on governments a duty to use their institutional power to compel citizens to conform to some grand vision of what an ideal good life is. Our view takes sides on some important elements of well-being, including a view of the kinds of moral relationships among persons that justice requires, but it does not entail a commitment to a strong expressivist role for the state. An expressivist account views the state as a set of institutional arrangements expressing, reflecting, and reinforcing a comprehensive conception of the good, for example, that of a particular religious tradition (Larmore 1987). The expressivist claim is that, because of the powerful, perhaps even unique, role of the state as an instrument of socialization, some of its citizens' deepest convictions require taking sides on these matters in order to sustain commitment. Apart from whether such claims are true, our view is incompatible. Our commitment to the importance of respect and self-determination is sufficient reason for the rejection of an expressivist account of the state. The proponent of political neutrality by definition opposes state imposition of a comprehensive conception of the good. That our view travels the same road on this matter as the proponent of political neutrality shows some inherent limits to the political neutrality doctrine itself, even under the weaker, neutral intent interpretation. No plausible principle of neutrality is neutral with respect to all conceptions of the good, and it is decidedly in opposition to conceptions of the good that foreclose cultural pluralism and individual diversity. Our commitment to self-determination, one item on our list that some may view as more controversial than, say, health or reason, turns out to be no more of a problem for us than for most other liberal theories. To the extent that they too reject the state imposition of comprehensive conceptions of the good, they cannot complain of our insistence on the importance of self-determination.

2.8 Justice and Basic Human Rights

Justice, as it is understood within moral and political theory generally, connotes a special branch of morality embodying claims of special moral urgency. They are often described as claims of absolute, or at least very significant, weight, such that they are not readily overridden by other moral concerns, or even overall social utility (Dworkin 1977). Such claims are often denominated as rights, and they impose duties on others for their satisfaction. To say that an action, government policy, institution, or social practice is unjust implies that some duties with respect to their satisfaction have been breached and that a rights violation has occurred. The language of rights, accordingly, is a frequent short expression for articulating the matters of moral significance central to justice.

The language of justice and rights supplies the common idiom for both legal and moral vocabularies, and their use within the law illustrates some of what many find puzzling about their use within morality. Legal rights, according to one familiar account, make claims on others, not because their justification can be found independently of human institutions, but solely because they are a matter of human convention (Hart 1963). Legal rights, then, are often claimed to be purely institutional in nature. Many legal rights are of a type known as relational rights. They arise in the context of some transaction involving a legally recognized relationship between specific parties. For example, rights might arise out of a contract between two parties. The law also recognizes some nonrelational rights that impose duties on everyone. These tend to be limited to liberty rights, or rights against interference with one's person or property, and not rights that impose duties on others for assistance in achieving some aspect of individual well-being.

Universal natural rights, or rights that are more commonly referred to now as basic human rights, often differ from the institutional, nonrelational model that is familiar in law. Basic human rights are noninstitutional in character. They have their origin in morality, and thus they are not strictly an artifact of institutional arrangements. Moreover, many discussions of basic human rights include some positive rights, or rights to assistance. They impose duties on everyone because they are claims based on one's universal humanity, not on any special relationship established between identifiable parties.

A defense of basic human rights requires work on two important fronts. The first issue regards the origins and basis for identification of the basic human rights, if, as most proponents claim, they are not of a purely institutional origin such that they might be known, for example, by reading statutes. The second concern is how such rights, especially the positive rights, can be understood as imposing duties on everyone, including persons who do not fall under some legal jurisdiction and on those persons for whom there is no clear relational connection. It is not our task to develop a comprehensive account of basic human rights. However, we think that our account of the dimensions of human well-being can serve as a useful starting point for answering these two questions.

Nature and Origin of Basic Human Rights

A defense of basic human rights requires an explication of the justificatory basis for those claims identified as urgent enough to be counted as rights. One way of explicating the basis of rights is known as the benefit or protected-interests conception. It supposes that the main function of rights is to give special weight to some interests in preference to others. As Joseph Raz defines it, "X has a right if and only if X can have rights, and other things being equal, an aspect of X's well-being (his interest) is a sufficient reason for holding some person(s) to be under a duty" (Raz 1986, 166). What such an account needs for completion is some way to decide what those especially weighty interests are. Many natural rights theories, for example, start with some such account of human good and argue for their special importance (Finnis 1980). Similarly, our account of the essential dimensions of well-being can be construed as possible candidates for explicating the underlying justificatory basis for basic human rights. One of the main reasons for thinking that our account of the essential dimensions of well-being might fill this theoretical role is that we think that each one meets a test Nussbaum set for her list of valuable functionings. Following Rawls's test for identifying primary goods, her claim is that the justification for each item on her list is "such that it is always rational to want them whatever else one wants" (Nussbaum 2000, 88–89).

One objection to the interest conception as an account of basic human rights is that it is not the best way of explicating the function of rights. The primary competitor is known as the choice theory. It supposes that the core function of rights is to secure individual liberty to make certain protected choices, free from the interference of others, not to license some positive rights to assistance. The case for the choice conception derives in part from the recognition that rights function as severe constraints on human action. As Ronald Dworkin puts it, if rights are not viewed as absolute constraints, they are at least "trumps" that set some threshold limits to trade-offs such that the pursuit of other aims, including greater social utility, are constrained (Dworkin 1977). Our list contains essential dimensions that would be the basis for both positive rights and liberty rights. The implication of expanding rights to include positive rights is that the pursuit of some goals will necessarily take priority over the pursuit of many others. While constraining certain forms of interference may seem worth the potential loss of social utility, some worry that an enumeration of positive rights unduly inflates the currency of rights and places too many constraints on the pursuit of well-being in all its forms.

Worries about rights inflation are significant, but so too are worries about unmet needs. Even the choice conception results in a system of liberty rights that imposes potentially large costs of compliance on parties, and ultimately it too must offer its own account of which interests are of such moral significance that they warrant treating some choices as protected against trade-offs in the pursuit of other goals. As H. L. A. Hart, a major proponent of the choice conception concedes, "the core notion of rights is neither individual choice nor individual benefit but basic or fundamental needs" (Hart 1982, 193). This is, in fact, the aspiration motivating our list of essential dimensions of human well-being.

Basic Human Rights as Nonrelational

A further difficulty for the line of argument we have proposed for justifying basic human rights, including some positive rights, lies in the fact that, if there are rights in virtue of our status as human beings, then by definition they must have their origins in some justification other than a relation between right-holders and those on whom a duty is imposed. Their origins must lie elsewhere, namely, in some account of human need that is universal in the way that Hart contends. Nonrelational rights are (a) needed by everyone, (b) against everyone, and (c) irrespective of differences in individual ends or projects (Lomasky 1987). Loren Lomasky claims that only liberty rights plausibly meet these criteria. The need for liberty rights is universal. We all need the noninterference guaranteed by liberty rights. Noninterference must be provided by all of us if its benefits are to be available to any of us. The value that noninterference has for each of us is wholly independent of the particular ends each of us seeks to advance. Liberty rights thus depend on our status as human beings, not on any relationship between specific right-holders and specific parties having duties to satisfy the claims of the right-holders.

The first argument against some positive rights, such as those pertaining to health or reasoning, for example, is that, while these claims might require something from others for their satisfaction, they can be provided by (or through the efforts of) particular persons. Hence, they fail to meet the second criterion of the nonrelational test. Their satisfaction does not require the imposition of duties on everyone. The second argument is that, because what we might need from others is not independent of our different projects and ends, such rights fail to meet the third criterion. In short, it is claimed that, if there are any basic human rights, they are strictly liberty rights because only they are fully nonrelational.

Both arguments rest on questionable assumptions. The first argument would be convincing only if it is the case that *everything* needed to satisfy a rights claim can be provided by oneself or by particular persons. For all of the dimensions of well-being we have detailed in this chapter, this claim does not seem plausible. For each dimension of well-being—respect, health, reason, and so on—we all require the assistance of others in the achievement of a sufficient level. We need a healthful environment, conditions conducive to learning, the respect of others, and so on. At minimum, we require favorable or advantageous circumstances, including social conditions that facilitate the development and preservation of each dimension of well-being. At most, what the critic's argument shows is that whatever positive rights we have are not necessarily rights to everything necessary to meet our needs. Any plausible rights conception would have to be compatible with a plausible account of individual responsibility, but the critic must have some argument about what the best account of individual responsibility is. He cannot help himself to the categorical rejection of positive rights by assuming that each of us must go it alone.

Moreover, our argument does not assume that the duties imposed on others must be identical for everyone. In fact, it seems reasonable to us to suppose that the specific obligations will differ among those under a duty to provide assistance. Some duties to provide assistance—for example, those in the form of ensuring favorable or advantageous social circumstances— can only be discharged collectively. Collective duties might fall upon only those entities best positioned to achieve collective ends. Such duties might apply to nation states possessing the wherewithal to discharge collective duties. When the rights claimants are citizens of weak or impoverished nation states, however, institutional entities having some global responsibilities may be better positioned to satisfy such claims through collective action. This possible differentiation among duties does not entail that individuals and nongovernmental entities have no duties. Individuals may have duties that Rawls labels as duties to support just institutions (Rawls 1971). Moreover, some parties may have additional responsibilities based on rights that are relational, or specific to particular right-holders and persons under a correlative duty. These additional duties may arise as a consequence of economic transactions or political interactions that impose duties in excess of those that are imposed on everyone.

The second argument would fail if the rights based on our list of essential dimensions of well-being meet Nussbaum's test, whereby they can be defended as ones that everyone "is presumed to want," whatever one's conception of the good. If this is the case, as we think it is, then we have no need to appeal to particular plans or projects of any individual in order to justify them. Our account of well-being is thus one that is meant to provide a basis for assessing the justice of the totality of institutions and social practices that make up the basic structure. Our next task is to articulate an account of the level and forms of protection and promotion for each dimension that is required by justice.

Justice, Sufficiency,
and Systematic Disadvantage

3.1 Varieties of Egalitarianism

Our claim is that justice is concerned with securing and maintaining the
social conditions necessary for a sufficient level of well-being in all of its
essential dimensions for everyone. Our theory therefore stands in stark
contrast to both utilitarian and libertarian alternatives described in chapter
1. Utilitarians are concerned about outcomes, as are we, but the utilitarian
aims at the maximization of some aggregate measure of utility. We are
neither maximizers nor proponents of a single measure of utility. Libertarians are concerned about the underlying social conditions and how they
affect certain ideals of human well-being, as are we, but libertarians are
concerned solely with limiting the adverse effects of governmental interference with the individual's ability to exercise control over her own life.
We are concerned about a broader range of social determinants of well-being
than strictly governmental ones, and the ideals of well-being are plural
rather than unitary. Our theory, then, is *egalitarian in the broad sense.*
Theories we call egalitarian in the broad sense embrace the notion that some
kinds of inequalities stand in need of moral justification. This commitment
alone distinguishes us from both utilitarian and libertarian theories. Neither
shares the view that inequalities of any sort stand in need of justification.
An important question, however, is how our theory stands in relation to
strict egalitarian theories of justice. Strict egalitarian theories contend that
an irreducible aspect of what justice involves takes the form of a *relational
ideal.* It holds that justice always involves a concern for how some fare in
comparison to others and not simply a concern for the worst off because
they are doing badly in absolute terms (Temkin 1993, 1995; Parfit 1991,
1998). The further claim of the strict egalitarian is that justice requires
equality as the ideal of how persons fare with respect to others. Equality is
thus said to be valuable for its own sake.

While strict egalitarians differ among themselves on whether the central concern of justice ought to be outcomes or means, many welfarist theorists, resource theorists, and capabilities theorists agree that the most plausible theory of justice is some form of egalitarianism that takes equality as its theoretical aim. The claim is that they simply disagree in their answers to the question, "Equality of what?" (Sen 1979; Dworkin 1981a; G. Cohen 1989).

Egalitarians in the broad sense, however, are not quite so uniform in their accounts as the strict egalitarian picture portrays. While equality may matter for some of their concerns, they are not so thoroughgoing in their substantive commitment to equality as the theoretical ideal for all concerns. Some, including Rawls, endorse equality of civil and political liberties, as well as an abstract or formal notion of moral equality or some similar notion of equal concern and respect, but deny that, when the focus is on welfare, resources, or capabilities, justice necessarily involves the pursuit of equality. Rawls, for example, argues for equal liberties and equality in the "social bases of respect," but when it comes to the primary social goods of wealth and income, he adopts the Difference Principle, a version of the "priority for the worst off" or prioritarian principle. Accordingly, equality may be *an* aim of egalitarian theories in the broad sense, but justice does not necessarily embody a unitary set of aims. The real issue, then, is whether, and in which instances, a substantive notion of equality is the most plausible conception of the aims of justice, or whether some alternative to equality for its own sake offers a more defensible account of some of the aims of justice.

Our answers to these questions are developed along two lines. First, sufficiency of well-being, not equality of well-being, is the central aspiration of justice within our theory. However, because our theory builds upon six separate dimensions of well-being, what sufficiency requires for each will differ. For some dimensions, we argue that sufficiency itself requires equality, and for others, in some concrete social circumstances, sufficiency is threatened by inequalities among persons in some of the essential dimensions of well-being. While there are powerful objections to the pursuit of equality for its own sake, the force of such arguments depends on what is taken to be the equalisandum, or object of equalization. Since our theory assumes that sufficiency sometimes entails equality, we therefore need to know when such objections are relevant and when they are not.

Second, while our theory takes outcomes, not merely the means to their achievement, as its ultimate concerns, the obligations of ensuring a sufficient level of well-being in our nonideal theory commits us to an ancillary concern also about inequalities in means. A nonideal theory that takes sufficiency of each dimension of well-being as its positive end, therefore, needs to develop an account of its implications for evaluating inequalities in the multiple and overlapping social determinants of those dimensions of well-being. The hallmark of many of the most familiar versions of sufficiency theories of justice is the claim that, above a certain threshold, justice requires no further concern for how some fare in comparison to others with regard to income, wealth, and other means to achieving well-being. An important part of our task is to show how our enriched sufficiency theory differs from these standard alternatives. Our task is to show how our theory, with its ultimate concern for ensuring sufficiency of outcomes, retains a concern for some inequalities in the means to their achievement without necessarily being committed to an objectionable version of the strict egalitarian's ideal of equality for its own sake.

3.2 The Leveling-Down Objection

A shorthand summation of the strict egalitarian view can be found in Derek Parfit's synoptic claim: "It is bad in itself that some people are worse off than others" (Parfit 1998, 3). Critics have mounted a number of objections against the idea of pursuing equality for its own sake. One of the most familiar and influential objections against the strict egalitarian position is known as the leveling-down objection. The heart of this objection centers on the prospect that equality can be achieved by reducing the well-being of the better off (leveling down), as well as by improving the well-being of the worst off (leveling up). If equality per se is the aim, what reason have we to reject instances of leveling down? The challenge, in a nutshell, is this: What is the moral basis for favoring a state of affairs in which all are more nearly equal in some respect, even if no one is made better off and some are made much worse off? The critic thus denies that anyone should think that equality itself has even prima facie moral value in cases in which there is no one for whom life is made better (Lucas 1965, 303; Lucas 1997; Raz 1986, 235; Parfit 1991, 1998; Goodin 1995, 248).

The critic, of course, need not object to all instances of leveling down, for example, when doing so makes the worse off better off. That the well-being of some may be lowered so that the well-being of others is improved is at least a plausible outcome of a variety of imaginable theories of justice, at least when the worse off can be made substantially better off and the better off are not made substantially worse off. The problem is that a strict egalitarian's commitment to equality for its own sake does not distinguish between cases of this sort, when leveling down is a plausible requirement of justice, and cases when it is not. Accordingly, the ideal of equality is open to the charge that it is absurd or repugnant.

The leveling-down objection is a general complaint against egalitarian theories whatever is taken to be the appropriate respect in which persons should be equal. Equality of resources, welfare, capabilities, or well-being otherwise defined are theories that are subject to whatever force the objection has. A thought experiment illuminating the challenge is captured in Derek Parfit's Divided World examples. He asks us to imagine two worlds, A and B. The worlds are said to be divided in the sense that we are to assume that nothing that happens in either is the cause or consequence of what happens in the other. In world A, everyone is equal in some respect, but conditions are so miserable that life is barely worth living. In world B, the degree of inequality is considerable, but even the worst-off person is vastly better off than everyone in world A. The critic will claim that it is coun-terintuitive to conclude that world A is prima facie better than world B. The challenge is to explain what reason anyone would have for asserting that equality in itself is an attractive ideal.

Intuitions in Divided World cases can run in differing directions. Con-sider another example frequently cited by both Derek Parfit and Larry Temkin. We are again asked to imagine two divided worlds, A and B. In world A half are blind and half are sighted. In world B, all are blind. If equality per se is thought to have moral significance, then we must also think that we have at least some reason to say that world B is better than world A in at least *some* respect. Egalitarians, of course, need not conclude that, all things considered, we have greater reason to prefer world B over world A. They surely are not committed to the further conclusion that we have an obligation to blind the sighted in world A in order to produce what we must admit is valuable about world B. Although egalitarians thus can still reach the same all-things-considered judgment as their critics would reach, a decisive difference between the two views remains. Egalitarians have to concede that there is some pro tanto reason to prefer world B. By contrast, proponents of the leveling-down objection view this concession as a decisive refutation of egalitarian ideals.

3.3 The Strict Egalitarian's Pluralist Defense

The clash of intuitions about moral phenomenology, however, is not so easy to adjudicate. Consider the following analogue. Within commonsense mo-rality, most take it that there is at least some moral reason to maximize the overall good. This is not to say that commonsense morality follows the utilitarian view that utility maximization is the exclusive goal of morality. The more modest claim of commonsense morality is that utility maximi-zation has some pro tanto moral importance, but competing considerations such as the importance of individual rights that might be violated—say, intentionally killing 2 to save 20 from dying from an accident—may lead us to a different all-things-considered judgment. When framed in this way, the ideal of utility maximization looks no more or less repugnant or problematic than the ideal of equality. Only the archest opponents of utilitarianism endorse the claim that utility maximization plays no role in our moral framework (Wiggins 1980). Other critics of utilitarianism simply assert that maximization of good consequences is not the whole of morality. It is sometimes required and sometimes prohibited. John Rawls, for example, claims that consequences sometimes do matter morally and that it would be crazy to suppose otherwise (Rawls 1971).

The thrust of the egalitarians' first line of defense, therefore, is that equality can be viewed as an independent, pro tanto good or defeasible moral ideal, but they can claim also that this ideal, like many other moral ideals, may be outweighed or defeated by other ideals. Egalitarians thus acknowledge that equality, if exclusively pursued, could have terrible implications, but the fact that the equality ideal may give way to other moral considerations such as the protection of liberty is no decisive objection to viewing equality as an appropriate distributive ideal within a theory of justice (Temkin 1993, 246–282; Arneson 1989, 77). Thus, the leveling-down objection based on its inherent phenomenological repugnance is, in our view, less than conclusive.

Even if this or some other argument can remove a well-known objection to the plausibility of the claim that justice must be in part a matter of equality, and that considerations of justice sometimes give way to competing moral ideals lying *beyond* justice, strict egalitarians must also defend the positive claim that equality for its own sake, rather than some other moral notion, plays an indispensable role *within* a theory of justice. By contrast, opponents need counterarguments showing that something other than the ideal of equality underlies our moral intuitions about what justice requires and what sometimes makes inequalities unjust.

3.4 Is the Appeal to Equality Unavoidable?

Rival accounts, such as a prioritarian principle of giving priority to the worst off, suggest that something other than equality is the underlying aim. The fact that some are very badly off in some respect or that the condition of the worst off falls below some level of adequacy or sufficiency is said to be the rationale for our central concern, not equality for its own sake (Parfit 1991, 1998).

However, some argue that equality ideals are unavoidable. One argument holds that some prioritarian alternatives must in the end presuppose a commitment to equality. Nagel argues that since a priority view narrows the conditions under which inequalities may be taken as morally justified, the underlying aim must be equality (Nagel 1979, 107). The Difference Principle, Rawls's version of a priority view, for example, does permit a sacrifice by the better off for the sake of the worst off, but it does not recommend taking from the better off when their sacrifice would do no good for the worst off. Because the point of the Difference Principle is improvement of the lot of the less fortunate, not redistribution for the sake of equality, it does not license any redistribution unless the worst off are thereby improved. Moreover, giving priority to the worse off does not necessarily compress the range of inequality within society. The priority view can allow the better off to benefit greatly and the worst off to benefit only slightly. In Rawls's view, for example, a small benefit to the worst off, coupled with a great benefit to the better off, is permitted as long as the worst off group benefits as much as any other available, morally acceptable social option would make possible.

Clearly then, the priority view, even with the rather stringent Rawlsian requirement that the worst off maximally benefit, does not care about equality for its own sake, for it is in principle compatible with extreme inequalities (Parfit 1991, 1998). For each increment of welfare, resources, capabilities, or whatever accruing to the better off, we can imagine scenarios in which the increment accruing to the less well off is but a small fraction of the increment enjoyed by the better off. The priority principle thus permits the less well off to gain in absolute terms while declining in relative terms. Nothing built into the priority principle commits it to any measure of concern for inequality per se, only a concern for the improvement of the condition of the worst off. Relative inequalities, or the proportional gap between the conditions of the worst off and the better off, are of no moral concern in a view that takes its cue from an exclusive concern for improving the condition of the worst off. While many Rawlsians may hope and expect that the Difference Principle (especially when operating in tandem with the principle of Fair Equality of Opportunity) will result in a decent minimum for the worst off, the achievement of that result is not its explicit rationale. The upshot is that prioritarianism is a genuine theoretical alternative to a commitment to equality per se.

Another principle that gives some priority to the worst off is known as the sufficiency principle. It also rejects equality per se as the exclusive aim of justice, but an added attraction missing from pure prioritarianism is its explicit aim of achieving a decent minimum for the worst off. However, the sufficiency principle also holds that the duty to improve the condition of the worst off applies only until the point that the worst off rise above some level of absolute deprivation. Harry Frankfurt's account is perhaps the most familiar. He claims that justice requires that everyone has enough, or a sufficient amount, of what contributes to a good life, not that everyone has an equal share. What is morally offensive for Frankfurt is not that "some of the individuals in those situations have *less* money than others but the fact that those with less have *too little*" (Frankfurt 1987, 32). According to Frankfurt's view, the needs of the worse off are not more urgent simply because they are the needs of the comparatively worse off. He claims that "[i]f everyone had enough, it would be of no moral consequence whether some had more than others" (Frankfurt 1987, 21). Whatever priority we accord to the worse off on the sufficiency view, we do so only to the extent that what anyone has falls below a minimum absolute level. Equality, or more precisely the compression of inequality, may be a by-product of implementing a principle of economic sufficiency, as for example when progressive taxation and social safety net legislation result in a transfer of wealth from the better off to the worst off. As it is in the case of a principle giving some priority to the worst off, it is the unfortunate condition of that group that is the exclusive, morally salient concern identified by sufficiency theorists, not any desire to reduce inequality for its own sake, and surely no direct concern for inequalities that arise above the threshold defining a minimal or acceptable standard of living. Sufficiency theorists thus see the job of justice as done when the evils of absolute deprivation have been addressed, and in the most familiar versions absolute levels of deprivation are defined in terms of an economic standard of living (Frankfurt 1987; Lucas 1965; Lucas 1977).

Sufficiency theories, then, sit somewhere midway between strict egalitarianism and pure prioritarianism in the redistributional demands they make. Sufficiency theories have an advantage over other prioritarian theories in that they set some explicit minimum standards for the worst off. However, their advantages are earned at some cost to their plausibility in another respect. Recall that in section 3.1 we distinguished between the strict egalitarian's commitment to a *relational ideal*, an irreducible concern for how some fare in comparison to others, and a second, more stringent commitment that the appropriate interpretation of that ideal is *strict equality* among persons. Sufficiency theories such as Frankfurt's reject both commitments.

Prioritarian views, by contrast, can embrace relational ideals, albeit ideals that are different from strict equality. Rawls's Difference Principle is a case in point. It makes the distributive share of wealth and income available to the better off dependent on whether it maximizes the share of resources available to the worst off. The maximizing requirement builds into the principle a relational ideal in which how some fare relative to others is a matter of moral concern apart from any worry about the absolute low well-being of the worst off. Unlike Frankfurt's sufficiency principle, the concern displayed for the worst off under the Difference Principle is not exhausted once the condition of the worst off has risen above what is required for a minimally decent life. No matter how well off the worst off become, as long as they can do better still, their claims against the better off remain at full force.

The two main theoretical alternatives to strict equality seem to be at an impasse. Prioritarian theories address the intuition that justice ought to care about inequality or how some fare relative to others and not just about alleviating the absolute bad condition of the worst off, but they do not embrace explicit ideals of what a decent minimum for the worst off would require. Sufficiency theories, by contrast, make sense of our intuitions that a decent minimum should be a central part of an account of justice, not simply that some priority to the worst off is required, but once a decent minimum has been achieved, they seem unable to address residual worries about inequality, including relative inequality. While the Difference Principle thus embodies some sort of relational ideal other than strict equality, it seems no better suited than a sufficiency theory as an account of those sorts of inequalities many find most troubling. Both are compatible with a great deal of relative inequality, or a very large gap in how some fare relative to others. One need not think that the positive aim of justice is equality in order to think that something is problematic about large relative inequalities.

Our strategy in the next section is to show how, once we shift the attention of a sufficiency theory to the essential dimensions of well-being, we can accommodate the powerful, indeed central, appeal of attending first to the needs of those whose absolute well-being is below some level of sufficiency, while at the same time explaining when, and which, residual inequalities, including relative inequalities in the various social determinants (including wealth and income) of well-being, are unjust.

3.5 A Sufficiency of Well-Being Approach

The focus of sufficiency theories need not be on individual income, wealth, or other available resources. They may instead focus directly on an account of well-being that may require some identifiable bundle of resources to achieve. Joseph Raz, for example, spells out the core concern of such a sufficiency theory, indicating why and under what circumstances the concern for the worst off should be taken as central to justice. "[T]heir hunger is greater, their need more pressing, their suffering more hurtful, and therefore our concern for the hungry, the needy, the suffering, not our concern for equality, makes us give them priority" (Raz 1986, 240). As Raz's language suggests, the same sort of points Frankfurt makes can be translated into a focus on morally desired outcomes rather than the resources instrumental to their achievement.

Martha Nussbaum proposes just such a principle as a minimal requirement of a sufficiency of well-being theory of justice. She claims:

> that in certain core areas of human functioning a necessary condition of justice for a public political arrangement is that it deliver to citizens a certain basic level of capability. If people are systematically falling below the threshold in any of these core areas, this should be seen as a situation both unjust and tragic, in need of urgent attention, even if in other respects things are going well. (Nussbaum 2000, 71)

Our account of sufficiency of well-being in all of its essential dimensions agrees with Nussbaum's assessment, but in our view, taking sufficiency as the central aim of justice has a number of important implications that need careful elaboration.

The first significant point to note is that our view does not have the same implications for the distribution of wealth and income that an economic sufficiency view does. Ours is not committed to the morally problematic claim that income inequality above the level of sufficiency is irrelevant to justice, nor is it condemned to silence on such questions. Because ours is a nonideal theory that is concerned with the totality of social structure having a profound and pervasive effect on the essential dimensions of well-being, any inequality in the social determinants contributing to persons falling below a level of sufficiency necessarily will be of derivative importance. Inequalities in wealth and income, for example, or how some fare relative to others with respect to these nonultimate concerns, may be unjust according to our theory insofar as they contribute to, reinforce, or perpetuate deprivations in any of the dimensions of well-being below the level of sufficiency. Whether a particular distribution of income is in fact incompatible with securing a sufficient level of any particular dimension of well-being is a contingent matter, about which we shall have more to say later by way of some illustrative examples. The upshot, however, is that a sufficiency of well-being theory does not share in the implications of the economic sufficiency view, which finds itself unable to condemn certain economic inequalities that many find problematic. Moreover, the sufficiency of well-being view offers an important explanation of when such inequalities are unjust without recourse to some strict egalitarian view of the value of economic equality for its own sake.

The superiority of a sufficiency of well-being account, however, should not be construed as a rejection of the utility of any effort to operationalize the sufficiency notion in economic terms. The calculation of an economic measure, however, is theoretically parasitic on the development of an antecedent definition of sufficiency measured against some minimum baseline of essential human well-being. Before economists can estimate the minimum level of resources each individual would need to meet their basic needs for the essentials of life, they need some prior notion of what those minimum essentials are. Fortunately, for many aspects of well-being there is frequently substantial agreement about the general range of normal functioning, permitting widely shared judgments that below some defined threshold, someone is malnourished, inadequately sheltered, or burdened by preventable disease or disability and a shortened life span. Thus, while absolute measures of sufficiency of the essential dimensions of well-being may be controversial at crucial points, there are many uncontroversial instances in which we know that the minimal level is not met. Economic measures of sufficiency accordingly must rely on some underlying account of the essential dimensions of well-being if they are to be meaningful tools of societal appraisal.

The second implication of the shift to a sufficiency of well-being view is that it offers an explanation of when relative economic inequalities, or the magnitude of the gap between the economic status of the better off and the worse off, matter. Economic sufficiency theories take it as a given that economic inequalities, even proportionally large inequalities between the better off and the worst off, are irrelevant as long as the worst off have enough. Even the Difference Principle, which exhibits concern for how some fare relative to others, is concerned only that the gains to the better off are tied to improvements in the economic condition of the worst off. That the gains of the former vastly outstrip those of the latter is of no independent moral significance on this view. Our view differs from both inasmuch as it has the theoretical resources with which to evaluate whether and when relative inequalities may be unjust. Relative economic inequalities are unjust in our view for the same reason that economic inequalities may be deemed unjust. In both cases, inequalities are unjust if they are contingently incompatible with securing and preserving a level of sufficiency for each of the dimensions of well-being.

The problem of accounting for the injustice of some relative economic inequality on a sufficiency of resources view, but not a sufficiency of well-being approach, is illustrated in the phenomenon of competitive utilization. Expanding on insights developed by Rousseau, Robert Goodin argues that the measure of how useful goods such as money are "to you in pursuing your ends depends on how much others have and use of it in bidding against you for scarce resources that you both desire but both cannot simultaneously enjoy" (Goodin 1995, 250).

A familiar example of competitive utilization is the gentrification of urban neighborhoods. A long-observed adverse consequence of an otherwise salutary return of prosperous young professionals to deteriorating inner city neighborhoods is that those at the lower end of the economic ladder can no longer afford housing because their rich new neighbors can outbid them many times over. Because both property values and property taxes skyrocket, home ownership becomes doubly more difficult for low-income persons. Such examples reveal difficulties in specifying the level at which someone has sufficient resources to secure enough of what contributes to a decent life without reference to how much others have. An account of how much is enough necessarily requires attention to how much others also have. In some cases, when the proportion of resources available to the poor declines, the poor experience a decrease in standard of living in absolute terms.

The point is not simply that the standard of living of the poor in the once-depressed community declines relative to their new, wealthier neighbors. The presence of rich urban professionals also means that the poor can no longer afford what they could afford before the gap between them and the better off in their neighborhood grew. If that gap grows significantly enough, the consequence is that the least well off can no longer afford not merely a house in the old neighborhood, but decent housing in any neighborhood. At some point, steeper gradients in the distribution of income are incompatible with the aims of a sufficiency of well-being requirement insofar as the basics of a decent life are placed out of reach. Short of that, relative inequality—or the widening gap between rich and poor—undermines, although not necessarily precludes, a sufficient level of well-being such as health, or the development of reasoning abilities. Education and health care, for example, may be priced out of reach of many with the predictable consequence that the well-being gap also widens. Although competitive utilization cases reveal circumstances in which the sufficiency of well-being view has income distribution implications similar to resource theories, the difference lies in the fact that the well-being view provides an independent way of determining what level of resources is sufficient, while the sufficiency of resources approach lacks such a standard. Moreover, such a standard offers a clear public criterion for debating the adequacy of any pattern of resource distribution. While such a standard might not compel agreement, it does articulate a plausible set of social purposes from which empirically informed arguments can be framed and assessed.

A third feature of the sufficiency of well-being theory is that it highlights an important qualification in the way the concept of an absolute level of well-being is to be understood. A sufficient minimal level of well-being is not something that can be defined apart from a particular social context. Philip Pettit offers a wonderfully elaborate account of some of the many complexities of what we call a context-relative measure of sufficiency as applied to reasoning:

> To function properly in a contemporary society you have to be able to read and write, to do basic mathematics, to have access to information about matters like work opportunities, medical facilities, transport services, weather forecasts.... And to function properly in such a society you need also to know how to ascertain and assert your legal rights in dealing with the police, with your children's school, or with your spouse.... As society has become more complex the demands of successful living have multiplied.... (Pettit 1997, p. 158)

Sufficiency for any dimension of well-being will be relative to the level of social organization and technological and scientific development in which that dimension must be realized. Because the ultimate focus of justice for us is on what persons "can do and be," there simply is no way that such judgments can be made apart from some understanding of the background conditions that define the parameters of legitimate aspirations for justice.

One important implication of context-relativity is that not all failures in the protection of essential dimensions of well-being are injustices. So, for example, when many people died of AIDS in the earliest years of the epidemic, before it was possible to develop effective treatments, these deaths were a human tragedy, but they were not an injustice. In such a circumstance, disparities in death rates do not constitute urgent inequalities since there are no immediate means to their being addressed.

The fourth implication of the shift to a sufficiency of well-being view is that the contrast between the requirements of a sufficiency theory and a strict egalitarian theory are not as sharp as they are when economic measures such as wealth and income are the focus of justice. We have said that, with a sufficiency theory, instead of an equal well-being account of the aim of justice, the demand is not necessarily for strictly equal well-being in every dimension but, rather, that every individual has enough of the essential dimensions of human well-being to be able to live a decent life. What that requires is not necessarily the same for each dimension of well-being.

For dimensions such as health, the injustice of a lack of sufficiency is judged by reference to the sheer awfulness of the conditions in which some, but not all, people live. This claim might seem to make facts about disparities or inequalities morally irrelevant information. However, given our third conclusion, that the very notion of an absolute measure of sufficiency only can be established relative to a particular social context, how some fare relative to others is always morally relevant information. How others fare is information necessary for judging when the conditions of some fall below the sufficiency level because it informs us of what is possible to attain. Sometimes, for example, the health gap between the better off and worse off is evidence that what counts as a sufficient level of health that is possible for a particular society or at a particular level of technological and economic development has not been accorded to some persons. That some fare worse *Suff* in terms of health outcomes is not, for that reason alone, necessarily unjust according to a sufficiency view; but health disparities may be deemed unjust when they are avoidable outcomes. Unlike the early days of the epidemic, in the present social context, some if not most of the differential death rates attributable to AIDS are not simply a tragedy; they are unjust. How some fare relative to others is not what makes it unjust. What is unjust is that some fall below the level of sufficiency, and how some fare relative to others is crucial information for determining what aspirations are legitimate for justice in any given social context.

While we do not think it is plausible to attempt to specify in the abstract precisely what constitutes a sufficiency of health, it is possible to illuminate the moral meaning of this objective in particular contexts. As we have argued in the paragraphs above and will elaborate still further in chapter 4, at the outer bound, sufficiency can be pegged to what is technologically feasible with regard to both length and health-related quality of life. The World Health Organization's Burden of Disease projects, for example, use the world's longest life expectancy, that of the Japanese, as the benchmark for measuring health burdens internationally. A less demanding account of sufficiency would require that each of us have enough health over a long enough life span to live a decent life. Efforts to measure life expectancy and burden of disease and injury for populations and relevant subgroups, as well as public health statistics generally, thus provide the raw data for evaluating how well we are doing on this one dimension of well-being.

We also think that for public health and health policy generally, groups matter, but we are not interested in the health, other dimensions of well-being, or rights of groups, per se. Rather, our focus on groups is contingent on what we understand to be true of how the world works. That is, we are interested in the well-being, flourishing, and rights of individuals, but in the real, historically situated world, how individuals fare is generally a function of the status, standing, and position within densely woven patterns of systematic disadvantage of the groups of which they are a part. For these reasons, the concept of sufficiency in health has its greatest theoretical value when it is used for comparisons between populations or population subgroups. Given the task of a theory of social justice as a basis for evaluating institutions and social practices in their totality, it is not the aim that the concept of sufficiency, perhaps measured in terms of personal health biographies, would aid us in reaching judgments about how to allocate scarce resources between two candidates for a public health intervention or medical treatment.

The focus of a theory of social justice therefore relies upon notions of sufficiency within health in a different way. Evidence of substantial health inequalities in a population, both within national borders as well as globally, is presumptive evidence of significant injustice. This presumption is defeasible. For example, if the inequalities are largely a consequence of factors that are neither preventable nor treatable, or if the inequalities exist among only adults and are largely a consequence of personal choice among people living otherwise decent lives, or if the resources needed to reduce the inequalities are better used promoting well-being in its other dimensions, even a substantial inequality in health may not be particularly troubling. Moreover, without knowing anything about who the different groups are and why they differ, it is not possible to make judgments about which inequalities are the most morally important to address. For example, we argue in chapter 4 that, although the life expectancy of American men is less than that of American women, at 75, it approximates any reasonable account of what constitutes a "sufficient" life span. Our point is not that we should be unconcerned about male life expectancy. Our point is that such differences do not automatically signal that men haven fallen below the level of sufficiency in life span. In addition, because our theory also takes special notice of health inequalities that figure in patterns of systematic disadvantage, the relative moral urgency of such gender inequalities in health would increase should the well-being of American men begin to fall across multiple dimensions.

Even when the notion of sufficiency is pegged to what is technologically feasible, and even when the primary application of the concept is carried out at the population level, the precise boundaries marking which health states are above or below a level of sufficiency are not fixed. However, in the world we inhabit there are many clear instances in which populations or population subgroups fall below a level of sufficiency in health. For example, some of the most profound inequalities in child health are between the wealthy and poor nations of the world, and there are many children living in rich countries who fail to achieve a sufficient level of health. Amidst affluence, most of these children are poor. As we elaborate in chapter 4, they are more likely to experience lead poisoning, less likely to be immunized, more likely to be obese, and thus at greater risk of developing diabetes and heart disease later in life than are affluent children. They also have higher rates of asthma and of asthma-related complications, including hospitalizations and permanently decreased lung capacity. Poor children are more likely than other children to die in childhood. Borderline cases, by contrast, are theoretically problematic in only a limited range of cases. Borderline cases are, by definition, of lesser moral urgency, and while such cases would become more of a theoretical concern were the sheer awfulness of health status relative to what is technologically feasible to be reduced, for the foreseeable future, we do not expect that the lack of usefulness of the theory at the margin to be a problem of the sort that we would be unhappy to have. Because our theory is meant to identify those inequalities that are morally most urgent, our theory can offer practical guidance in a substantial range of cases in the world as we now know it.

Although we argue in chapter 6 for a special priority for children in health and other dimensions of well-being where the requirements of human development necessitate interventions and protections at critical junctures early in the life course, it is our view that a well-developed view of sufficiency in health reveals domains of health that matter equally throughout all life stages. Ensuring a sufficiency of health is not in our position simply a matter of ensuring comparable lifetime health prospects across a population. Such a goal matters greatly, of course. However, any plausible account of sufficiency in health must be able to accommodate some distinction among those domains of health that matter equally at any age (e.g., pain and depression levels) *and* those that arguably are more urgent to address at younger ages in order to ensure sufficient lifetime health prospects.

A plausible understanding of sufficiency will vary across the different dimensions of well-being. Lack of equality will trigger quite different threshold concerns. While a much more complicated story needs to be told before the presumption of injustice attaches to observable differences in health status, absent any other factors that suggest the need for heightened scrutiny, inequalities in other dimensions raise different threshold concerns. By the very nature of some other dimensions of well-being, what is required for minimal sufficiency lessens the degree of inequality that, under any conceivable social arrangement, can be considered just. A clear example is respect. Respect is a dimension of well-being that has its value for any individual or group of individuals only when the social conditions that promote and sustain it are equal for all persons. For example, no society can be counted as just when some persons are accorded less respect based on their membership in a racial or ethnic group or on the basis of gender or sexual orientation. Such systematic differences in respect are always unjust.

Similarly, when the capacities of some persons to develop and sustain personal attachments are compromised by cultural factors, for example, rigid gender roles that devalue and discourage the expectation of equality and mutuality in friendship and love, then the judgments of a sufficiency of well-being approach would not seem to diverge from what an equality of well-being theory concludes. To the extent that specific persons or groups bear the burden of externally imposed norms of self-sacrifice in personal relationships and a deformed sense of self and self-worth makes a critical stance toward these norms unlikely, such inequalities of well-being would bear a heavy burden of justification from the vantage point of a sufficiency theory.

As the above examples suggest, the reason that sufficiency is incompatible with substantial, and certainly systematic, inequalities in dimensions of well-being such as respect and attachment is that these essential dimensions of well-being simply cannot be realized in conditions in which some fare much worse than others. Systematic differences in the capacities of some persons to respect themselves and others and to be respected by others, inequality in the protection of personal security, or systematic differences in capacities for developing meaningful personal attachments are as morally condemnable from within a sufficiency approach as they are from a strict equality approach.

How much inequality in dimensions of well-being of other kinds is compatible with the very idea of sufficiency is a matter ranging beyond our task in this book. As we shall argue at greater length below (in 3.7), sufficiency with regard to self-determination does depend a great deal on how others fare in that regard, but it need not require anything approximating equality. We can say that our sufficiency of well-being theory does not rest upon a commitment to achieving strict equality among persons in every aspect of their lives, and that what sufficiency requires will be a function of many contingent features of the social structure that bear on any judgment of the sufficiency of any dimension of well-being. For some dimensions, however, anything other than a rough equality among persons is unlikely to be enough to count as what sufficiency of well-being requires. Just as we maintain that there are multiple dimensions of well-being that matter independently to justice, we maintain also that sufficiency judgments for each dimension present different burdens of justification.

3.6 Toward a Unified Theory of Social Determinants and Well-Being

Patterns of economic distribution are important social determinants of the development of each of the dimensions of well-being. A sufficiency of well-being approach within a nonideal theory of justice would lack the intended practical value were it unable to offer guidance in evaluating whether the distribution of resources within a society, based on its effects on the essential dimensions of well-being, met the requirements of justice. Economic distribution, however, is not the only social determinant having a profound and pervasive effect on each of the dimensions. Capacities for respect for self and others and for attachment, for example, while influenced profoundly by economic inequalities, are affected every bit as much by social practices and norms. Likewise, cultural and political barriers, as in apartheid or the Taliban rule, can produce ill health, lack of control over one's own life, and the inability to develop one's cognitive skills. Our theory is intended, therefore, as a unified account that is concerned with all of the social determinants having profound and pervasive effect on the development of each of the dimensions of well-being.

A nonideal theory, moreover, is not only interested in assessing how each dimension is affected by each major social determinant, but also in how each is affected by multiple, overlapping social determinants, and how clusters of effects on more than one dimension are produced by various social determinants, singularly or in combination. Our task in this and the next section is to provide a framework for that assessment in the real, imperfect world in which unjust inequalities of all sorts are not only the norm, but often are systematically related to one another. That framework consists of four representative scenarios, based on whether a single social determinant or multiple, overlapping social determinants are involved and whether a single dimension of well-being or clusters of different dimensions of well-being are affected by them. The following table summarizes the distinctions characterizing each of the four scenarios, and we consider illustrative examples of each in the remainder of this section and in section 3.8. We argue that a real-world, nonideal theory of justice has to expect scenarios in which there are overlapping social determinants and clusters of effects on multiple dimensions of well-being. Moreover, these overlapping determinants are often systematically related in ways that make their effects more burdensome and their escape less likely than we would expect under ideal conditions of perfect justice.

1. One social determinant with profound and pervasive effects on one dimension of well-being	3. One social determinant with profound and pervasive effects on a cluster of dimensions of well-being
2. Overlapping social determinants with profound and pervasive effects on one dimension of well-being	4. Overlapping social determinants with profound and pervasive effects on a cluster of well-being dimensions

The first and most familiar approach to understanding what justice requires directs our attention to a particular social determinant and some particular outcome such as health or reasoning for which it is hypothesized to be especially important. Often, this hypothesis is made in conjunction with the further assumption that the outcomes of interest play a special strategic role in bringing about some other, more fundamental requirement of justice, such as equality of opportunity. If one social determinant is presumed to be of special strategic significance to the development of one and only one particular dimension of well-being, then reflection on what justice requires can proceed in isolation from any concern about the impact of other aspects of the social structure and without regard to any further effects on other dimensions of well-being. We might consider justice in the allocation of health care resources, for example, if, contrary to much empirical evidence, access to care is plausibly thought to be the primary determinant of health outcomes. Such an assumption is not unreasonable when the aim of theorizing is to determine what justice in health care requires under conditions in which just background institutions are in place. That, however, is not the task of a nonideal theory. Our theory is interested in evaluating which inequalities, if any, pose the most urgent issues of justice, given the more complicated, real-world conditions of the sort represented in the other three scenarios of this framework.

There are numerous examples of the second scenario in which multiple or overlapping social determinants have profound and pervasive effects on some particular dimension of well-being. If, for example, it should turn out that access to medical care, or at least access to certain forms of care, has significant impact on some health outcomes, but some other social determinants play equal or greater causal roles in most health outcomes, then our nonideal theory of justice would require that the full range of relevant social determinants be taken into account in assessing what justice demands with regard to health. Other social determinants that arguably play such roles include environmental and occupational hazards, agricultural policies, the criminal justice system, clean water and sanitation infrastructure, and any number of possible factors that similarly have a profound and pervasive effect on health. These are considered in more detail in chapter 4.

However, an important theoretical point about this kind of scenario is that the reason that our theory attends to the various elements of the social structure causally related to the development and preservation of each dimension of well-being is that such information is relevant to answering questions about which inequalities are most urgent to address. Consider two illustrative examples of when inequalities instrumentally relevant to well-being may be more urgent. One case involves circumstances in which the combined effect of two social determinants is a magnification of the adverse effects on a dimension of well-being. Neighborhoods or countries lacking proper sanitation, coupled with lack of basic primary preventive care, including the necessary immunizations, can increase both the probability and severity of communicable diseases among a population. In a second, slightly different kind of case, overlapping social determinants can reinforce the adverse effects and make them harder to ameliorate. For example, those with elevated levels of environmental exposure to carcinogens can experience a greater prevalence of cancer than the general population, and if they also lack adequate and timely medical care, they can experience delays in diagnosis and treatment that might have made the course of illness less burdensome.

Instances in which negative effects on a dimension of well-being are the result of overlapping social determinants, and are thereby magnified or reinforced, are more likely to result in some persons falling below the level of sufficiency possible in that society. In our view, the point is not simply that acknowledgment of overlapping social determinants requires us to attend to a broader slice of the social structure when thinking about justice in the nonideal world. The further point is that such circumstances demand a heightened level of moral scrutiny. Overlapping social determinants affecting a particular dimension of well-being, therefore, raise matters of special moral urgency when they form a constellation of inequalities that systematically magnify and reinforce the initial adverse effects.

The third scenario in our framework is one in which any given social determinant, such as the distribution of income or wealth, or even lack of access to health care, profoundly and pervasively affects more than one dimension of well-being, causing some to fall below a level of sufficiency in multiple respects. There are several common variants of this scenario. In one variation, the problem is simply additive. Profound and pervasive adverse effects on more than one dimension of well-being are produced in tandem as a joint consequence of a single social determinant, causing some to fall below the level of sufficiency for more than one dimension of well-being. If deprivation in one essential dimension of well-being below a level of sufficiency is unjust, deprivations of still more dimensions of well-being below sufficiency levels are additional injustices creating particular moral urgency.

The simplest example of clusters of effects flowing from a single social determinant involves institutions and social conventions designed primarily to affect one dimension of well-being, but which simultaneously have profound and pervasive effects on other dimensions of well-being as well. For example, the effect upon health alone is not the sole criterion on our view for evaluating the justice and injustice of a health care system or public health policy. That such systems or policies result in substandard health for some is a major ground for moral concern, but so too is the impact of those systems and policies on capacities for respect for self and others, self-determination, and the ability to form bonds of attachment. If a health care finance and delivery system, for example, excludes some persons in ways that signal second class citizenship, or undermines their ability to shape even the basic contours of their own fate, or renders impossible their ability to care for dependent children and loved ones in ways the more fortunate take for granted, these effects are additional sources of injustice. Accordingly, what justice requires in the appraisal of each social determinant is an appreciation of its contribution to the development of well-being in all of its essential dimensions. In these instances, clusters of effects are produced in tandem as a direct result of the design and structure of a catalytic social determinant affecting multiple dimensions of well-being simultaneously.

There are further systematic causal patterns that can arise under this third scenario in which a more complex causal chain is set in motion, eventuating in some persons systematically falling below levels of sufficiency for several dimensions of well-being. We consider two illustrative examples.

The first one involves social determinants that constitute what Michael Walzer calls "dominant goods" (Walzer 1983). From inequalities in dominant goods flow further inequalities in those things that are the primary social determinants of several dimensions of well-being, and the result at the end of this causal chain is a systematic pattern of insufficiencies in multiple dimensions of well-being. For example, Walzer argues that when monopolistic control is exercised over a dominant good, then virtually all other socially valuable goods are controlled. Waltzer understands dominant goods in a broad sense:

> Physical strength, familial reputation, religious or political office, landed wealth, capital, technical knowledge: each of these, in different historical periods, has been dominant; and each of them has been dominated by some group of men or women. And then all things come

to those who have the one best thing. Possess that one, and the others come in train. (Walzer 1983)

The implication of Walzer's account of dominant goods for our sufficiency of well-being theory of justice is that, in a social structure where goods of one sort are allowed to dictate the distribution of all other social advantages and disadvantages, the life prospects for some are greatly diminished compared to what would otherwise be possible, given the level of social and economic development. Just as those who fare well in one sphere of dominant goods fare well in all, those who fare badly in one will fare badly in all. Thus, inequalities in the goods that are primary social determinants of one dimension of well-being ultimately can translate into social conditions in which some fall below the level of sufficiency for several dimensions of well-being.

Rousseau is notable for thinking that differences in income and wealth play much the kind of role Walzer contemplates in his analysis of dominant goods. From initial distinctions he called the natural inequalities—"age, health, strength of the body, qualities of mind and soul"—flow differences in political power, and then social status and rank, and finally, "wealth is the last to which they are all reduced because wealth, being the most useful to well-being and the easiest to communicate, can be readily used to buy all the rest" (Rousseau [1755] 1984, 132). Suppose, for the sake of argument, that Rousseau is right about the role of income distribution within modern, highly interdependent, technologically advanced forms of social organization. If those who control great wealth thereby gain control of the political process, restrict access to health care and dictate decisions about protection of the public's health and education, then vast inequalities in wealth eventually result in some segments of society falling below the level of sufficiency for both health and the development of reasoning abilities possible in that society.

The advice a sufficiency of well-being theorist offers for the distribution of wealth and income is not straightforward, even if income and wealth do play the role of the dominant good within a particular social structure. What justice demands with respect to the distribution of wealth and income is not a matter, for example, of what hypothetical, disinterested parties would agree to in advance. Instead, it is a matter contingent on a variety of additional considerations. If it is feasible to devise a social structure in which vast inequalities in wealth can coexist with other spheres of distribution such that the goods and opportunities necessary for development of the essential dimensions of well-being are not dictated by wealth, then those resource inequalities are morally benign.

The point is that justice, in a well-being sufficiency theory, can be achieved under such conditions either by lessening the differences in wealth and income or by lessening what can be done with wealth and income, for example, with regard to such things as financing political campaigns and causes, buying organs for transplant, and gaining entrance to elite educational institutions. If, however, circumstances are such that wealth inevitably determines how each person fares with respect to the social basis of some dimensions of well-being, then differentials in wealth and income are unjust because they cause some to fall below levels of sufficiency for multiple dimensions of well-being.

The special prominence of economic distribution is not the only empirical hypothesis regarding which social determinants qualify as dominant goods. Aristotle and Walzer tend to place more emphasis on the pivotal role of the concentration of political power, from which both the increased temptation and opportunity to amass greater material goods are said to flow and are more reliably assured. Aristotle noted that "men do not become tyrants in order to avoid exposure to the cold" (Aristotle 1946, 1267a). By that he meant that the desire for political and personal domination seems to be a powerful and innate motivating force in its own right, independent of the longings for material comforts and satisfaction of consumer desires. As such, concentrations of political power need to be curbed for the protection of the well-being of citizens whose interests are most likely to be ignored or trampled upon.

We need not adopt any particular view of which, if any, aspect of the social structure in any given social context acts as a dominant good and thus functions as a catalytic social determinant of any or all of the essential dimensions of well-being. Nor do we need to assume that a single dominant-goods thesis must be correct with respect to all dimensions of well-being. It may be the case that winners in some spheres will exert more control over how some fare with respect to some dimensions of well-being, and winners in other spheres will exert more control over how losers fare in regard to other dimensions of well-being. The upshot of the dominant-goods thesis, and its main implication for a sufficiency of well-being theory, is that justice will demand vigilance against the development of social structures that permit the winners in some spheres from determining the winners and losers in all other spheres. The ultimate concern of our nonideal theory of justice is all of the essential dimensions of well-being, but as the empirical plausibility of the dominant-goods thesis shows, a unified theory of well-being and its relation to the primary social determinants requires attention to the causal pathways that influence the outcomes that matter centrally to justice.

A second complex causal chain arising under the third scenario in our framework resembles the dominant-goods thesis, but the mediating factors are slightly different. This variant of the scenario involves a cascading and interactive causal chain initiated primarily by a single social determinant. The initial negative effect of some aspect of the social structure on one essential dimension of well-being, in turn, becomes the primary social determinant of an adverse effect on another dimension of well-being. The two effects interact to magnify and reinforce the negative effects on both, and the result can be a cluster of effects on multiple dimensions of well-being such that more than one dimension is systematically brought below a level of sufficiency.

There are notable examples from the social science literature on the way educational deficits and poor health display this pattern of cascading and interactive effects. Deprivations of reasoning abilities cannot help but spill over and cause or reinforce deprivations in health. Equally consequential for the prospects of developing one's reasoning capacities are deprivations in health. Development of one's intellectual ability is undermined when learning is undertaken under conditions of neurological impairment, illness, or pain. While the claim is that some initial social determinant may play an especially prominent, or catalytic, role, it is important to note that the approach described here is an interactive model, not simply a linear model in which one single causal sequence all the way down the line is assumed. The development of each dimension of well-being provides both opportunities for and constraints on the development of the other dimensions of well-being. Poor health is not just added to poor reasoning abilities. Each can be made worse by the presence of the other. Poor education not only leads to the underdevelopment of reasoning capacities but also plays a further, well-documented role in producing poor health. Not only does lack of access to health care for children undermine children's health, but the conventional public acceptance of their widespread exclusion from access to care also can adversely affect capacities for respect and affiliation for both parents and children.

There are thus instances in which social structures can compound the adverse effects on well-being in all its dimensions and mutually reinforce the probability of their production. A cascade of deprivations greater in their magnitude than each would have been in isolation is set in motion. Inequalities in such social structures are among those most urgent to address. They thus warrant a heightened level of moral scrutiny on our theory.

The phenomenon of interactive and cascading effects has some interesting implications for how we answer questions about which inequalities are most urgent to address. In Nussbaum's view, we must satisfy each and every item on her list, and a life falling below a minimum level of each is said to be a seriously deficient life and an injustice. That approach, in which we concur broadly, builds a floor under each distinct dimension of well-being contributing to overall well-being, and it thereby provides a greater bulwark against the prospect that any dimension of well-being might fall below a level of sufficiency. Justice demands attention to all the dimensions of well-being. But the cascading and interactive causal model adds a twist to this logic. In some cases, it is conceivable that sufficiency of some dimensions of well-being (e.g., health) may be promoted best by attention to other dimensions (e.g., reasoning development). In such cases, the answer to which inequalities are most urgent to address may be that we should give priority to addressing inequalities in those social determinants in which the potential adverse effects on more dimensions of well-being are at stake. No simple algorithm is possible, but some additional moral guidance for public policy arises out of an awareness of how the various dimensions of well-being and the social determinants affecting them can interact.

3.7 Densely Woven, Systematic Patterns of Disadvantage

Jon Elster notes that, "To a large extent, life itself is a series of uncorrelated stochastic events.... By the nature of chance events, some individuals will miss every train..." (Elster 1992, 134). In many cases, however, the inequalities that arise are not simply the consequence of unrelated instances of bad luck; they are predictable consequences of some forms of social organization that are within the power of human agency to alter. Some are likely to miss every train as a consequence of the way basic social structure is arranged. Elster agrees, noting that there times when "the total effect of local decisions is to create a pattern of burdens and benefits that seems unfair, inefficient, or both" (Elster 1992, 132). The causes and effects in such situations are structural and systematic: they are artifacts of the interactive workings of the overall social structure, and the pattern of advantages and disadvantages that emerge are often the consequences of activities of numerous overlapping institutions, social practices, and individuals.

We have seen a variety of such patterns in scenarios two and three. In some cases, adverse effects on a single dimension of well-being are magnified and reinforced because they are brought about by overlapping social determinants. Adverse effects on multiple dimensions of well-being can be produced in clusters, simultaneously, by a single social determinant. Catalytic social determinants can disproportionately account for the negative impact on other social determinants, which then produce a cluster of adverse effects on multiple dimensions of well-being. Catalytic social determinants can set in motion an initial adverse effect on a dimension of well-being, which, in turn, adversely affects the development of a second dimension of well-being, resulting in a cascading and interactive pattern of adverse effects, each compounding the severity of the effects on multiple dimensions of well-being and reinforcing their probability.

Each of the above causal models is but a contingent possibility, of course, and each rests on some simplifying assumptions about how social structures in the real world can work. In many instances, however, it is more plausible to suppose that, while all these systematic patterns are characteristic of real-world social structures, very often matters are still more complicated. The fourth scenario is one in which, in addition to the foregoing, there are both overlapping social determinants and clusters of adversely affected dimensions of well-being. Such cases are multicausal in origin and multidimensional in effect. As we move from the second and third scenarios to the fourth, these patterns are both increasingly more difficult to avoid or escape and more burdensome in their detrimental effects.

In our view, the point of a nonideal theory of justice, expressed positively, is to achieve a level of sufficiency for each of the dimensions of well-being. Those inequalities that are most urgent to address, for a theory that aims ultimately at a sufficiency of dimensions of well-being, are ones that are a consequence of systematically related overlapping social determinants affecting multiple dimensions of well-being. Justice, therefore, requires both obligations to remedy existing systematic patterns of disadvantage that profoundly and pervasively undermine the prospects for well-being, as well as prospective obligations to design social institutions and structures in order to prevent such patterns of disadvantage from arising.

The fourth scenario represents a more robust and more densely woven pattern of systematic disadvantage, increasing its moral urgency. All of the systematic patterns of disadvantage found in causal variants of the second and third scenarios of our framework, which are matters of special moral urgency in their own right, figure in this fourth scenario. One source of disadvantage, such as inequality of economic resources, can create and exacerbate deficiencies in several, if not all, dimensions of well-being. Adverse effects on any dimension of well-being can have spillover effects on other dimensions of well-being and set a cascading and interactive causal chain in motion. Poor reasoning development can contribute to poor health and vice versa. Well-being deficiencies of one sort can fuel inequalities in the social basis of other dimensions of well-being. For example, deficiencies in respect for self and others can undermine one's economic prospects. Similarly, poor health and intellectual underdevelopment can in turn perpetuate disparities in economic resources, further undermining self-determination and respect. And so on. Inequalities beget inequalities, and existing inequalities—in the social determinants of well-being and ultimately, in the essential dimensions of well-being themselves—can compound, sustain, and reproduce a multitude of deprivations in well-being, bringing some persons below the level of sufficiency for more than one dimension. The disadvantages associated with inequalities in the social basis of well-being in all of its dimensions are various; they often travel in tandem; and they can mutually reinforce and perpetuate one another. In turn, they can and often do affect a whole range of dimensions of well-being. Taken in their totality, the interactive effects of multiple sources of disadvantage add up to markedly unequal well-being, leaving some with greatly decreased prospects in every major aspect of their lives. As inequalities of well-being multiply, they reinforce one another. Any one sphere of deficiency in well-being becomes harder to escape, the disadvantaging effects harder to overcome, and the aim of sufficiency for all persons on all dimensions of well-being harder to achieve. The achievement of sufficiency, then, is simply incompatible with densely woven patterns of systematic disadvantage of this sort.

In the remainder of this section we discuss three illustrative examples of these densely woven patterns.

First, forms of oppression and subordination, including racism and sexism, are paradigm cases of the multicausal and multidimensional social structural barriers to achieving a level of sufficiency for all of the dimensions. Our theory is offered as an account of the injustices inherent in these phenomena.

However, our theory also takes account of a second kind of systematic disadvantage that is not based on animus toward persons because of group membership. In particular, our theory accounts for systematic patterns that involve especially powerful effects on self-determination.

In some instances, to be sure, what the worst off lack that the better off have is the option of saying no. Nevertheless, the social constraints under which many of the worst off live their lives virtually guarantee diminished futures for reasons that are more foundational than a lack of suitable choices in their adult lives. Many of the social structural constraints that our theory takes into account affect *children and their futures*, but not initially or even primarily through constraints on choices.

Our theory, then, differs from some prominent accounts of justice where the concept of domination is understood primarily as a set of social constraints on self-determination, either of socially identifiable groups or less rigidly defined members of powerless, low socioeconomic classes. For us, the real diagnostic test of all three of these patterns is whether the totality of social relations imposes systemic constraints on the development of the essential capacities in ways that guarantee profound and pervasive adverse effects on all aspects of the well-being.

One prominent form of systemic disadvantage is variously labeled as oppression, group domination, or subordination. Whatever the label, this particular pattern of systematic disadvantage is linked to group membership. Perhaps the most acute and most visibly manifested instances of that phenomenon are exhibited in racism, sexism, and ethnic conflict. Such patterns typically involve (a) lesser respect accorded to some persons because they are members of an identifiable group; (b) which often translates into lower respect for self and a reduced sense of personal efficacy and capacity for self-determination among members of the lower status group; and (c) members of higher status groups benefit (or believe they benefit) from a social arrangement in which members of subordinated groups are held in lower regard (Cudd 1994; Young 1990).

Domination or oppression based on shared characteristics of a group have some features in common with other forms of systematic disadvantage. Wealth, power, and opportunities may be concentrated in the hands of a few. Domination can take many forms, including political dominance, cultural dominance, intellectual dominance, market dominance, or any number of other ways in which the life prospects of some are profoundly diminished, often by virtue of the better life prospects of others within a society. Dominance can be achieved through multiple means and overlapping social determinants. It can involve physical restraints, coercive legal structures, psychological impediments arising out of social conventions and customs, the structure of markets and political processes, and the many other ways in which power, prestige, and social advantages enjoyed by some contribute to the lack of development of the capacities others need to live a decent life.

Perhaps because of these commonalities, accounts of domination often concentrate on the adverse effects of overlapping social determinants on some aspects of what is required for self-determination. In one such approach, nondomination is offered as an alternative account to negative conceptions of freedom, by which freedom is understood as noninterference with the choices of others. Phillip Pettit, for example, takes such a view, arguing for a nondomination account of freedom in which a person is free to the extent that another agent does not have the power to interfere arbitrarily and at will with the choices a person is in a position to make (Pettit 1996; Pettit 1997).

As important as self-determination is, it is not the full story of what dimensions of well-being are at stake in systematic patterns of disadvantage that attach to group membership. Iris Marion Young, for example, distinguishes between domination and oppression. Domination is used to refer to conditions in which self-determination are thwarted, while oppression is a broader term, referring to systematic constraints on dimensions of well-being other than self-determination (Young 1990, 37–38).

Our account of systematic patterns of disadvantage is meant to be inclusive, recognizing that self-determination is always at stake in such patterns but also that particular forms of systematic disadvantage have some distinctive characteristics. Characteristic of group domination is the fact that disadvantages such as lack of resources are compounded by, and often preceded by, differential respect accorded members of the group. Some voices simply do not get a hearing because they are the voices of persons who are members of groups whose claims are not judged worthy of concern by the larger society. Similarly, both resource disparities and disparities in respect are bequeathed from initial power differentials between individuals, nations, ethnic groups, or genders based largely on brute force and the physical ability to impose the will of one group on another. The hallmark of these patterns of disadvantage is animus to some group, an intentional harming of members of that group, and a belief that the dominant group gains thereby. However, the multidimensional character of racial and gender-based domination means that, in addition to adverse effects on respect and self-determination, there are almost always profound and pervasive effects on capacities for attachment, as well as reasoning abilities and health. The central moral evil of reduced respect, accompanied by the overlapping and mutually reinforcing nature of effects on dimensions of well-being of all kinds, justifies a heightened level of moral scrutiny and a commitment to the eradication of the self-perpetuating constellations of disadvantages that result. For these reasons, the job of justice is not one in which it is enough to focus on some factors, such as disparities in wealth and income, and hope that as a contingent matter, all else of moral significance will come in its wake. Our theory does not ignore the prominent causal role that resource inequality may have in group domination, or minimize the profound effects of the overlapping social determinants on self-determination. However, because it takes the capacity for respect for self and others and capacities for attachment as morally important concerns in their own right, our theory comprehends a full range of distributive and nondistributive concerns as equally important elements of systematic patterns of disadvantage, for which it is the job of justice to remedy.

Not all patterns of systematic disadvantage involving overlapping social determinants and clusters of effects on multiple dimensions of well-being conform to the characteristics of group domination or oppression. Self-determination, in many instances, plays a pivotal role in an individual's ability to achieve a bare minimum of the other dimensions of well-being, at least for adults. The pivotal importance of self-determination, then, lies in the fact that in many instances, many of the adverse effects on other dimensions of well-being are often achieved and consolidated through the mediating role of decreased capacity for self-determination, which is, in turn, produced by a constellation of overlapping social determinants.

What is additionally striking about self-determination is that the more that some persons are able to exercise control over their own lives, the more they are likely to be able to exercise substantial control over the lives of others. Some have more resources, greater political clout, more understanding of the world around them, and greater confidence in their abilities to devise and execute strategies to achieve their own goals. The more that some are insulated from the adversities of social, natural, political, and economic contingencies, the more others may be buffeted by the very means the more fortunate can employ on their own behalf.

Rousseau, for example, suggested that no man should be so rich that he could buy another, and no man so poor that he should be tempted to sell (J. Cohen 1989). Although this is a fairly modest standard, much of the developing world and pockets within the developed world are in this condition. And it is not lack of resources alone that makes for an inadequate level of self-determination. We can add much more to Rousseau's suggestion, including the idea that as long as some are far more powerful politically, or have better health or have fewer unmet needs (remember Rousseau's reminder that necessitous men are not free men), some will enjoy a relative advantage over others in their abilities to control their own destinies. These advantages pose structural barriers; they constitute systematic patterns of deprivation that are achieved, in very large degree, via the ill effects on self-determination, from which much else that matters ultimately to a sufficiency of well-being theorist follows.

In some instances, what the better off have that the worse off lack is the option of saying no, or at least the option of holding out for better terms in both private and public spheres. Some individuals are faced with (what was known in *The Godfather* as) "an offer you can't refuse." Those who command a proportionately greater share of the community's economic resources are better off, not simply by virtue of having a higher standard of living, but in having disproportionate influence in public affairs, augmented bargaining power in private transactions, and the full measure of respect and esteem of others. Indeed, the worst off may have little option but to do the hardest work, with the greatest threat to health and safety, at the least convenient times, with the greatest risk of ruin by a turn of bad fortune, and for wages that can never raise them above their current state. All of that can translate into some falling below a level of sufficiency for multiple dimensions of well-being, from which escape requires heroic effort, good luck, or both. The moral bottom line in such cases is that the guarantee to everyone of a sufficient level of each dimension of well-being is not readily compatible with a social system that permits some to exercise highly asymmetric power over the choices of others. It is the systematic patterns of disadvantage flowing from the differences in material resources, political power, and social standing within a culture that produces a constellation of well-being deficiencies and disadvantages that makes it increasingly improbable that individuals can improve their own situation through their own efforts. The crux of the matter, then, is not that self-determination is the central or definitive dimension of well-being through which unjust patterns of systematic disadvantage are woven. Rather, the importance of self-determination in some scenarios is that without it, it is one escape route, for adults at least, that is systematically foreclosed, allowing the adverse effects to compound and consolidate their hold over one's life prospects.

A sufficient level of self-determination thus depends upon no one having too much political power or cultural approbation relative to what others have. Sufficiency of this particular dimension of well-being may not demand near equality, as some other dimensions of well-being we considered earlier in this chapter might. But how some fare relative to others—in terms of self-determination and the social determinants that profoundly and pervasively affect it—are matters that a sufficiency theorist must take seriously, if, as we claim, part of the aim of justice is to police patterns of systematic disadvantage. Aristotle and Rousseau each summarize what is at stake for our view of justice with regard to what sufficiency of self-determination implies about inequalities in its primary social determinants. Aristotle notes that, where some enjoy too many advantages and some too few, "Men will not even share the same path" (Aristotle 1295b). Rousseau reminds us also that "when a giant and dwarf walk the same road, every step each takes gives an extra advantage to the giant" (Rousseau [1755] 1984, 105). The guarantee of sufficiency in all the dimensions of well-being requires social conditions for which there must be ways out without having to depend on improbable good luck or heroic efforts. For that, we must at least walk the same path, without some acquiring too much extra advantage with every step.

Patterns characteristic of oppression and group domination and similar patterns through which the routes of escape by one's own efforts and choices are foreclosed are not the only kinds of social arrangements our theory takes into account. Some patterns of systematic disadvantage form densely woven webs of constraint on the development of well-being in all of its dimensions where neither group animus nor impediments to self-determination are centrally at issue. We have in mind the kinds of systematic constraints that typically lock in the life prospects of some at an early age. For example, children living in adverse social circumstances "are more likely to be of low birthweight, be exposed to poor diets, experience passive smoke exposure, and have worse educational opportunities" (Ben-Shlomo and Kuh 2002, 287). In such cases, we find overlapping social determinants leading to socially patterned clusters of impairments to well-being such as those affecting health and reasoning abilities. For some social conditions and life events, the production and the magnitude of their adverse effects on well-being are dependent on their timing and sequence within particular developmental stages in life. Often, their most profound effects are not manifested until much later in life. Like other unjust patterns of systematic disadvantage, they are made harder to escape, and the burdens are often magnified and compounded, as a consequence of the way those disadvantages were locked in.

Evidence of the importance of the timing and sequencing of disadvantage on well-being is increasingly available in what is called the "life course" approach in the fields of epidemiology and health services research (Halfon and Hochstein 2002; Ben-Shlomo and Kuh 2002; Davey Smith 2001). Some events that occur during critical developmental periods produce adverse effects on health over the course of a life time. Poor nutrition and environmental exposures before and soon after birth can produce permanent and sometimes irreversible damage to organs, tissues, and body systems that can predispose people to such conditions as cardiovascular disease, developmental disabilities, noninsulin-dependent diabetes, and hypertension (Leon 1998). In the case of asthma, exposure to allergens or inadequately treated infections at a sensitive developmental stage in early childhood, when immune, neurologic, respiratory and endocrine systems are being programmed, may have a larger effect on the frequency and severity of disease than if those exposures occur later in life.

The life course conception has a number of important implications for the way our nonideal theory of justice approaches problems of deprivation and disadvantage. First, while the life course approach within the field of epidemiology deals primarily with health, the implications extend equally to the development of reasoning abilities, abilities to form attachments with others, and the development of respect for self and others. Some opportunities for development of emotional capacities and reasoning abilities are effectively missed if not seized early in life.

Second, given that the relative influences on the development of some dimensions of well-being differ according to life stage, public policy choices of the appropriate targets for interventions greatly matter, not simply for the sake of efficiency, but for the sake of the development of the essential dimensions of well-being our theory takes as the ultimate focus of justice. Just social systems will not simply be ones in which patterns of resources are not maldistributed, but will require concentration of resources at the right time and in the right ways. For example, family environment is thought to have a relatively greater effect on the long term-health development of young children, peer influences are thought to have disproportionate effects on behavioral and emotional development of adolescents, and social networks are the main influences on the abilities of older persons to adapt to functional loss (Halfon and Hochstein 2002, 439).

Third, the way we understand the interactive and dynamic aspects of how health disparities and other differences in the development of well-being emerge, and thus what justice in concrete terms demands of the social structure, may be altered by what we learn from the life course approach. Leon notes that "the assumption that inequalities in health today, whether between or within countries, are caused by contemporaneous differences in circumstances of life is not sustainable for a range of important diseases that appear to be driven by poor socioeconomic circumstances in early life and childhood" (Leon 2000). Thus, our judgments about the justice of social arrangements necessarily involves adoption of a long horizon, and in many instances, a special degree of concern for those disadvantages that occur early in life and for the welfare of children, generally.

Group domination and patterns of disadvantage that foreclose escape by constraining self-determination are thus but illustrative examples of how overlapping social determinants can produce clusters of effects on multiple dimensions of well-being. Following Amartya Sen's crisp expression, "what we can be and do" is not simply a matter of what we can choose, or even the social conditions under which our options are determined. Our life course model reflects the notion that much of the way our prospects are dominated by social structural conditions is not simply a matter of lack of more or better choices, but of constraints that guarantee diminished futures from an early age. Dimensions of well-being, therefore, are not reducible to what mature, autonomous, self-interested adults can choose; they refer also to the underlying unchosen conditions that determine the extent to which we are able to flourish.

3.8 Conclusion

The framework we have developed in this chapter is in some respects both more encompassing than many accounts of justice and less guided by fixed guideposts. In this regard we find much affinity with Hume's observations on justice. As we see it, the job of justice in its most pressing role demands a permanent vigilance and attention to social and economic determinants that compound and reinforce insufficiencies in a number of dimensions of well-being. For the most part, their importance is tied to a careful empirical appraisal of social institutions as a whole and their potential for profound and pervasive effects on those dimensions of well-being. What may be required by our approach is, therefore, dependent on contingent and shifting constellations of human vulnerabilities rising and falling in significance under particular forms of social organization. Empirical inquiry is essential to working out what a nonideal theory of justice requires and for answering questions about which inequalities, if any, matter most. Some of that inquiry, of course, may well come from social scientists, economists, and other empirically oriented researchers. The voices and perspectives of those whose life experiences reflect the cumulative weight of multiple disadvantage are also of critical importance, and thus the working out of our theory in concrete situations is therefore never simply a matter of deference to expert opinion.

The permanent background condition of the job of justice is, as Hume also reminds us, the enduring tensions of cooperative living in a world characterized by limited resources, limited imagination, and limited sympathy. In one historical context, it may be the monarchical state that poses the gravest threat. In another context, it may the hierarchy of an official religion, the tyranny of the uneducated masses, or the unchecked power of concentrated capital.

The job of justice under any of these conditions often involves the remedial task of ensuring that the basic social structure is one in which each person has a sufficient material, cultural, and political basis for the pursuit of his or her own life through the development of all of the distinctly human dimensions of well-being that are the central focus of justice. Our nonideal theory, then, defines a positive aim of justice in terms of a sufficiency of each of the dimensions of well-being, and the vigilance against systematic patterns of disadvantage define its remedial aims. It is only when we consider what sufficiency requires in real-world, concrete social circumstances that we can say which inequalities are most urgent and which are morally benign from the point of view of justice.

Social Justice and Public Health

4.1 Introduction

The theory of social justice that we have thus far presented is not designed to focus solely on one aspect of human welfare, public policy, or social organization. Quite the opposite. We have built our account around six distinct dimensions of well-being, each of which illuminates a uniquely salient moral consideration. Although distinct, these different dimensions often have common social determinants and are frequently intertwined in complex webs of disadvantage and privilege. Our theory thus emphasizes the importance of keeping all the dimensions in view when evaluating the justice of social organizations and public policies. Although health figures prominently in our theory as one of these six dimensions, it is no more or less important than the others. At the same time, as we noted in chapter 1, we came to develop our theory out of an original concern with questions of justice in public health and health policy, questions which have never quite left us. Accordingly, we turn now to some of the health-specific implications of our theory. In this chapter, our focus is on the social institution of public health. In chapter 5, we examine the implications of our account for a central issue in health policy and public health: how justly to organize and finance medical care services. In chapters 6 and 7 we examine the ways our theory informs the problem of how to justly set priorities among competing public health programs and health care policies.

We begin in this chapter by arguing, contrary to much of what has been written about the ethics of public health, that the foundational moral justification for the social institution of public health is social justice. In particular, we put forward multiple related reasons that social justice as explicated in our theory provides a fine, if not perfect, fit with the commitments and practice of public health. Moreover, making public health directly a matter of social justice strengthens its moral claim in the basic social structure. Next we consider how our account of both the negative and positive points of justice provides guidance for public health policy. The negative point of justice, which in our view requires a commitment to policing patterns of systematic disadvantage that profoundly and pervasively undermine prospects for well-being, shines the spotlight of moral urgency on the health needs of oppressed and subordinated groups, on people whose prospects for well-being, including for health, are so limited that their life choices are not even remotely like those of others, and on children whose prospects for well-being, not only in childhood but throughout life, are at risk because of the locking in of systematic constraints at an early age. By contrast, the positive point of justice is to secure a sufficiency of the dimensions of well-being for everyone. While we argue that it is not possible to specify in the abstract precisely what constitutes a sufficiency of health, it is possible to illuminate the moral meaning of this objective in particular contexts. Our theory thus provides guidance as to how to think about health inequalities both within nations and globally, as well as the role of public health policies and practices in the service of dimensions of well-being other than health.

4.2 Moral Justification for Public Health

We view social justice as the foundational moral justification for public health. This is not the standard way in which the ethics of public health is understood.

Commentary on ethics and public health is, at best, thin. The importance and variety of emerging views on the moral foundations and commitments of public health are changing as we write (Anand, Peter, and Sen 2004). However, insofar as a standard view of the moral justification or moral point of public health has emerged, it goes something like the following. Public health is the social institution charged with promoting human welfare by bringing about a certain kind of human good, the good of health. The moral foundation for public health thus rests on general obligations in beneficence to promote good or welfare. Depending on the interpretation, public health is further understood as having utilitarian commitments to bring about as much health as possible. Concerns about justice, like concerns about respect for individual liberties, are understood as ethical considerations external to the moral purpose of public health that serve to balance public health's single-minded function to produce the good of health with other, right-making concerns. In these discussions, justice is almost entirely presented as a distributional principle. Justice is thus introduced in the standard view about the ethics and justification of public health as a reminder that the moral imperative in public health to produce health must be tempered with concern for who experiences these health benefits as well as who is exposed to hazards that harm health (Kass 2001; Childress et al. 2002).

Our theory of social justice easily accommodates what the standard view gets right about the moral justification for public health. Social justice as we understand it is about well-being and about outcomes. Justice in our view requires ensuring for everyone a sufficient amount of each of the essential dimensions of well-being, of which health is one. Thus, in our account, bringing about health is a specific objective of social justice. What the Institute of Medicine defines as the purpose of public health—bringing about the conditions necessary for people to be healthy—is precisely what we understand to be one of the *direct* requirements of social justice.

What the standard view of public health gets wrong is that it frames public health as if the enterprise is solely concerned with outcomes. Unlike either beneficence-based or utilitarian justifications for public health, by situating the focus on well-being within a theory of social justice, we capture what we believe are the twin moral impulses that animate public health: to improve human well-being by improving health and to do so in particular by focusing on the needs of those who are the most disadvantaged. A commitment to social justice, as we explicate it, attaches a special moral urgency to remediating the conditions of those whose life prospects are poor across multiple dimensions of well-being. Placing a priority on those so situated is a hallmark of public health.

The first reason, then, that our theory of social justice provides a fitting moral justification or grounding for public health is that it captures both the outcomes or welfarist orientation of public health *and* the commitment of public health to the needs of those whose welfare is the lowest, a commitment that we take to be as foundationally constitutive of what public health is as the commitment to promote health generally. There are also other reasons, however, that our theory of social justice provides a fitting moral underpinning for public health as well as guidance for public health and health policy.

Our account rejects the separate spheres view of justice in which it is possible to speak about justice in public health and health policy without reference either to how other public policies and social environments are structured or to how people are faring with regard to the rest of their lives. Public health reaches the same conclusion. Public health historically, and public health today, recognizes that there are multiple causes of ill and good health, that policies and practices that affect health also affect other valued dimensions of life, and that health itself is sometimes a causal factor with regard to other important human goods. Our theory sharpens this orientation of public health to a wide net of potential influences and interactions and gives it particular moral intensity. As we argued in chapter 3, our account emphasizes the importance of recognizing how each dimension of well-being is affected by multiple, overlapping determinants, as well as how the different dimensions affect one another. We also underscore that these determinants are not restricted to political, economic or legal institutions but extend as well to social conventions and customs, an observation not lost on public health or some of the more recent contributors to the debates (Anand, Peter, and Sen 2004).

Moreover, our account provides a moral framework for what is sometimes referred to as the boundary problem in public health. While the broad scope of public health is often interpreted, we think rightly, as the correct perspective, public health is sometimes viewed as being so expansive in its compass as to have no real core, no institutional, disciplinary, or social boundaries. Everything from war, terrorism, and crime to genetic predisposition to disease; from environmental and occupational hazards to income inequality; and from personal behavior to natural disasters has been claimed as a public health problem. As we noted in chapter 1, the World Health Organization's definition of health as a state of physical, mental, and social well-being takes this broad brush approach to public health to perhaps its most extreme. What the WHO definition wrongly conflates is precisely what our theory emphasizes. On the one hand, health, as an essential dimension of well-being, is of independent moral concern whenever it is threatened. Part of what may make such diverse things as war, social responses to natural disasters and environmental hazards, and political oppression unjust is their effects on health. In this sense, they are all public health problems. Arguably, a central social role of public health, grounded in social justice, is to draw attention to any aspect of the social structure that exerts a pervasive and profound effect on the development and preservation of health. At the same time, however, health is one of six different lenses through which the justice of social institutions, practices, and policies are to be evaluated. In some cases, the effects on other dimensions of well-being may be as or more important in making determinations about injustice as the effects on health. Calling attention to war's impact on health is not the same as reducing all war's negative effects on well-being to its health effects. That war undermines personal security, attachment, and self-determination is not, for example, reducible to the impact of war on mental health. Each identifies a separate kind of injustice and each may be invoked in attempts to provide a moral argument against war in particular contexts. Because many determinants of the dimensions of well-being are shared, they are of concern to multiple social institutions and professional communities. That war has a profound and pervasive effect on health does not mean that international relations and diplomacy are to be considered tools or strategies of public health. As we noted in chapter 2, there is no reason to suppose that social institutions and public policies always rest on a single moral foundation.

Public health and health policy have a unique relation to one dimension of well-being. Arguably, educational institutions and policy have a similarly unique relation to the dimension of reasoning. These institutions have stewardship over particular determinants that have a special strategic effect on health and reasoning, respectively. However, we know that determinants such as access to primary medical care and schooling have pervasive effects on well-being that go far beyond their impact on health and reasoning. Just as public health has an obligation to call attention to any aspect of the social structure that has a significant effect on health, so too must public health evaluate the impact of its policies and practices, not only on health, but on all the dimensions of well-being. As we argue in chapter 5, access to medical care affects not only health but also what is necessary for being respected as a moral equal. Control over reproduction improves health, but, depending on the context, may do more to advance well-being by improving the ability to form bonds of attachment and to make basic decisions about one's life. Justice in health policy does not rest solely on its implications for health but on the totality of its effects on well-being in a particular context in which people likely vary in how well their lives are going, generally.

Yet another element of our account of social justice that works well with public health is that, as a nonideal theory, our focus is on the empirical particulars of specific contexts. As we argue in chapter 3, the questions of what inequalities matter most, and what constellations of determinants are most important, cannot be answered in abstraction. Empirical inquiry is necessary to identify both how well people are doing and what elements of the social structure are having the most profound effects on the different dimensions of well-being. Arguably, empirical inquiry of just this sort with regard to health is the job description for public health surveillance and research. Global and local efforts to measure life expectancy and burden of disease and injury for populations and relevant subgroups, as well as public health statistics generally, provide the raw data for evaluating how well we are doing on this one dimension of well-being. Research in public health by epidemiologists, toxicologists, biologists, behavioral and social scientists, and others provides a basis for understanding the complex factors that affect health in different settings, an understanding that necessarily shifts as social circumstances shift. While empirical inquiry is thus essential to working out the implications of the requirements of our nonideal theory in the real world, it is a mistake to equate this empirical understanding exclusively or even primarily with expert opinion. As we argue in chapter 2, while each of the elements of well-being should matter centrally to everyone, we do not maintain that each matters equally to everyone. Especially in contexts of pervasive disadvantage, where serious deficiencies exist across multiple dimensions, but in less urgent cases as well, the perspectives and preferences of those whose lives are most affected matter centrally. Their empirical understanding of what most depresses their well-being and what might be most useful to change is critical to the overall empirical appraisal. Moreover, any theory that takes seriously respect and self-determination as essential elements of well-being, as ours does, places a high value on according a central role to those who would be most affected by any policy decision or public health intervention. Our approach emphasizes that what matters morally is not only what state of well-being we experience, but also what we can do for ourselves and for our children—that is, the active role we play in bringing about the desired states.

Our theory also has something to say about what is perhaps one of the most contested, and most important, moral concerns of public health: whether there is a fundamental right to health. Many in public health accept that there is such a right, either as an article of faith or perhaps by relying on the United Nations Universal Declaration of Human Rights (United Nations General Assembly, 1948), even in the absence of a broadly accepted justification of the right or what it might mean. Public health has correctly understood that rights are claims of particular moral urgency and thus the recognition of a universal moral right to health is of considerable strategic importance. As we noted in chapter 2, our theory is one way of justifying a "protected interests" account of basic human rights of the sort that arguably underlies the United Nations Declaration. Health, along with the other five dimensions of well-being, are weighty interests of special enough importance to be given protection as basic human rights, assuming we are correct in our claim that it is rational for everyone to want these six dimensions, no matter what else we want.

Also in chapter 2, we lay out our response to critics of interest-based accounts of rights who believe that the only claims that are worthy of designation as rights are claims to be left alone or rights of noninterference. Of particular relevance here is our analysis of on whom fall the duties entailed by a right to health. From the standpoint of our theory, the human right to health generates a duty to ensure that the social conditions necessary to achieve a sufficient level of health are in place. As we argue shortly, with respect to children there is a more stringent duty to ensure, insofar as possible, that children actually experience a sufficient level of health. Many of the duties entailed by these health rights require positive, collective action and thus fall upon those entities that are best positioned to achieve collective ends. The most obvious candidates are governments, but social institutions of all sorts, formal and informal, professional and community, can be understood as having collective duties that bear on the right to health. Taken together, any society that fails to ensure for its members the conditions necessary to achieve a sufficient level of health is an unjust society that in our view has violated a basic human right. Moreover, as a basic human right, the claims of the right to health are not bounded by national borders but bind the human community, as a whole. Justice does not require equality in health, and what constitutes a sufficient level of health involves specification in particular contexts. However, as we discuss shortly, certain health inequalities are clearly unjust and are of particular moral urgency. These include the enormous gaps in life expectancy and child survival and health that currently divide the rich and poor nations of the world. In much of the developing world, governments are impoverished, corrupt, or otherwise unable or unwilling to provide for their citizens the conditions necessary for health and thus the means to narrow these disparities. It is the duty of the global community to ensure that the needs of the people living under such governments are met. Once again, collective action is required, but the best strategies for eliminating the injustice involve much more than what global public health institutions, both public and private, can provide. For example, the philosopher Thomas Pogge, who approaches the problem of world poverty from a negative rights standpoint, has cogently argued for the need to restructure the global economic order if severe poverty in the developing world, with its devastating consequences for health, is ever to be significantly reduced (Pogge 2002, 2004).

By focusing on collective action and thus on those institutions that are best positioned to achieve collective living ends, we do not mean to suggest that the right to health never entails duties on the part of individuals. In chapter 3, for example, we introduced the Rawlsian notion that individuals may have duties to support just institutions. This notion can be extended to include an individual duty to take steps to reform institutions that are unjust, if only through the exercise of the franchise. Arguably, public health professionals who, by virtue of their professional roles, are in a position to know when injustices with respect to health are occurring and why, have at very least a duty to share that knowledge with others. The institutional changes required to redress injustice in the real world often require the awakening of the consciences of large numbers of people, or at least large numbers of people in positions of influence.

 Our view that social justice is the foundational moral justification for public health is, we believe, congenial to those who argue that the values that underlie public health practice are the values of human rights (Rodriguez-Garcia and Akhter 2000). Pioneered by Jonathan Mann, the links between violations of human dignity and poor health are increasingly understood (Mann 1995, 1997, 1998). In an influential commentary defending human rights as the foundation for public health, Rodriguez-Garcia's and Akhter's views on health and justice are similar to our own. They assert that health has an intrinsic value, that there is an undeniable relationship between dignity and health, and that "Health is a necessary element in improving people's lives, but health alone, disassociated from social, political, and economic developments and social justice, cannot foster human developments or improve the human condition" (693). Rodriguez-Garcia and Akhter call on public health professionals to make a difference in the global struggle for social justice and human rights: "Vigilance to *prevent* human rights violations and to ensure social justice for all people is essential to the advancement of human development and the prevention of human suffering" (693). Numerous World Health Organization reports similarly echo the connection between human development, human rights, social justice, and health (Gunatilleke and Hammad 1997; WHO 2003b, 2003c; Bankowski, Bryant, and Gallagher 1997; Cook 1994).

Although the language is less direct, the United States-based Public Health Leadership Society's "Principles of the Ethical Practice of Public Health" also evidences the fit between our account of social justice and public health. Referred to as a "living document," it is the product of town hall meetings, professional conferences, and Internet feedback intended to capture the morally relevant values, beliefs, and principles of public health professionals. The document begins by affirming that humans have a right to the resources necessary for health as proclaimed in Article 25 of Universal Declaration of Human Rights and that the primary concern of public health lies with fundamental social structures. It also emphasizes that public health is particularly interested in those members of a community who are underserved, disenfranchised, or marginalized. The document further asserts that in some instances the fundamental value and dignity of each human being may demand the implementation of public health policies that are neither optimally efficient nor cost-beneficial (Public Health Leadership Society 2002).

4.3 Public Health, the Negative Point of Justice, and Systematic Disadvantage

As we have noted throughout, our theory of social justice draws a distinction between what we have called the negative, or remedial, point of justice and the positive, or aspirational, point of justice. We have also throughout maintained that our theory helps identify which inequalities are most morally urgent to address. It is now time to link these themes together in the specific institutional context of public health. The negative point of justice requires the policing of patterns of systematic disadvantage that profoundly and pervasively undermine prospects for well-being across multiple dimensions. Densely woven patterns of disadvantage are both more difficult to avoid and escape and more burdensome in their negative effects. For us, inequalities in health that are a part of such systematic patterns of disadvantage are the inequalities that are most morally urgent to address. Justice here demands aggressive public health intervention to document and help remedy existing patterns of systematic disadvantage and their detrimental consequences. Justice also, however, imposes prospective obligations to ensure that, at very least, public health policies do not exacerbate such patterns and that they contribute to preventing such patterns from arising.

One important implication of our theory is that whether any particular inequality in health is among those most morally pressing to address requires consideration of both how the people affected are faring with respect to the rest of their lives as well as how any public health interventions interact with other dimensions of well-being. Following chapter 3, we here argue that inequalities involving systematically disadvantaged social groups as well as those who are so profoundly disadvantaged that their life choices are not even remotely like those of others are of particular moral urgency. We also include in this most morally pressing category children whose prospects for well-being, not only in childhood but throughout life, are at risk because of the locking in of systematic constraints at an early age.

Disadvantaged Social Groups: Disparities in health statistics take on different moral meaning when those disparities identify differences between socially dominant groups and socially disadvantaged groups. Whether the term used is oppression, domination, or subordination, as we argued in chapter 3, patterns of systematic disadvantage linked to group membership are among the most invidious, thorough going, and difficult to escape. They generally engage all the dimensions of well-being, but perhaps most centrally the dimension of respect. Group membership becomes sufficient reason for failing to treat people as dignified human beings worthy of equal moral concern. In its extreme, group domination entails wholesale violations of human dignity and regard, virtually ensuring that members of the demeaned group will suffer insufficiencies of well-being across the board. Even when patterns of group domination are lessening in their intensity, the life prospects for those in the dominated group generally remain well below those of others.

One critical moral function of public health as we see it is to monitor the health of those who are experiencing systematic disadvantage as a function of group membership, to be vigilant for evidence of inequalities relative to those in privileged social groups, and to intervene to reduce these inequalities insofar as possible. As we argue shortly, inequalities in health of many sorts can provide useful information and thus are of interest to public health. Establishing the extent to which there are inequalities in health between dominant and subordinated groups is, by contrast, a particular moral imperative, for such inequalities are among the most urgent to address. Thus, for our nonideal theory of social justice—and, we think, for public health—groups matter. Social justice is not only a matter of how individuals fare, but also about how groups fare relative to one another whenever systematic disadvantage is linked to group membership. Depending on the context, the groups of particular concern may be defined by different characteristics such as gender, ethnicity, race, religion, caste, citizenship, sexual orientation, or disability. Whatever the common characteristic, the members of the disadvantaged group are accorded less respect, which frequently translates into reduced self-respect, reduced expectations, and reduced capacity for self-determination. They face numerous, overlapping obstacles to achieving a decent level of well-being that are rooted in any number of sources including social conventions and custom, legal constraints, and the structure of political systems.

One of the most compelling recent examples of work in public health on behalf of an oppressed group involved documentation of the disastrous impact of the Taliban rule on the health of women. Research conducted by the group Physicians for Human Rights provides powerful evidence that the denial of basic human rights to women resulted not only in horrible injustices with regard to respect, affiliation, and personal security, but also with regard to health (Rasekh et al. 1998). It is not necessary, however, to point to the horror of the Taliban regime to find examples of public health research documenting the impact of oppression of women upon their health. In the developing world, as well as in some communities in the United States, the vulnerability of women to HIV is attributed in large measure to women's lack of political and social status and their dependence on men (Gollub 1999; Sanders-Phillips 2002; Buseh et al. 2002; Wyohannes 1996). Public health research has also helped direct the world's attention to the impact of violence against women on women's health (Pan American Health Organization 2003), as well as to the enormous health problems of many indigenous peoples (Pande and Yazbeck 2003; Wiseman and Jan 2000; Roubideaux 2002).

In American public health, much attention has been paid to disparities in health between white Americans and nonwhite Americans, particularly African Americans, Native Americans, and Hispanics. The implicit assumption, which we believe to be correct, is that these disparities are of particular moral concern. Although precise assessments of the impact on health of ethnic disparities are difficult to establish, one study estimates that 886,202 deaths would have been averted if the mortality rates of African Americans and white Americans had been equalized in the decade from 1991 to 2000 (Woolf et al. 2004). Some considerable effort is being expended in an attempt to identify the causal patterns responsible for ethnic disparities (Committee on Understanding and Eliminating Racial and Ethnic Disparities in Health Care 2003; Goldman 2001). An empirical understanding of why ethnic disparities in health outcomes and other indicators of well-being persist is needed to guide the implementation of effective interventions. However, from the standpoint of our theory of social justice, it is not necessary to establish a direct causal connection between specific health disparities and specific acts of injustice, such as overt discrimination in access to advanced medical technology or primary health care, to hold that these inequalities are of significant moral urgency. Nor are we arguing that addressing these inequalities is of significant moral urgency as a matter of compensation for some kind of "trans-generational debt" (Loury 2002; 2003, 337). Rather, we maintain, in line with the work of Glenn Loury, that social and cultural factors that have historical roots but that remain persistent have resulted in continuing disparities in human development and flourishing. Combating overt racism and racial discrimination, although important to root out where they exist, is not sufficient to addressing this gap in well-being. Thus, for us, a different kind of causal story is required, a causal story about how a disadvantaged group's staying in relatively poorer health continues to contribute to decreased well-being overall. What is needed then, is, on the one hand, evidence, readily available in these cases, that people continue to be systematically disadvantaged by virtue of their membership in minority groups in ways that significantly undermine their prospects for well-being and, on the other hand, reason to believe that interventions directed at reducing the health-related inequalities will contribute to the alleviation of these group-related burdens.

Making the health needs of disadvantaged groups a public health priority advances the remedial aims of justice in at least two ways. Insofar as such policies actually improve the health status of dominated groups, the negative point of justice with regard to health is advanced. In addition, however, policies that target the inequalities of dominated groups may have positive effects on other elements of well-being. For example, such policies are public expressions of respect. Specifically, they are public expressions that members of the disadvantaged group are entitled to equal regard as full moral persons. They are public acknowledgment that the failures of respect that underpin a web of negative determinants and consequences, including health inequalities, are unjust and must be addressed.

Focusing on respect is particularly important in public health policies and programs directed at disadvantaged groups. Sometimes it is the enabling of respect by others, as well as of self-respect, that is public health's biggest contribution to well-being. Consider, for example, people with physical or cognitive disabilities. Although the most acute and visible instances of systematic disadvantage attached to group membership are evidenced in the phenomena of racism, sexism, and ethnic conflict, people with disabilities often experience systematic hardship by virtue of their identification as disabled. Efforts on the part of public health to reduce the stigma attached to various disabilities and to advocate for accommodations and assisting devices in public spaces and in the law are all examples of ways in which public health contributes to reducing inequalities in well-being through the dimensions of respect and self-determination (American Public Health Association, APHA, 1950, 1983, 1988, 1993; WHO 2003a).

Poverty and Disadvantage: In many contexts, it is arguably the case that the poor, especially the desperately poor, are a dominated group whose members suffer from the same kinds of systematic disadvantages associated with racism and sexism. It is not necessary to make this claim, however, to maintain that the inequalities in well-being associated with severe poverty are inequalities of particular moral urgency. Those who have a proportionately tiny share of available economic resources are worse off, not simply by virtue of having a much reduced standard of living, but in having disproportionately little influence on public affairs and in the marketplace, all of which translates into their having little control over their own lives. As we argued in chapter 3, the systematic patterns of disadvantage that flow from dramatic differences in material resources produce a cluster of deficiencies in well-being that makes it extremely unlikely that individuals can improve their life prospects through their own efforts.

Also, in chapter 3, we drew on a metaphor offered by Aristotle illustrating how large inequalities are unjust because they undermine the ability of all to "walk the same path." With regard to the dimension of health, perhaps the starkest indicator of the inability of all to walk the same path is found in differentials in life expectancy. Here, we live in a world of radical inequality (Pogge 1998). Despite significant improvements in life expectancy in low-income countries since 1960 (Jha et al. 2002), there is currently as much as a forty-year differential in average life expectancy between those who live in major industrial countries and those who live in southern Africa. Even if mortality in early childhood is not considered (a topic we will address shortly), in 2000, the average fifteen-year-old boy living in the United States can expect to live well into his seventies, if not beyond, while the average fifteen-year-old boy living in Uganda will be lucky to reach his fiftieth birthday. With life prospects, indeed the very prospect of living at all, so radically different, it is hard to conceive of these two youths as in any respect walking the same path. The magnitude of this source of extraordinary injustice cannot be overstated. It is estimated that each year as many as twenty million people in severe poverty in the developing world die young, by the standards of the rest of the world, from malnutrition and diseases that can be inexpensively prevented or treated.

Whatever other inequalities are moral priorities for public health, none are more pressing than the inequalities associated with severe, life-long poverty, which has such crushing, grinding effects on all the dimensions of well-being. Thomas Pogge comes to effectively this same conclusion arguing from a somewhat different standpoint. Citing statistics in support of the conclusion that world poverty is by far the most important factor in explaining health deficits, Pogge argues that because world poverty is largely the outcome of global economic institutions which those of us in the developed world in relevant respects uphold, citizens of developed nations as well these nations themselves have a direct, relational, responsibility for ameliorating health deficits among the world's poor, and global poverty more generally (Pogge 2004).

While the severity of poverty in the developing world is of staggering dimensions, poverty is also present in unfortunate abundance in the world's wealthy nations. Within the United States, poverty and poor education, often coupled with additional, compounding disadvantaging properties, can also produce conditions that make it impossible for the economic least well off to walk the same path as the rest of us. Here, too, differentials in mortality loom as stark, if less dramatic, indicators of the impact of profound inequality on well-being. For example, for men between the ages of twenty-five and sixty-four, the age-adjusted death rate is 591 per 100,000 for those with less than twelve years of schooling but only 217 for those with thirteen or more years; for women, the comparable rates are 409 and 172 (Minino et al. 2002). The loss experienced by the poor is far greater, however, than merely fewer years of life. In the 1980s, before it was established that antiretrovirals could prevent the transmission of HIV from mothers to newborns, we interviewed women to ascertain their views about HIV and pregnancy. All the women were HIV positive, and most were poor and of color. In contrast to the public commentary of the time, in which HIV-AIDS was presented as a dreaded death sentence, these women were not particularly concerned about developing AIDS. Although they understood the seriousness of AIDS, they did not expect to live long enough for the disease to manifest itself. The prospect of violence and violent death, homelessness, and drug overdoses had robbed these women of any capacity to envision futures for themselves past the next few years. They were not walking the same path as other Americans of the time who, with realistic expectations of long life and thus with something of value to lose, were more open to public health interventions promoting safe sex practices. The social science and health literature is replete with examples in which the seemingly irrational, self-destructive patterns of the poor are made comprehensible against a plausible expectation of limited options, hopelessness, and early death (Gold et al. 2002; Sullivan 1993; Jacobs 1994; Freeman 1989; Galea and Vlahov 2002; Boardman et al. 2001).

As some of these examples illustrate, those among the poor whose life prospects are the most bleak are frequently also members of socially stigmatized groups. The inequalities that they experience in view of the dense web of disadvantaging properties in which they are caught make their plight all the more morally urgent.

Children: From the standpoint of our theory, social justice demands that, insofar as possible, all children achieve a sufficient level of health. With adults, depending on the context and the particular dimension of interest, we may be as concerned with securing for them the capability to achieve a sufficient level of well-being as with the state itself. By contrast, with children, what matters most in terms of justice is that the social order secure for them sufficient levels of each dimension of well-being. As we noted in chapter 2, with adults the emphasis in justice is sometimes on capabilities and sometimes on functioning. In the case of children, however, we are always concerned with *actual* functioning. As a developmental matter, unless children experience a state of sufficient well-being in their young years, their capabilities as adults, and thus what they will be able to do with their lives, will be compromised. We are concerned about the actual health, reasoning abilities, and attachment of children, in part because these dimensions of well-being will develop properly, if at all, only if they are nurtured and secured in appropriate developmental stages. Moreover, the value of the dimensions of well-being to children does not depend on what children can do for themselves, as it sometimes does for adults. Securing the well-being of children can be achieved only through the actions of others and through the existence of a social order conducive to their development. Thus, for our nonideal theory of social justice—and, we think, for public health—children matter differently than do adults. Social justice is not only a function of how individuals and groups that suffer systematic disadvantage fare, it is also in special ways about the actual well-being of children across childhood's developmental stages.

Our theoretical position on the privileged status of childhood in social justice provides a line of justification for human rights documents and conventions that accord special status to children. In 1990, these documents were concretized in writings emerging from the United Nations' World Summit for Children, which affirmed the principle mandating "first call for children":

> [A]ction and co-operation must be guided by the principle of "first call for children"—a principle that the essential needs of children should be given high priority in the allocation of resources, in bad times as well as in good times, at national and international as well as family levels. (UNICEF 1990, paragraph 33)

A decade later, in 2001, this principle was reaffirmed at a global summit: "[Leaders] also promised to uphold the far-reaching principle that children had 'first call' on all resources, that they would always put the best interests of children first—in good times or in bad, in peace or in war, in prosperity or in economic distress" (Annan 2001, 1–2). The 2001 report of this summit goes further, providing a rationale for s "first call" principle whose themes align closely with our own:

> It is children whose individual development and social contribu-
> tion shape the world's future—and it is through children that en-
> trenched cycles of poverty, exclusion, intolerance and discrimination
> can be ended. This is the vision that inspired the World Summit for
> Children—and generated a global principle of a "first call for children"
> as a guide to public policy, allocation of resources and practical
> activity. (102)

Nowhere is the impact of well-being in childhood on the prospects of well-being in adulthood more clear than with regard to the dimension of health. As we surveyed in chapter 3, there is overwhelming evidence that compromised health in childhood has profound effects on health later in life. Diseases as diverse as cancer, lung disease, cardiovascular disease, and arthritis have all been associated with poor health in childhood (Halfon and Hochstein 2002; Wadsworth 1999; Wadsworth and Kuh 1997; Blackwell et al. 2001).

Compromised health in childhood also has profound effects on dimensions of well-being other than health, most notably on the potential to develop the skills necessary for reasoning. It has long been established that severe intrauterine growth retardation, maternal malnutrition, extreme prematurity, and prenatal exposure to toxins are associated with poorer cognitive performance later in life (Andersson, Gotlieb, and Nelson 1997; Goldenberg et al. 1996; Emory et al. 2003; Schantz, Widholm, and Rice 2003; P. A. Fried 2003). There is increasing evidence that growth and development in infancy and early childhood may be equally critical to the development of cognitive capacities (Gale et al. 2003). Malnutrition in the early years as well as exposure to toxins such as lead can have a profound and permanent effect on brain development and cognitive capacity (Grantham-McGregor 1995; Finkelstein, Markowitz, and Rosen 1998). Failure to diagnose and treat disorders such as phenylketonuria can result in permanent mental retardation.

Perhaps the most obvious way in which compromised health in childhood forecloses options in adulthood is through child mortality. Despite significant reductions in child mortality in the 1980s and early 1990s, in 2003 more than 10 million children under the age of five years died (Gillespie et al. 2003). Almost all of these children lived in low-income countries or in poor communities in middle-income countries. Most of these deaths could have been prevented by interventions that in 2003 were available, reasonably cheap, and in widespread use (Jones et al. 2003). By any plausible account of social justice, and certainly by our own, these deaths constitute injustices of the gravest sort (Victora et al. 2003). Diarrhea, pneumonia, and malaria—the principal killers of young children, abetted by undernutrition—are all eminently treatable or preventable conditions.

Among the world's poorest, many children never survive long enough for us to even begin to speak meaningfully about their capabilities, well-being, or flourishing. Even those who survive past infancy face a staggering chance of dying by comparison to children born in high-income countries. In 2000, 25 of every 100 children born in Angola and Niger died before the age of five; in Europe, this rate was less than 1 in 100 (Gillespie 2003). The effect of poverty on child mortality is evident *within* low- and middle-income countries as well. In Indonesia, children born in the poorest quintile of the population are four times more likely to die by age five than children born to the wealthiest quintile (Gillespie 2003).

For all of these reasons, inequalities in the health of children are among the most morally urgent for public health to address. Without a sufficient level of health in childhood, systematic constraints on well-being that are inescapable are locked in at an early age. Although, once again, the most profound inequalities in child health are between the wealthy and poor nations of the world, many children living in rich countries fail to achieve a sufficient level of health. Amidst affluence, most of these children are poor. In the United States, for example, poor children are more likely than other children to die in childhood (Jones et al. 2003). They are more likely to experience lead poisoning (Rabito, Shorter, White 2003) and less likely to be immunized (American Academy of Pediatrics Committee on Health Services 2003). They are more likely to be obese, and thus at greater risk of developing diabetes and heart disease later in life than are affluent children (Alaimo 2001). Poor children have higher rates of asthma and of asthma-related complications, including hospitalizations and permanently decreased lung capacity (Aligne et al. 2000). Some of America's poorest, and least healthy, children are also members of minority groups.

The focus in social justice on securing the well-being of children also requires placing a priority in public health on the health of parents. Maternal nutrition, maternal health, and prenatal care are profoundly important to the health of babies and children, as well as to their mothers (Sanders-Phillips and Davis 1998; Alexander, Kogan, and Nabukera 2002; Kogan et al. 1998). That the health of children and their subsequent well-being turns critically on the well-being of women during pregnancy and childbirth is only the most obvious way in which the health of parents are important to the health of their children. Being orphaned, either by the death of parents or by abandonment, is among the most significant setbacks to children imaginable. Not all deaths of parents are preventable or otherwise a matter of injustice. But in some cases, the fact that particular diseases will with certainty result in the creation of large numbers of orphans increases the moral urgency associated with that disease. The most obvious such disease today is AIDS. According to the United Nations Children's Fund, more than 3.5 million children in sub-Saharan Africa have lost both their parents to AIDS, and 11 million have lost at least one parent. It is estimated that by 2020 there will be about 20 million children, or 15% in the region, missing at least one parent as a consequence of AIDS (Lafraniere 2003; UNICEF 2003). The well-being of these orphaned children is, not surprisingly, terribly poor. Their life prospects are dismal. They are frequently unschooled, suffering from malnutrition, and living on the streets. Prostitution and crime are often these children's only sources of income. Many of them will themselves become infected with HIV. It is hard to envision a pattern of disadvantage more overwhelming than that facing these children. They have little or no personal security and the most important bond of attachment in childhood, that between parent and child, has been irrevocably severed. They have little opportunity to learn about the world and no control over their lives. They are hungry and sick. The utter terribleness of their plight is overwhelming. If there are any inequalities of special moral urgency, surely the inequality in well-being between these children, other desperately needy children, and the rest of us count among them.

4.4 Public Health, the Positive Point of Justice, and Health Inequalities

As we see it, the job of justice in its most pressing role looks first to conditions of the most profound disadvantage. Justice's first concern requires permanent vigilance and attention to determinants that compound and reinforce insufficiencies across multiple dimensions of well-being in ways that make it difficult if not impossible to escape. Although our theory thus concentrates the attention of public health on those gaps in well-being that are the most urgent, there is a positive as well as a negative point to our theory, one that sets aspirations for achieving a sufficient level of well-being in all of its essential dimensions for everyone. For the dimension of health, it is not possible to specify with precision what sufficiency requires, nor is it possible to establish precise numerical targets. At an outer bound, sufficiency can be pegged to what is technologically feasible with regard to both length and health-related quality of life. The World Health Organization's Burden of Disease projects, for example, use the world's longest life expectancy, that of the Japanese, as the benchmark for measuring health burdens internationally. A less demanding account of sufficiency would require that each of us have enough health over a long enough life span to live a decent life.

Depending on how they are framed, many questions of social justice in public health seem to address either remedial concerns, positive concerns, or both. One central such question is how we should think about inequalities in health that are not so obviously matters of moral urgency as those we have just surveyed. Unlike the dimension of respect, where a sufficiency of well-being requires that each be accorded equal regard, our theory of social justice does not require for health that there be precise equality between persons. That some fare better in terms of health outcomes is not, for that reason alone, necessarily unjust. At the same time, however, our theory does provide guidance as to how to think about inequalities in health.

In some cases, such as those we have just surveyed, there is no need to look to inequalities for guidance as to whether a profound injustice exists. The sheer awfulness of the conditions in which some people live—the absolute deprivation across multiple dimensions of well-being including health—is enough to make the judgment about injustice. In other cases, however, health inequalities help inform judgments about justice and public health. Evidence of substantial health inequalities in a population, both within national borders as well as globally, is presumptive evidence of significant injustice. This presumption is potentially defeasible. For example, if the inequalities are largely a consequence of factors that are neither preventable or treatable, or if the inequalities exist among only adults and are largely a consequence of personal choice among people living otherwise decent lives, or if the resources needed to reduce the inequalities are better used promoting well-being in its other dimensions, even a substantial inequality in health may not be particularly troubling.

Consider table 1.

Table 1. Average Life Expectancy

75.0 vs. 63.2 (+11.8)
75.6 vs. 66.6 (+9)
74.8 vs. 68.2 (+6.6)
79.5 vs. 74.1 (+5.4)
79.7 vs. 75.8 (+3.9)
77.6 vs. 73.8 (+3.8)
77.3 vs. 31.6 (+45.7)
80.9 vs. 34.3 (+46.6)

From the standpoints of both public health and the positive or aspirational point of justice, any inequality in a health outcome, including all the comparisons on this table, are potentially of interest. That one group fares better than another group suggests that it may be technically possible, now or in the future, to improve the health status of some people. Any inequality is potentially informative to justice with regard to its positive aim. Depending on why the inequalities exist, that some experience better health than others tells us something about what it is possible to achieve with regard to health. For public health, evidence of inequality provides data points and insights for intervention. If it is possible to reduce the burden of disease from cardiovascular disease in one state, it may (and indeed likely should) be possible to do so in another. The positive aim of social justice thus provides the moral underpinning for the imperative in public health to improve health where ever reasonably possible. In line with its aspirational point, improving health status is always a goal of justice in public health.

Improving health status, and thus narrowing inequalities, is not always a morally urgent matter, however. Whether an inequality in health assumes the sort of moral priority attached to the negative point of justice is a separate issue. We cannot tell simply from the numbers reported in table 1 which, if any, of these disparities are the sort of inequalities that, as a matter of justice, should become public health priorities. That the life expectancies of some is as much as a decade less than that of others is concerning, and a differential of almost fifty years is alarming. Nevertheless, without knowing anything about who the different groups are and why they differ, it is not possible to make judgments about which inequalities are the most morally important to address.

Now consider table 2:

Table 2. Average Life Expectancy for Selected Population Groups

75.0 vs. 63.2 (+11.8)	U.S. African American males: 13+ years of education vs. 8 years (Crimmins and Saito 2001)
75.6 vs. 66.6 (+9)	Right-handed vs. left-handed people (Coren and Halpren 1991)
74.8 vs. 68.2 (+6.6)	U.S. white males vs. African American males (Arias 2002)
79.5 vs. 74.1 (+5.4)	U.S. females vs. males (Arias 2002)
79.7 vs. 75.8 (+3.9)	Oscar-winning actors vs. matched controls (Redelmeier and Singh 2001)
77.6 vs. 73.8 (+3.8)	Japanese males vs. American males (Lopez et al. 1999)
77.3 vs. 31.6 (+45.7)	People without cystic fibrosis vs. people with cystic fibrosis (Cystic Fibrosis Foundation 2003)
80.9 vs. 34.3 (+46.6)	Japanese citizens vs. citizens of Sierra Leone (Lopez et al. 1999)

Here we begin to have a basis for making judgments about which inequalities matter most from the standpoint of justice. Often in public health, evidence of inequalities is sought or identified between groups that are otherwise of interest for reasons that, we argued earlier in this chapter, matter morally. Even in the absence of the systematic patterns of profound disadvantage associated with severe poverty and the group animus of racism, residual clusters of negative determinants can remain that make it more difficult for some groups to achieve a sufficiency of well-being. In the United States, for example, we are rightly more concerned about questions of justice when we identify health inequalities between social classes than between those who live in small and large states or between those who identify as Protestants and Catholics.

That African American men who have at least some college education have an average life expectancy that is over a decade longer than African American men who have little education is exactly the sort of inequality that according to our theory should be a moral priority. Reasoning as well as health is no doubt compromised for these poorly educated men. Indeed, it is likely that these men are living with a cluster of disadvantages that result in setbacks with regard to all six essential dimensions of well-being. Moreover, the absolute difference in life expectancy—fully a decade—is clearly substantial.

The size of the disparity is not by itself, however, sufficient to determine whether an inequality in health should be a moral priority. Although according to at least one study (albeit a flawed one) there is also almost a decade differential in life expectancy between right-handed Americans and left-handed Americans, it is unlikely that the handed-ness inequality rises to the same level of moral concern. If this difference is real, it is of public health interest for the reasons already detailed. However, unless it can be established that being left handed is still, as it was in centuries past, associated with multiple social disadvantages and abuses, or it can be established that the differential in life expectancy is a consequence of right-handed engineering in machinery and consumer products, then this inequality should not be among those that matter most in American health policy.

Consider next the inequalities in life expectancy between African American and white American men, and between American men and women. We suspect that intuitively most people would be more concerned about considerations of justice in the racial inequality than in the gender inequality cases, and not because in these particular studies the race differential is greater by one year. Moreover, we believe that such intuitions are correct. Inequalities in health are of most importance when they are avoidable and when they co-travel with clusters of disadvantaging determinants that undermine multiple dimensions of well-being. The characterization fits well the inequality between African American and white American men. By contrast, although the life expectancy of American men is less than that of American women, at seventy-five it approximates any reasonable account of what constitutes a "sufficient" life span. Moreover, in almost all other dimensions of life, men fare at least as well and frequently far better than do women. Our point is not that we should be unconcerned about male life expectancy, or that we should not mount research and clinical programs to extend men's lives. Once again, we underscore that any inequality is of interest to public health and to the positive point of justice. Our position is merely that in the developed world gender inequalities in life expectancy, or even in disability-adjusted life expectancy, are not matters of relative moral urgency (Tsuchiya and Williams 2005). They may become so if, for example, the size of the disparity were to become more dramatic, or if the differential were to reverse, significantly favoring men rather than women, or if the social context were to alter dramatically and men's lives were as a group to fare far worse than the lives of women. We are not here suggesting that dimensions of well-being should be traded off for one another; indeed, below a level of sufficiency, such trade-offs are clearly unjust. Rather, our point is that should the well-being of American men begin to fall across multiple dimensions, the relative moral urgency of gender inequalities in health would increase.

That actors who win Academy Awards live on average fours years longer than other actors, or that the same is true of Japanese men relative to American men, is of no account whatsoever from the standpoint of the negative point of justice. Our theory does not require strict equality in health and, in the absence of evidence of systematic disadvantage in the other dimensions of well-being, these inequalities are not of particular concern. In sharp contrast to a disparity of four years, a differential in average life expectancy of forty years is of enormous concern. The Japan-Sierra Leone disparity, in which the nations with the longest and shortest life expectancies are compared, is a morally easy case. The people of Sierra Leone are desperately poor; the people of Japan are among the most prosperous in the world. As we argued earlier in this chapter, inequalities in well-being associated with severe poverty are inequalities of highest moral urgency. By contrast, the inequality in life expectancy associated with cystic fibrosis is more morally complicated. If, contrary to fact, the disease were preventable or easily and effectively treated, and people were still dying young for lack of medical care, then this inequality would rival that experienced by the people of Sierra Leone in its moral urgency. However, if even with the finest medical care and social services this were the best average life expectancy it is currently possible to obtain for people with cystic fibrosis (which it is not), then this dramatic inequality in life expectancy, however tragic, would have different implications for justice. It remains a matter of moral importance, but for biomedical research as compared to public health.

Note that all of our judgments about the relative urgency of inequalities in health and their relationship to the negative and positive points of justice, reflect not only the particular commitments of our theory but also the empirical particulars in which these inequalities occur. As relevant features of the world change, so too do the implications for justice and public health. While the positive aspiration of public health—to strive for all lives that are healthy and long—remains a constant, what it is possible to obtain in terms of health is ever changing. So too are the concrete demands of the negative aim of our theory for public health. Here also the moral job of public health remains constant: to document and help remedy existing patterns of disadvantage and their detrimental effects and to ensure that children achieve sufficient levels of health so that well-being in adulthood is possible. However, as patterns of social organization and systematic disadvantage alter and the greatest threats to health sufficiency and other dimensions of well-being shift, the specific moral priorities for public health also will shift. And that is as it should be.

Medical Care and Insurance Markets

5.1 The Moral Foundations of Markets

Markets are a central pillar of almost every social structure throughout the modern world, especially since the end of the Cold War. Official ideologies may cling to contrary views, or markets in underdeveloped nations may not resemble the complexity and sophistication of mature markets, but markets do play a prominent role almost everywhere. International organizations such as the World Bank and International Monetary Fund often condition loan guarantees to developing nations on commitments to increase their reliance upon private markets as an alternative to state-owned industries and public welfare programs. Many developed industrial nations that have relied upon public programs for provision of health and other social services are considering or have embarked upon policies that introduce market mechanisms into areas where markets have not played a major role in the past. Supply-side restrictions of services by managed care organizations and user fees (co-payments) for medical care that once were available without cost to the individual are becoming more common in developed and developing nations alike.

Every culture and every nation, of course, recognizes the need to impose some restrictions on markets. At the very least, each expresses some moral reservations about the extent to which certain aspects of life ought to be governed by market norms. However, in many contexts, reliance on markets is frequently considered to be the presumptively best policy. Contrary proposals face a heavy burden of justification, especially against two prominent types of argument. First, neoclassical economists and many utilitarians argue that greater consumer choice in the market is instrumentally valuable. The cumulative effect of our individual market choices is *allocative* efficiency, or the allocation of scarce resources within the overall economy that best satisfies our varied, individual wants and needs. Moreover, informed, self-interested consumers seeking their individually optimal mix of goods and services will spur competition on the basis of price and quality. The expected consequence of this market response to consumer demand is *productive* (or technical) efficiency, or a situation in which particular goods and services that are most desired by consumers will be produced with the least expenditure of resources. When more of us get more of what we want and less of what we don't want (allocative efficiency), and when what we do want is produced with less of our resources and efforts (productive efficiency), then individual utility, and ultimately aggregate social utility, is increased. Indeed, the maximization of aggregate social utility, which is the goal of utilitarian moral theory, is explicated by a more general criterion of economic efficiency by many neoclassical economic theorists (Powers 1992). Second, even if it is debatable whether efficient markets always maximize the sum of individual utilities and hence overall social utility, or whether it is even always a good thing to do so, many theories of justice, most notably libertarian theories, value markets because they offer opportunities for individual choice that are judged intrinsically valuable. To the extent that markets increase consumer choice and limit the sphere of social decisions made collectively by the state, markets allow persons greater individual control over many of the conditions that affect their well-being and shape their lives most profoundly. For those whose central moral commitment is freedom of choice, markets are valuable because they let individuals make more choices according to their own values and preferences, whether or not utility is maximized or efficiency is achieved.

However much there is to be said on behalf of markets, markets have been subject to substantial moral criticisms. It is important to consider these criticisms especially given the continued development of global markets and the increasing frequency with which markets are touted as the remedy for all social ills. From the vantage point of our theory, criticisms of markets can be distinguished by their rationales and by the implications of those rationales for proposals to remedy the perceived problems that markets create.

Karl Marx offered perhaps the most famous and the most sweeping line of criticism of markets, condemning markets of all kinds, including most notably the labor markets that are at the heart of modern capitalism. One rationale Marx offered for this critique was based on the inherent potential of such markets to result in systematic disadvantage for the working classes. He argued that capitalist labor markets result in the immiseration of the proletariat as a consequence of the inherent logic of the capitalist mode of production. Owners of capital, Marx noted, have both strong incentive and superior bargaining position, allowing them to drive down wages to a bare level of subsistence. In this judgment, Marx was not unique. For example, Locke explicitly assumed that a modern system of wage labor would produce the same consequence, but he found no injustice in this. Marx also argued that workers, who have only their labor to sell, have comparatively little power with which to improve their economic condition because capitalists also control both the apparatus of the state and the main institutions of education and public information.

Moreover, in Marx's view, the systematic disadvantage is not confined to the lowest socioeconomic classes. The lower rung of the middle class would tend to sink to the level of proletarians once capital became increasingly concentrated and large corporate interests overtook small merchants and independent tradesmen. The result would be the exacerbation of class differences, along with differentials in market influence and political power. For Marx, the remedy for wholesale injustice is wholesale change. Nothing short of a proletarian revolution overthrowing the entire capitalist mode of production would eliminate the systematic disadvantages that flow from markets.

A second line of criticism agrees with Marx's assessment that inherent in markets is a tendency to work to the systematic disadvantage of some. However, this line of reasoning concludes, unlike Marx, that markets alone need not be determinative of how well those who are thus disadvantaged ultimately fare. Rousseau, for example, argued that the effects of natural inequalities in age, health, and qualities of mind, body, and soul are magnified as the opportunities for acquiring material goods increase with advances in civilization (Rousseau [1755] 1984). In particular, Rousseau saw as a likely consequence of the development of specialized knowledge, combined with modern modes of economic organization, an increase in the differential rewards available to the best off and the worst off and a greater increase in differences in political power and social standing. However, Rousseau (as well as Aristotle) thought that political systems might be structured to prevent economic elites from capturing the machinery of government and thereby cementing an all-encompassing grip on the life prospects of the less fortunate.

This second line of criticism thus appreciates the inherent potential for markets to adversely affect those at the bottom, but it recognizes that other powerful social determinants, such as governmental regulation, the social ethos, and cultural or professional norms have the potential either to compound and reinforce market-induced inequalities or counterbalance them. For example, in the modern context, such policies as minimum wage laws, occupational safety regulations, and collective bargaining schemes stand against Marx's sweeping conclusions and his worries that in capitalism all of society's cards are stacked against wage laborers. In this second view, then, the ultimate moral assessment of markets rests on a more complex moral rationale. It does not stop with the recognition of the inherent potential of markets to impose systematic disadvantage, but instead requires an assessment of how markets function within the totality of specific social arrangements. The case for the abolition of markets in general, or of markets for particular goods and services, is made only if no feasible modification of social arrangements are adequate to counteract the inherent tendencies of markets to disadvantage some segments of the population.

A third line of criticism does not locate its objections in the inherent potential of markets to produce unjust economic and political consequences, nor in the failure to mitigate those consequences through offsetting societal arrangements. Instead, the complaint is that markets are dehumanizing.

Marx, for example, notes that even if he is wrong in his dire predictions, and even if social legislation does improve the lot of the working class, the consequence is but a well-paid slave. A slave, nonetheless, Marx concludes, for the core of his objection is that markets undermine human flourishing and especially those aspects of human flourishing that depend on the kind of relationships we have with one another. The commodification of labor, largely seen by others both then and now as morally benign, inherently alienates human beings from their true selves. Marx's alternative vision to a system of wage labor is one in which each can be hunter in the morning and critic in the evening without ever being merely the sum of a person's paid occupation. This is, of course, a rather romantic vision, born of a belief that technological advancement and increased productivity will make the "many-sided development" of the human species a practical reality. Market commodification also alienates persons from others by transforming all human relationships into market relationships. Markets of all kinds should thus be resisted, lest they displace all other valuable forms of human relationship, including the bonds of love between spouses and between parents and children.

Some critics who share worries about the effects of markets on human relationships are less sweeping in their condemnation of markets. They do not view the commodification of labor as necessarily dehumanizing, nor do they fear that acceptance of markets per se will lead us down a slippery slope to the corruption of all of our human relationships. Rather, the complaints tend to be more discrete and more qualified. A familiar objection of this sort lies against the existence of specific markets—for example, for sexual and reproductive services—on the grounds that commodification of these dimensions of life can be dehumanizing, especially when they occur within a broader unjust social context of sexist norms and practices that compound and reinforce disadvantages to women. This more circumscribed version of the third rationale for objecting to markets is that the existence of some kinds of markets can corrupt human relationships and human flourishing by undermining such things as mutual respect, respect for self and others, and the ability to form attachments.

In sum, we have distinct rationales underlying three lines of criticisms of markets. There are objections based on the inherent tendencies of markets to create patterns of systematic disadvantage to various distributive interests. There are more qualified objections against the reliance on markets under particular forms of political and social organization that compound and reinforce, rather than mitigate, these systematic disadvantages. And there are objections that rest on the negative effects of markets on nondistributive aspects of human well-being.

Our nonideal theory of justice is concerned with any aspect of the basic social structure that has potential for systematic disadvantage on any of the essential dimensions of well-being, including but not restricted to health. That markets have inherent potential for such effects, is, for us, however, never the whole story. Markets or any other element of the social structure need to be evaluated in light of how they contribute to and interact with other social determinants of well-being. Justice will then be a matter of how any given market functions within a particular political, social, and economic context. We also are interested in how markets, thus embedded within a specific social context, can affect the nondistributive aspects of well-being. Our particular interest in this chapter lies in markets for health insurance, and we focus on the United States whenever a specific context for our argument is needed. We will define and consider in turn a variety of forms of insurance, including both indemnity insurance, varieties of managed care, and public insurance plans. Given the presence of certain background social and economic conditions, we examine the adverse effects of various alternatives for the financing of medical care on the essential dimensions of well-being.

In 5.2, we begin with an examination of how economists since Kenneth Arrow have explained what in theory makes markets for medical care different from markets for most other goods and services. We then show how those hypothesized differences have been used to explain the proliferation of various arrangements for financing medical care that emerged in the industrialized nations in the last century. As Arrow's theory predicted, and as a large body of empirical literature has confirmed (especially within the United States), some fundamental features of health insurance markets (as contrasted to some specific features of the U.S. market) explain the tendency of these markets to fail or at least produce results that differ greatly from the efficient outcomes expected by neoclassical economic theory. These tendencies toward failure in health insurance markets undermine one of the most powerful arguments in favor of financing health care through health insurance markets, and they also reveal some problems that the organization of alternative health care financing arrangements face.

Our ultimate concern, however, is not simply the prospect that utilitarian and efficiency-based arguments for reliance on health insurance markets might not succeed on their own terms (either within the U.S. context or more generally). Indeed, our primary focus is on how predictable responses to the prospects of market failure have produced consequences that, from the perspective of our own theory, are unjust. In 5.3, we examine such responses within the United States, where there has been a far greater reliance on markets than upon systems of public provision. In particular, we examine the roots of moral hazard and adverse selection, two forms of potential market failure in insurance markets associated in substantial part with the unavailability of, or the asymmetric distribution of, information about relevant features and prices of health care goods.

Some additional features of the new medical marketplace specific to the U.S. context further compound and exacerbate the potential for systematic disadvantage associated with these twin threats of market failure. In 5.4, we examine the moral significance of the employment-insurance nexus for health and other dimensions of well-being, especially for the most vulnerable or already most disadvantaged members of society.

In 5.5, we consider some moral challenges posed by the combined effects of mixed systems of private insurance and public safety nets for health care, with particular focus on the nondistributive aspects of human well-being, including respect for self and others, self-determination, and attachment.

The conclusions we reach do not constitute a broadside against markets in general, or even a categorical rejection of markets within the medical and health care arenas. Such noncontingent judgments are not possible in our nonideal theory of justice. There are four conclusions that we do reach, however. First, because of the *inherent* tendencies of markets to have a systematically disadvantaging impact on well-being (especially on those already multiply disadvantaged), the justice of a market system of health care depends on the existence of background conditions that mitigate, rather than compound, its ill effects. Second, market-based health care finance under some specific social and economic conditions, especially employer-based insurance arrangements, add to the problems inherent in health care markets and thus pose additional challenges to any efforts to make markets conform to the minimum requirements of justice. Third, whatever role markets may play, justice requires a system of universal, continuous access to a reasonably comprehensive level of medical care. Fourth, many currently accepted ways of combining private markets and public safety nets are unjust, and they are unjust for reasons of their negative effects on all of the dimensions of well-being, not on health alone.

5.2 Sources of Market Failure

In an influential article published in 1963, economist Kenneth Arrow argued that health care is unlike many other goods in the marketplace. His claim is that many of the standard assumptions of neoclassical economic theory do not hold in the case of health care and health insurance markets. Arrow explained that inherent problems in health care markets tend to skew normal market operations, thus leading to widespread inefficiencies or market failures. Arrow's analysis also highlighted ways in which problems inherent in health care markets also tend to undermine efficiency in health insurance markets. In this section, we present a brief explanation of four sources of potential market failure and their conceptual connections to the utilitarian moral foundations of neoclassical economic theory. We describe some of the pivotal changes in the health insurance marketplace in the United States since Arrow's article as a way of illustrating some of the most inherent challenges any attempt to organize health insurance markets must address, and in some instances we show how those problems affect not only market-based systems of health care finance but other systems as well.

Arrow's extraordinary contribution was to apply principles of microeconomics in order to show how markets for medical care and health insurance differ from ordinary markets for other goods and services. It is an article of faith in most economic circles that the aims of efficiency are met when markets conform to certain assumptions and that such markets are more efficient than any other methods of allocating scarce resources. However, as Arrow famously observed, markets can only be superior in terms of efficiency to other means of allocation if in fact they meet the minimal conditions of those assumptions.

Two assumptions are crucially important for our discussion. First, for the efficient operation of markets, both buyers and sellers must be able to evaluate hthe utility-enhancing features of all the goods and services available in the market place. To the extent that there is imperfect information or substantial uncertainty about the utility to be derived from those goods and services, then the expectation of achieving efficiency through consumer choice is undermined. Arrow's argument is that there are numerous, highly significant sources of informational uncertainty that prevent health care markets, and derivatively health insurance markets, from functioning efficiently. Second, efficient markets require that the information that does exist about the utility-enhancing features and price of all goods and services be available to all market participants. Insofar as there are substantial asymmetries between buyers and sellers in the distribution of information, inefficiencies are introduced. The prospects for the consumer-driven utility-maximization is undermined when consumers are not comparable judges of the value of the goods and services offered by producers who possess specialized professional expertise not readily available to consumers. Arrow's conclusion is that both uncertainty and asymmetry of information are endemic to medical care markets, creating the potential for market failures and opening the door to extensive debates about the consequences of relying on market responses to those failures and the proper role of government intervention to correct them.

Uncertainty and Asymmetry in Medical Care Markets

Uncertainty pervades medicine. In this respect, much of medical care is unlike many other commodities. One source of that uncertainty lies in the nature of medical needs. Some medical needs are episodic, highly variable, and often unpredictable, both in their timing and in their severity. By contrast, needs for other essential consumer goods such as food and housing are regular and predictable. The basic requirements for nutrition and shelter are relatively similar among persons, but what is required to meet health needs is highly variable among persons and within different periods of any individual's life. The degree of that variability is often unknown and unknowable. The consequence is that there are substantial limitations in the basis upon which individual consumers must judge the kinds and quantities of medical care that are optimal for them.

Many medical needs generate what economists call unplanned consumption. Knowledge of current health status offers only a limited basis for predicting future needs. Individuals often cannot predict the nature or quantity of specific services they will need in the future. Moreover, they do not know the full range of alternatives that will become available for any medical condition that they currently have or may develop. When need does arise, individuals often have little realistic opportunity to shop on the basis of price and quality comparisons. The ability to anticipate and budget for the satisfaction of many medical needs is made more difficult because of the inelastic character of demand for some services. Inelasticity of demand can occur when the satisfaction of needs can only be achieved by specific goods and services in contexts in which changes in price do not substantially alter the level or urgency of the demand. For such needs, satisfaction cannot be achieved by substituting other, less costly alternatives. The point can be made clear by a contrast to transportation markets. Consumers can decide whether to buy an economy car or just forgo buying a car altogether and take the bus or walk. If there is a lack of available funds to meet transportation needs, or other needs are judged more pressing, then consumers can make rational priority decisions and the consequences are not generally disastrous. By contrast, in medical care markets, some specific kinds of services cannot be foregone without great costs to physical, emotional, and economic well-being.

Uncertainty regarding price is another crucial impediment to the kind of prudent planning and budgeting that is essential to an efficient allocation of resources. Much of medical care, especially the types of treatment that may have quite high utility for many consumers, not only generates unplanned consumption, but is expensive and not amenable to prudent budgeting. The cost of treating a catastrophic illness or injury can leave even the affluent unable to pay for care out of current income or savings. Increasingly, the price of medical care is beyond the reach of many, even for routine and relatively predictable costs of care for chronic illnesses. Although an increase in income or the accumulation of wealth can insulate many individuals from other deprivations of life's necessities, except for the richest among us, the same cannot be said of health care. In an age of rapid and costly technological innovation, this is an even greater problem than it was when Arrow first described it in 1963. For all but the truly wealthy, an increased risk of chronic illness or extended disability from an acute illness or injury also increases the risk of reducing income and wealth to the point where quality of life is seriously threatened.

Most important perhaps is the fact that the actual benefit from medical treatment is uncertain. Individuals with the same medical conditions differ in numerous possible ways. For example, they differ in age of onset, severity of illness, the presence or absence of co-morbidities, the impact of complications, stage of diagnosis, and responsiveness to particular treatment regimens. These differences translate into uncertainties regarding the effectiveness of therapies for the medical conditions of particular patients. Medical care is thus not like other market commodities, such as a stereo, lawnmower, or refrigerator, where the main differences relevant to consumer choice are largely matters of personal taste.

In sum, an usually large degree of uncertainty associated with both the utility and price of goods is a pervasive feature of medical care markets, making the goal of consumer-driven pursuit of efficiency difficult to realize.

In addition to genuine uncertainty—matters about which all participants have imperfect information—medical care markets are further complicated by the asymmetric distribution of information. Arrow points to the fact that for many medical care services, patients must rely upon professional judgments for assessing both the existence and nature of the need and the proper means to its satisfaction. If medical care markets were highly efficient, patients would have "as good or nearly as good understanding of the utility of the product being produced as the producer" (Arrow 1963, 951). Goods and services that do not exhibit the more symmetrical distribution of information presupposed by neoclassical economic theory are often described as credence goods (Sloan 2001). Consumers must defer to the expert judgments of others, and the basis of that deference is often the trust borne of the belief that others possess both the superior knowledge and the requisite fiduciary integrity necessary to advise them of their best interests. The degree of deference to professional judgment, of course, differs depending on the kinds of care, the level of knowledge and personality of the individual patient, and the extent to which the patient is a frequent purchaser of a particular service or has prior experience that informs the decision-making process, which differs, for example, with a chronic condition and an acute event (Pauly 1978; Sloan 2001). Such differences notwithstanding, consumer's judgments, even in routine matters about which a patient has substantial prior experience, depend much more heavily on the advisory role of professional judgment than in many other markets, making the model of rational individual consumers, knowledgeable and capable of maximizing their own utility, an unreliable vehicle for achieving efficiency.

Arrow's claims should not be misread, as they often are. Three important caveats must be noted. First, there is no claim that medical care markets are unique. Nor do the implications for understanding his insights about the inherent tendencies to market failure in medical care markets depend on such a claim. Other markets involve credence goods, and to the extent that they do so, they also exhibit inherent tendencies to market failure (Sloan 2001; Robinson 2001a).

Second, Arrow's analysis should not be read as attributing all inefficiencies in actual health care markets (or the health insurance markets that build upon them) to the imperfect and asymmetric character of information inherent in medical care as a market commodity. Inefficiency can also be a consequence of the specific ways markets are organized. Competition itself, for example, can produce "transaction costs" that are associated with ancillary matters such as billing, collection, or marketing, and these costs can inflate the aggregate health care bill of a nation. Such costs result in a loss of productive efficiency: for the same amount of resources, care could be provided for more citizens, or more of the resource expenditures would be available for improving health, rather than funding activities with less social utility.

Additionally, Arrow points out that among the main sources of inefficiency in health care is the fact that health, more than most other goods, is something that is often valued so much that we routinely provide health care on the basis of need, independent of the usual market norms of willingness and ability to pay. He seems to suggest, as many since have argued as well, that health care is unlike other commodities for the additional reason that health is valued differently from other aspects of human well-being. In an often-cited comment, Arrow notes that, "[t]he taste for improving the health of others appears to be stronger than for improving other aspects of their welfare" (Arrow 1963, 954).

Third, Arrow does not claim and his analysis does not support the conclusion that it is impossible for markets to be organized in ways that reduce the presence or impact of uncertainty or that reduce asymmetry of information. However, Arrow's analysis does support the claim that such attempts face great difficulties. Moreover, even if responses to the threats of market failure do make markets more efficient, they bring in their wake a number of other consequences that must be evaluated in light of what justice requires.

Arguably, as the scientific basis of medical care improves, some areas of uncertainty will diminish (Sloan 2001; Robinson 2001a). Equally plausible, however, is the possibility that, as we learn more about the natural history and etiology of well-described but poorly understood constellations of medical symptoms, the emergence of new treatment modalities will constantly introduce new sources of uncertainty into the medical marketplace. Uncertainty thus seems to be an enduring fact of life in medical care markets and a built-in source of potential market failure.

Asymmetry of information also seems similarly resistant to elimination. That many asymmetries can be eliminated is a reasonably optimistic position to hold. Indeed, their elimination is precisely the aim of many proposals for better measurements of quality and effectiveness of medical care. In addition, many new developments such as public access to Internet databases may change the patterns of information distribution such that some asymmetries between patients and professionals are lessened. For example, some patients are notably better informed about treatment options for chronic disease management than many nonspecialist physicians. Nonetheless, the explosion of medical knowledge and the tendency toward extreme specialization introduces new asymmetries (even among professionals), just as some of the old asymmetries between patient knowledge and professional knowledge recede.

The more modest points we make are that inherent to medical care markets (although not uniquely so) are uncertainties and asymmetries of information. Those informational characteristics are sources of potential market failure in medical care and health insurance markets alike, whatever other sources of inefficiency may arise as a consequence of any particular configuration of those markets. These claims seem to us a reasonable distillation of the enduring lessons of Arrow's justifiably influential paper.

Arrow's paper also points up some of the implications of the pivotal choices available to policy makers. Given the inherent potential for market failures in the delivery of medical care, virtually all developed modern economies have had to choose between two broad policy options for institutional design. The first option is to remove some allocation decisions from the exclusive province of the market. Medical care markets have given way either to some form of government-administered social insurance arrangement for financing access to medical care (e.g., Germany) or to some national health service responsible for the direct public provision of care (e.g., United Kingdom). The second option is to maintain primary reliance on private insurance markets (e.g., United States) and through a combination of market responses and government intervention attempt to address the fact that, as Sherry Glied observes, "health insurance induces its own set of market failures" (Glied 2001, 957). Because the United States offers a textbook example of how the informational problems inherent in medical care markets contribute to new sources of potential market failure in health insurance, we illustrate the problems of health insurance markets through the lens of the U.S. experience.

Uncertainty and Asymmetric Information in Health Insurance Markets

Neoclassical economic theory tells us that for individual consumers to maximize their individual utilities and therefore for society overall to achieve maximum utility, it is necessary for consumers to evaluate what bundles of health care services represent individually optimal amounts for them. Ideally, healthy persons at low risk for future illness would allocate less of their incomes to health services, and less healthy persons or persons at greater risk for future illness or injury would allocate a greater share. We have seen that imperfect information explains why that optimal allocation mix of medical care and other goods is difficult to achieve. The same problem applies to markets for insurance where an optimal mix of insurance and other goods and services is desired. Insurance, if the level of risk protection is adequate, allows individuals to meet the costs when need does arise, but because it is still the case that individuals simply do not know what their future needs or the costs of their satisfaction will be, they are no better equipped to decide the optimal mix of insurance coverage relative to other goods and services than they are to decide how to balance medical and nonmedical needs. The uncertainty that tends to make medical care markets inefficient thus tends to result in inefficiency in health insurance markets. The point is not that consumers must have the market equivalent of a crystal ball in order for the market to work well. Rather, the point is that health insurance markets inherit all of the inherent problems of planning that plague medical care markets and make both medical care and health insurance unlike most other commodities.

It is important to note that the problem of uncertainty in health insurance markets is one that affects both traditional and managed care plans. Uncertainties regarding future need, available therapeutic modalities, and price cannot be eliminated entirely. Such uncertainties are facts of life affecting both kinds of insurance products. Under indemnity insurance contracts, insurers contract to provide partial or full indemnification for the fees paid to independent physicians. Under typical managed care plans, especially the staff-model health maintenance organization (HMO), insurers contract to provide their enrollees access to medical care services from the physicians on staff or from other cooperating physicians who have contracted with the HMO to deliver the needed care for enrollees. Both forms of insurance are examples of contingent claims contracts: the performance obligations of the insurer are dependent upon medical contingencies not within the control of the insurer. This is true whether the insurer is an indemnity insurer or a managed care plan.

Under neither type of insurance contract can the insurer predict or control the full range of medical contingencies its enrollees will experience. Unknown individual health risks, the unknown benefits and costs of treatments, and the unknown character of the treatments that might be available at the time of need introduce a considerably large number of variables into the underwriting equation. Moreover, no matter how precisely the managed care contract seeks to specify in advance the services for which it will provide, it fares no better than indemnity insurance in knowing precisely what form of care will be required. The problem of uncertainty therefore still looms large under any contractual form of insurance for the simple reason that not all of the risks, not all of the services, and not all of their attendant costs are knowable, and thus controllable, even to the experts.

Asymmetry of information is also a problem in health insurance markets. Just as there is an asymmetry of information between patients and physicians in medical care markets, there is an important asymmetry of information between insurer and enrollees. Some individual enrollees, at least at some points in their purchasing history, have some ability to predict increased needs for services. They may have illnesses or have reasons to suspect that they are at increased risk for contracting or worsening of certain conditions. They thus may possess information that insurers may not have, thus making the appropriate match of risk and premiums difficult to accomplish. While asymmetric information in medical care markets generally favors the providers of medical care over the less well informed consumer, the asymmetry of information in insurance markets favors the consumer over the insurer. This disparity of market position is true whether the insurer is an indemnity insurer, managed care organization, or self-insuring employer who bears the risk and contracts with underwriting professionals for management.

Uncertainty and asymmetric distribution of information are important within health care markets in large part because they also contribute to two additional sources of market failure: adverse selection and moral hazard. Adverse selection and moral hazard arise, in part, as a consequence of the uncertainty and asymmetry that Arrow claimed inherent in medical care and health insurance markets. The connections among these four concepts are best understood against the backdrop of debates about the purposes of insurance as they have been reflected in the evolution of insurance markets in the United States.

Insurance, whether funded by taxes and administered by governments, or funded by individual premium contributions and administered by commercial insurance companies (or other entities such as self-insuring employers), is a way to pool resources and share risks. All individuals within the pool (or someone on their behalf) make financial contributions, and only those with medical needs of the sort for which risk protection is provided draw upon the pooled resources. The question, then, of how best to understand the underlying purposes of insurance can be further divided into two component questions: (a) How should the composition of the risk-sharing pool be determined? and (b) for what goods and services ought risk protection be provided?

Adverse Selection: Determining the Composition of Risk Pools

The U.S. insurance market in 1963, at the time of Arrow's influential paper, suggests very different answers to both questions than we find in the market for health insurance at the start of the twenty-first century. After World War II, health insurance was increasingly sold to groups of employees as a benefit of employment. The individual insurance market, in which each applicant undergoes some sort of medical exam, medical history, or medical questionnaire designed to rate each individual's health risk, declined for most Americans. By the 1960s, with a few notable exceptions, individual risk-rated insurance became a relatively small proportion of the overall health insurance market in the United States (Stone 1993).

In the postwar period up until the early 1960s, the not-for-profit Blue Cross group health plans relied upon community rating as a basis for determining membership in the risk sharing pool. Under community rating schemes, all employee groups are charged the same premium. Employees of large and small firms, in both high or low occupational risk industries, and healthier and sicker employees alike within a geographic region paid the same amount. Community rating thus assumes the appropriateness of cross-subsidization of high risk enrollees by low risk enrollees.

The for-profit, commercial plans that emerged during the postwar period adopted a different model; they shifted from community rating to experience rating. Under an experience-rating scheme an established pool, typically one constituted by the employees of a single firm, is charged on the basis of their recent claims history. The "experience" of the group's claims in previous years is thus used as a basis for predicting and setting the premiums for subsequent years. As Deborah Stone has observed, this shift had a profound impact. "Corporate benefit managers and small business owners would naturally choose to buy insurance from companies that offered them cheaper rates. So they would withdraw from the large Blue

Cross/Blue Shield (BC/BS) pool, leaving a slightly less healthy group of people (on average) in the pool" (Stone 1993, 301). In time, BC/BS followed their lead, and virtually all group insurance was underwritten for increasingly fragmented pools on the basis of their claims experience (Starr 1982).

By the end of the twentieth century, the official industry view of how risk pools for organizing health insurance should be formed came to be known as "actuarial fairness" (Stone 1993; Light 1992). The principle of actuarial fairness is a deceptively simple one: like risks should be treated alike and no one should be required to share or subsidize anyone else's risk. According to this view, an insurer has the "responsibility to treat all its policy holders fairly by establishing premiums at a level consistent with the risk represented by each individual policyholder" (Clifford and Iuculano 1987, 1806, quoted in Light 1992, 2507 and Stone 1993, 293). More precisely, the principle of actuarial fairness, as applied to the group health market, cannot be read as an endorsement of a wholesale return to individual risk rating (i.e., setting premiums on the basis of an individual's age, gender, occupational status, and health status). Instead, the principle of actuarial fairness requires that the risk level of a particular group be identified as finely as possible so that no one in one risk group would share the risks of persons in another group whose aggregate risks were higher. Actuarial fairness thus represents the polar opposite position of the community-rating view of how membership in risk-pooling groups ought to be conducted. As Stone comments, "insurance underwriting, far from being a dry statistical exercise, is a political exercise in drawing the boundaries of community membership" (Stone 1993, 299).

The actuarial fairness view, as well as the achievement of efficiency in health insurance markets, would be undermined by any scheme in which low risk individuals would subsidize high-risk individuals. The rationale of those worried about efficiency, however, is not that such subsidies are unfair, but that such subsidies are to be avoided because they fail to maximize the sum of individual utilities. Under pooling arrangements that require persons with lower risks to subsidize persons with higher risks, resources that could be used to satisfy other needs and preferences are diverted from healthier individuals. If the healthier persons were in a market with risk-sharing pools composed of persons at their own lower, average risk, they could have purchased individually optimal mixes of goods and services with their limited resources. Subsidization is thus condemned by neoclassical economics as inefficient, whereas subsidization is condemned by those of a more libertarian political orientation as "a forced subsidy from the healthy to the less healthy" (Clifford and Iuculano 1987, 1811). Both in principle reject all forms of cross-subsidization: if risk pooling is to be a part of any health insurance market, these pools should approximate individual risk rating as nearly as economically feasible to achieve.

Community rating and other heterogeneous risk-sharing schemes are not the only examples of cross-subsidization. While such schemes are designed with the deliberate aim of redistributing the economic burden of health risks, even with the best efforts to distinguish among risks, pooled risk arrangements often contain persons with heterogeneous risks who nonetheless are charged the same premiums. For example, the widely used risk category of age fails to predict whether insureds will have comparable utilization rates because within-group variations are so great relative to between-group variations (Light 1993, 2505). To be sure, medical underwriting techniques that seek actuarial fairness constantly refine the informational basis in the hope of achieving a more fine-grained segmentation of risks. But because of imperfect information about the health risks of any individual, there are limits to the ability of insurers to readily distinguish between high-risk individuals, who otherwise would be charged a higher premium, and low-risk individuals, who would be charged a lower premium. From a libertarian perspective, such results are unfair, if avoidable. From the perspective of neoclassical economics, it is inefficient insofar as it fails to produce individually optimal mixes of health insurance relative to other utility-producing goods and services.

Uncertainty is not the only culprit, if, as some argue, the proper aim of risk-pooling arrangements is actuarial fairness and efficiency. Asymmetry of information is another source of potential market failure. Those who know or believe themselves to have higher risks, if they are rational utility maximizers, have strong incentives to obtain extensive insurance coverage at the best possible premium rate. Community-rating schemes are individually optimal for the less healthy, but their gains come at a cost to others who are healthier. Once community-rating schemes are replaced by experience-rating schemes, the incentives of the less healthy take a distinct form. The individually rational strategy for higher-risk persons is to obtain insurance from a group whose experience rating is such that it provides more coverage for the same or lesser premium costs. The sicker enrollees or those at greater risk of expensive illness thus become "free riders" from the perspective of the actuarial fairness principle.

The prospect that higher-risk enrollees will be attracted into risk sharing pools composed of persons who are on average of lower risk is known as adverse selection. The phrase is suggestive of the fact that the selection of an insurance plan is "adverse" or opposed to the economic self-interests of those members of the pool whose average risk is lower. Insurers, of course, naturally worry about deliberate free riders who capitalize on asymmetry of health risk information. Insurers' interests are served by seeking low-risk enrollees who constitute a "favorable selection."

Moral Hazard: Determining the Scope of Risk Protection

If protection against financial loss from unplanned need is a central purpose of health insurance, then the scope of the coverage would necessarily be limited to coverage for infrequent, acute events, not the relatively routine events for which individuals could in principle budget and pay for out of earnings and savings. In addition, if the central purpose of insurance is only the protection against large or catastrophic financial losses, then the coverage would be limited still further to high-cost medical care.

However, the evolution of the insurance market in the United States reflects a more comprehensive risk protection that covers expenditures both large and small, for events both unanticipated and relatively routine. For much of the 1950s, available health insurance coverage was for hospitalization expenses as the original Blue Cross policies provided. Later, with the addition of Blue Shield, increasingly expensive physician services were covered. Even in the 1960s, when insurance coverage moved toward greater comprehensiveness, such things as medical services for normal routine deliveries were not covered. Not until the 1990s were benefits for prescription drugs widely included. Normal childbirth and delivery and prescription drugs were routine expenditures and they were viewed as not requiring insurance (Glied 2001).

What then explains the movement toward comprehensiveness of risk protection in health insurance? Many have argued that factors specific to U.S. labor markets and tax policy accounted for the shift, at least as much as any other explanation. Favorable tax policy toward employer-provided health insurance offered a tax-sheltered form of employee compensation that employers and labor unions alike found attractive (Melhado 1998). Notably, however, most insurance policies placed limits on their own losses through annual and lifetime expenditure caps, thereby leaving their policyholders "vulnerable to the financial costs of long-term illnesses" (Glied 2001, 961). The coverage thus became comprehensive or broad (covering expenses for routine and unanticipated care) but shallow (with little or no economic protection against catastrophic expenses). From the earliest stage of this trend, critics objected that such policies are an inappropriate form of risk protection (Feldstein 1973). One problem is that the shallowness of the coverage "left consumers exposed to risks they could not hope to budget and induced them to avoid seeking care that was expensive" (Melhado 1998, 242).

The comprehensiveness of insurance that emerged in the marketplace was and continues to be criticized as "overinsurance" (Pauly 1974; Sloan 1993). The comprehensiveness of insurance, now expanded to include many routine expenditures, was said to stimulate overutilization of services, often of marginal or even negative utility, leading ultimately to uncontrolled price inflation. When the existence of insurance causes consumers to demand benefits in excess of what they would otherwise seek to receive, the result is known as moral hazard. Moral hazard, according to Mark Pauly's definition, is present "whenever an individual's behavior that affects the expected loss is altered by the quantity of insurance he obtains" (Pauly 1968, 630). The term connotes the industry concern "that insured persons would take advantage of (or abuse) insurance" (Melhado 1998, 231). One reason for the increased utilization is that the existence of insurance itself stimulates demand by lowering the price of care. As Pauly observes, increased utilization may be an individually rational response to the fall in price (Pauly 1968, 535). Moreover, it is not just the existence of private insurance that can trigger increased utilization. National health insurance can have the same effect (Pauly 1971). Insofar as care is free, such schemes "will encourage all use, whether appropriate or not" (Pauly 1980, 204).

Moral hazard is not just a theoretical possibility. The empirical literature provides rich documentation in a wide range of settings, in both public programs and in private markets (Cutler and Reber 1998). Increased utilization, of course, would not be so problematic, at least from the point of view of those interested in achieving efficiency, if the existence of insurance (or national health care) induced a more appropriate level of utilization, or one that actually resulted in a gain in utility. Insurers (and taxpayers within a national health care context), however, may see things differently. They are interested in controlling utilization in order to protect their own economic interests and thus may worry about such increases in any case. By contrast, economists worry that insurance-induced utilization results in a "welfare loss" or reduction in overall utility for the simple reason that the existence of insurance (or free national health services) can stimulate both beneficial and nonbeneficial (or marginally beneficial) utilization indiscriminately. The so-called "welfare loss" argument is predicated on the belief that, because patients lack the information to discern the difference between the two, the perceived high social valuation that many place on health will result in nonoptimal levels of insurance protection (Melhado 2000; Manning and Marquis 1996). Hence, the explanation of the term "overinsurance." More of our resources are thus spent for insurance, and in turn, more resources are spent for medical care, without more utility being realized.

The ultimate source of the problem of moral hazard lies in the presumed informational deficiencies that Arrow identified in 1963. Consumer ignorance is partly a function of genuine uncertainty regarding the expected benefits or the efficacy of some intervention or diagnostic test. More often, however, moral hazard is described in many discussions as an artifact of indemnity insurance. The refrain is familiar. Because insured patients can expect to be indemnified for the services they use, they are not cost-sensitive. They demand services independent of the costs, and the aggregate consequence of such decisions is a lack of control on prices, and hence, a greater use of resources than might otherwise be necessary to achieve the desired health benefits (i.e., productive inefficiency). Fanning the flames of that indiscriminate use of care is the influence of physicians. Under fee-for-service medicine, combined with indemnity insurance, there are strong economic incentives for physicians and hospitals to provide medical services, however marginally beneficial. Not only does the economic self-interest of physicians and health care institutions favor provision of more services, so too do the ethical norms of medical practice that place the best interests of patients in the forefront of a physician's duties, along with the natural human desire to respond to need, however remote the possibility of benefit.

To be sure, asymmetry of information, coupled with the alignment of physician economic incentives and moral aspirations to do more rather than less under indemnity insurance arrangements, does help explain why the problem of moral hazard can be as big as it is. However, moral hazard is not simply a problem of asymmetry of information within the context of indemnity insurance. Uncertainty, coupled with the high social valuation on medical care, has the inherent potential to stimulate utilization. Under any financing arrangement in which medical services of even marginal health benefit are offered at free or substantially reduced prices, there are powerful incentives to utilize them. The significance extends beyond market-based systems. Citizens of countries that have instituted a national health service providing free care, as well as enrollees in managed care plans that provide medically necessary services for a pre-paid annual per-patient fee, reflect the same set of patient (and physician) incentives (Pauly 1980). Such plans differ largely in the ways that they curb or of fail to counterbalance the incentives to use more services, whether useful or not.

5.3 Responses to Market Failure: Some Examples from the U.S. Experience

The potential for market failure is a source of concern from the perspective of neoclassical economic theory for reasons having to do with its adverse social consequences. Inefficiency means lower aggregate social utility. Insurers themselves, including self-insuring employers, have reasons of self-interest for responding to the potential for such failures. Students of microeconomics—the study of economic behavior from the perspective of the incentives of decision makers within a competitive economy—observe that market failures threaten the competitive, cost-saving objectives of the firm. Uncertainties regarding onset and severity of need, medical effectiveness, and costs at time of utilization, combined with lack of health status information that may be known to enrollees, tends to undermine the ability of insurers to establish the appropriate price for each level of risk. Having too many high-risk enrollees (adverse selection) likely to utilize more services than they would have without insurance (moral hazard) are problems that any cost-conscious insurer cannot ignore. Risk minimization is thus a business imperative if and when pricing strategies alone are inadequate to ensure profitability (or solvency in the case of not-for-profit insurers).

While these details of strategies to minimize risk that are observed in U.S. markets do not exhaust the possibilities, they are illustrative of the general types of market response, either alone or in combination, that are available to insurers. They include: (a) traditional pricing strategies that make those who are likely to use more services pay more in premiums, if, in fact, the underlying informational problems can be overcome sufficiently; (b) underwriting strategies meant to exclude from coverage altogether the highest risk or highest utilizers who are not excluded; (c) supply-side underwriting strategies meant to limit the scope of coverage or supply of services available to those with higher health risks or higher utilization rates; and (d) demand-side strategies that depress demand for services by passing on a greater share of the costs of utilization to employees.

In most markets, some mixture of all four strategies are present. Even within some public programs, the demand-side, or cost-sharing, strategy is increasingly promoted in some policy circles as a way of introducing an element of market discipline into nonmarket systems (Flood 2000). The emphasis on a particular strategy will depend on a variety of factors, including the presence or absence of other market considerations, the legal regulatory climate, and the currency of various proposed solutions offered by economists, health policy researchers, and management theorists.

Pricing Strategies

From both an economist's societal perspective and an insurer's self-interested view, a pricing strategy is preferred to minimizing risk. From the perspective of microeconomic theory, insurers should seek to enroll persons of all levels of risks as long as those risks can be identified accurately and premiums can be priced at levels commensurate with individual risk. No reasonable insurer would seek to restrict the size of the market as long as the insurance product can be priced appropriately. Neoclassical economists would agree: it is a market failure and a loss of social utility when people would prefer to have a good or service, including insurance against some risk, and there is unmet demand (Glied 2001, 964).

However, the pervasiveness of uncertainty and the asymmetry of information between insurer and enrollee are among the main reasons for doubting that accurate pricing in health insurance is achievable. In addition, some suspect that individual risk rating inevitably involves sufficiently high transaction costs such that whatever efficiency gains are possible through risk rating are overtaken by the costs of gathering the information necessary for the risk rating (Light 1992). Whether informational deficiencies or transaction costs make individual risk rating and pricing strategies unfeasible in any context is a matter that is both speculative and beyond our expertise to assess. Both are open empirical questions (Sloan 2001; Robinson 2001a).

There are, however, other reasons in some specific contexts that may make it difficult to implement pricing strategies designed to make those who are likely to use more pay more. Prominent among these other reasons are economic considerations such as U.S. tax policies that favor employer-based group insurance over the individual, risk-rated market and the existence of legal restrictions on the use of differential pricing strategies. For example, some state laws set uniform rates for all groups in a jurisdiction or prohibit individual risk rating among enrollees within a single group.

If inherent informational impediments, competitive considerations, legal reasons, or some combination of concerns, make reliance on differential pricing strategies less attractive to insurers, then insurers face a new set of decision parameters. Absent an ability to price risks appropriately, risk minimization strategies gain in importance. Insurers must either restrict those to whom they sell or change the nature of what they sell whenever pricing is not a viable option.

Exclusionary Underwriting

When pricing strategies are not an adequate option, exclusionary underwriting is often the first line of defense. It is easier to limit the entry of high-risk enrollees into the risk-sharing pool than to contain the costs of increased risks once those with greater needs are insured. Indeed, exclusion was an important early strategy as commercial health insurance made major inroads against the community-rated, nonprofit Blue Cross and Blue Shield insurers. For example, it is well known that the shift from community rating to experience rating in the United States resulted in a segmentation of groups based upon (real or perceived) differences in health risks (Starr 1982). One result was that groups of like or similar risks were priced similarly, thus approximating the results of individual risk rating. However, greater actuarial fairness was not the only consequence. The process of market segmentation of risks was also used to redline, or exclude, employees of entire industries thought to be at health risks too great to insure (Stone 1993; Light 1992). Given the phenomenon of uncertainty, coupled with worries about the asymmetry of information between enrollees and commercial insurers, avoiding certain high risk groups altogether emerged as a prudent business strategy.

That some insurers would choose exclusion of risks over attempts to price higher risks more accurately turned the expectations of many theorists on their head (Newhouse 1996). The prevailing wisdom had been that supply would respond to demand, just as it is predicted to do for markets generally. That meant that the more people need coverage, the more they would have to pay. What is more, the prediction was that, given the existence of pooling arrangements, the demands of those at higher risk who presumably want extensive coverage would be met, while the demands of those with lower risks who presumably want less coverage would not. The reason for that prediction was that risk-sharing pools make these differences in preferences and needs less visible to individual enrollees and thus make subsidization of the worst off easier. Hence, what becomes available in the marketplace is skewed toward benefits packages that better match the preferences of those whose needs are greatest (Rothschild and Stiglitz 1976). Indeed, some continue to speculate that today's relatively comprehensive group health plans exhibit a similar phenomenon called "middle-class capture." These comprehensive plans provide a degree of risk protection that is more in line with the preferences of enrollees who have more resources to spend on health insurance than the preferences of those who are poorer and would prefer to spend their limited resources on other goods (Shapiro 1998).

The operative principle in practice tends to be the opposite, however. The greater the demand the less the supply. Instead of getting what they want, while having to pay more for their insurance, there is a mountain of empirical evidence showing that high-risk individuals have greater difficulty in obtaining insurance of any kind (Newhouse 1996). The circumstances leading to the creation of Medicare, the federal program established in the 1960s to provide insurance to the elderly is an important, often-cited example of high-risk disenrollment. By the 1960s commercial insurers had virtually stopped selling insurance to the elderly. Demand by those with greater potential needs tends to cause supply to contract, unlike what would be expected in other markets.

There are a number of possible explanations for the failure of supply to respond to increased demand, including the possibility that insurers are simply acting with a degree of risk-aversiveness that is not warranted by the real magnitude of the economic threat posed by high-risk enrollees (Robinson 2001b). Another possibility is that the market for insurance for high-risk populations simply disappears when medical care costs rise so much that the expected costs of their premiums surpasses the resources available to enough of that population to make marketing to them economically feasible. The lack of resources was surely one important factor among others when Medicare was enacted. Less than half of all seniors had health insurance, and more than a quarter were below poverty levels. Commercial insurers dropped coverage of the elderly in order to pursue more lucrative, less risky group insurance for employees and their families (U.S. House of Representatives 1999). No doubt, all of these factors played some part in the explanation.

In addition, the necessity of responding to the threat of moral hazard plays some role in some high-risk persons being excluded from coverage. At the very least, the threat of moral hazard explains their being excluded from the level of coverage they would purchase if supply responded to demand. In instances in which more generous insurance plans have been priced commensurate with the higher expected needs of the enrollees, the result has been greater adverse selection. When given a choice of plans, each priced according to expected risk, sicker and older employees opt for more extensive coverage and the healthier and younger employees opt for less expensive and less generous plans. While in principle, this is precisely what efficiency-minded observers would hope for, choice turns out to be a "two-edged sword" according to Victor Fuchs. "It is a fundamental principle of health insurance that more choice implies more adverse selection—that is a greater proportion of enrollees with potentially costly health care needs" (Fuchs 2002, 1822). Greater choice leading to greater adverse selection often sets in motion a chain of events eventuating in what is known as the premium "death spiral" (Newhouse 1996; Cutler and Reber 1998).

The death spiral refers to the fact that the more generous plans experience more adverse selection relative to the less costly plans, and as a consequence the difference between average risk of the members in the more and less costly plans widens, setting off still further differences in premiums. The ensuing upward premium spiral for the more generous plans then results in their being eliminated from the market altogether. They become too expensive for enrollees, who no longer enjoy the subsidy of the lower risk enrollees, and too costly for employers to administer, given the smaller pool. Insurers themselves become increasingly risk averse when contemplating underwriting for a high-risk population. The upshot is that more consumer choice, designed to combat moral hazard by making consumers bear the greater costs of their greater needs, can undermine risk pooling mechanisms to such a degree that markets become less likely to respond with differential pricing strategies for different risks, and higher risks become effectively uninsurable.

Greater consumer choice is not the only way some people become effectively uninsurable. Improvement in the insurer's ability (or a belief in that increased ability) to identify those at higher risk also leads to greater market segmentation according to risk. Higher premiums are charged for the higher-risk groups, and if they rise enough, whole groups emerge as less favored candidates for insurance and become uninsurable in much the same way that they are driven out of the market by the death spiral set in motion by enhanced consumer choice. This is what happened to the elderly prior to the enactment of Medicare. Other groups in the U.S. market experienced a similar fate. Availability of dependent health coverage as a benefit of employment dropped precipitously in the 1990s (Etheredge, Jones, and Lewin 1996). Being employed is a reasonable proxy for being an average health risk, but a dependent's risk profile is an unknown. The availability of Medicare supplement insurance as a benefit for retirees and the availability of group health coverage for early retirees (those who retire prior to the age of Medicare eligibility) also dropped dramatically (Iglehart 2002b). Their greater potential health needs place them on the higher end of the risk spectrum and thus add greatly to the costs of insuring younger, presumably healthier workers.

The groups who are considered uninsurable, of course, may differ from time to time. Uninsurability is not a brute fact of nature; there are no risks that are in principle beyond underwriting. Whether to engage in exclusionary underwriting is determined by a variety of factors. Some undesirable risks may be ones that insurers are legally required to insure as a condition of doing business. Some high risks may be economically worth insuring if doing so provides the market opportunity to insure the more profitable risks as well. Also, there are practical limits to the use of exclusionary underwriting as a means of warding off adverse selection. No insurance market can survive without enough potential customers. In the case of self-insuring employers, some may be partially motivated by a desire to minimize the extent of their own involvement in the insurance of their workers and families. They, too, may find that limiting financial liability in some other way often may be preferable to outright exclusion.

Supply-Side Strategies

If not all high risks can be eliminated by exclusionary underwriting, then one way of reducing the potential financial liability is to reduce utilization through controls on the supply of services. The theoretical basis of managed care reflects in large degree this supply-side approach. If, as the threat of moral hazard demonstrates, consumers are not sufficiently motivated to restrict utilization, and in fact utilization may increase when insured, then contractual arrangements that limit which services consumers will receive may accomplish what consumers themselves are not motivated to achieve.

Typical supply-side solutions involve managed care restrictions on the kinds of care received by patients. They include having primary care physicians act as gatekeepers, thereby limiting access to costly specialist services; setting pharmacy and practice guidelines that limit physician discretion in treatment and diagnosis; and requiring pre-utilization review and approval of services. While these and other supply-side solutions are primarily intended as responses to moral hazard, they also provide an additional hedge against the consequences of the limited ability to control adverse selection. As long as services are constrained sufficiently, a few more higher risks can enter the pool without doing profound damage to the overall profitability or solvency of the plan. Exclusion of coverage can be a partial substitute for exclusion of persons.

For a variety of political and cultural reasons, many of the supply-side solutions most favored by managed care theory were abandoned or severely limited after their U.S. heyday in the mid-1990s. Insurance practices altered so much that some market observers have declared that the era of managed care is over (Robinson 2001b). Many of the usual tools of managed care cost containment did not survive for very long in the marketplace, and real competition between plans never materialized in any widespread manner, making comparisons with traditional alternatives within the same populations (i.e., the employees of large employers) even more difficult. An industrial purchasing model, in which large corporations limit consumer choice in order to achieve cost-savings from economies of scale associated with having only one or a small number of insurance plan providers, became the norm. Smaller firms from the very beginning of the decade moved quickly to reduce choice even further for similar reasons (Maxwell and Temin 2002; Marquis and Long 1999; Etheredge, Jones, and Lewin 1996). Prospective utilization review of services also went by the wayside in many large plans, as did the primary care physician's gatekeeping role and other direct controls on the supply of medical goods and services (Sullivan 2000). As James Robinson observes, the essence of the managed care bargain was never fully implemented. The aim of managed care is to offer comprehensive benefits in return for limits on some forms of care established within a process of utilization review, thus providing the enrollees with most of their care with minimal out-of-pocket costs. Instead, the public interpreted the bargain as "a promise to unrestrained access to all relevant services" (Robinson 2001b).

While supply-side restrictions within traditional managed care rely upon mechanisms of controlling the exercise of medical judgment, not all supply-side solutions are unique to managed care, and not all supply-side solutions require management of medical judgment as a means of restricting access. Many looser variants of managed care that have both in-network and out-of-network options (point-of-service plans), as well as traditional indemnity insurance plans, also restrict supply by incorporating explicit expenditure limits within the insurance contract (Robinson 1999). Lifetime or annual expenditure "caps" or ceilings on coverage for certain diseases or conditions such as HIV/AIDS or diabetes, exclusions of coverage for specific services such as organ transplants, and payments only for generic drugs or other set treatments are examples. The advantage is that the contract itself can achieve the same sort of cost-saving objectives that might otherwise be achieved by relying on practice guidelines and other direct controls on physician judgment. The physician may have to tell the patient that "your insurance policy does not pay for that," but he or she does not have to tell the patient "you cannot have that." In effect, managed care gives way to a system of managed costs.

Moreover, there are virtually unlimited opportunities for managing costs through modifications of the insurance contract. For each group policy, such as those underwritten for a particular employer, modifications can be made at each renewal date to eliminate or reduce coverage for precisely those services that, in the previous year, proved to be among the most costly for that specific group of enrollees. These risk-management strategies do not require the exclusion of identifiable persons based on individual health risks. Those very same persons can be excluded from effective coverage through more carefully tailored means that reduce both moral hazard and the worst effects of an inability to control adverse selection (Light 1992; Powers 1997; Robinson 1999).

Demand-Side Strategies

Pure managed care arrangements were overtaken by new forms of insurance in the late 1990s as willingness to control physician behavior dwindled and the emphasis on cost control by any feasible means replaced the original managed care theory. These new forms of insurance represent a kind of hybrid of indemnity and managed care (Hellander 2001; Inglehart 2002a). Looser variants of managed care provide one set of benefits, as well limited copayments and deductibles, for patients who choose physicians and hospitals within the network of approved providers, and less generous reimbursements, as well as higher co-payments and deductibles, for out-of-network services (a "point of service" option). Hybrids emerged in importance also after adverse selection resulted in the premium death spirals within multiple-choice employer benefits, which, in turn, eradicated many of the more generous indemnity insurance plans (Cutler and Reber 1998). These hybrid plans still exhibit some of the supply-side features of the purer managed care approach, especially the contractually established expenditure limits, but the risk-management emphasis changed (Strunk, Ginsberg, and Gabel 2001).

In contrast to the theory that favors competition among managed care plans, many of the hybrid plans and more recent proposals for altering the marketplace suggest greater reliance on strategies to curb demand as a way of restraining utilization, and less reliance on the combination of physicians having incentives to do less and the expertise of plan purchasers to make judgments about quality of care on behalf of their enrollees. The current emphasis has its roots in proposals of the 1970s. Some economists frankly doubted that the enthusiasm for evidence-based medicine or comparison of health outcomes held out sufficient promise as a constraint on utilization (Pauly 1971). Relying on empirical studies that showed that higher co-payments, higher deductibles, and larger co-insurance requirements (proportions of the total bill not paid by insurance) depressed utilization, they favored these demand-side curbs over supply-side curbs. Armed also with evidence that, for much of medical care, the depressed utilization resulted in no aggregate differences in health outcomes (except for the poor), they concluded that it would be better to let consumers, not the plan manager experts, decide what care is most beneficial (Melhado 1998, 2000). The problem of asymmetry of information between physician and patient, they concluded, was perhaps not the problem it had seemed if consumers, when given the proper economic incentives, make choices that do not result in worse outcomes on average.

The fact that health outcomes did not vary substantially, even after medical utilization dropped, was taken as confirming their belief that on average most of the U.S. population is overinsured and could as well be left to make their own decisions in the way traditional market theory recommends. The proponents did not assume that consumers could make all of their medical decisions in this fashion. The proposal was that full coverage be retained for large, catastrophic risks from acute events, but that more costs be shifted to the individual purchaser in paying for small and routine risks.

A renewed emphasis on these 1970s-style proposals for cost-sharing strategies became evident in both practice and theory in the decade beginning in 2001 (Galvin and Milstein 2002; Inglehart 2002a). Depression of demand through greater cost-sharing has become an important strategy. It is, for many, an attractive strategy, especially when uncertainty and asymmetry of information make identification of higher risks unfeasible, or when the greater exclusion or limitation of coverage is legally prohibited, publicly unpopular, or judged to involve the insurer too heavily in assessing medical utility of the services about which their enrollees have differing opinions. Indeed, surveys of employers throughout the 1990s and beyond reveal increasing reservations about their capacity to assess the quality of care offered by insurers, as well as doubts about the validity and utility of quality-of-care information. Insurers themselves expressed increasing anxiety about the consumer response to their efforts to manage physician medical judgment and behavior (Epstein 1995; Jensen et al. 1997; Agency for Health Care Research 1997; Maxwell 1998; Hofer and Haywood 1999; Lo Sasso et al. 1999; Krumholz and Rathore 2002; Hargraves and Trude 2002; Draper et al. 2002; Galvin and Milstein 2002). Added to the incentives for shifting away from supply-side curbs is the dissatisfaction many physicians express over having to participate in the process of vetting which services are provided. Indeed, the American Medical Association is on record in favor of replacing managed care with some sort of system of medical savings accounts so that resource decisions would be made by patients, rather than through a process of protracted negotiation between medical professionals and insurers (Bodenheimer 1999b, 587).

For reasons discussed already, concerns about potential economic and medical consequences of supply-side curbs mirror those of demand-side curbs. There are additional issues associated with demand-side curbs, however, and their potential for adverse consequences depend on a host of considerations. For example, if applied across the board to everyone in the population, the economic and health effects are likely to fall disproportionately on the poor. The evidence from the most comprehensive studies of the issue found no generalized adverse health impact associated with a system of extensive cost-sharing, but it did find an adverse impact on the health of the poor (Newhouse 1994). Moreover, significant cost-sharing requirements, if imposed on the poor, function like a regressive tax, and early proponents argued for cost-sharing only for the middle- and upper-income insureds (Pauly 1971). Even if cost-sharing is the "next big thing" in health care finance policy, it may not be the right approach for the entire population. As James Robinson notes, "The new paradigm fits most comfortably the educated, assertive and prosperous and least comfortably the impoverished, meek, and poorly educated" (Robinson 2001b).

Overinsurance or Underinsurance?

Both supply-side and demand-side curbs can reduce utilization. The question is whether they limit utilization in ways that is harmful to those affected. Some argue that the result has been a growing phenomenon of underinsurance (Farley 1985; Light 1992). According to one definition, underinsurance occurs when "medical needs...either are not covered by health plans or covered but with high co-payments that force beneficiaries to forego treatment" (Kuttner 1999b, 165). On the one hand, longer-term trends toward greater comprehensiveness in health insurance coverage show increasing protection against financial hardship. A far greater proportion of medical expenditures are paid for by insurance than they were at the time Arrow wrote his famous paper: 83% in 1998 compared to 46% in 1963 (Glied 2001). The share of total medical expenditures paid for out-of-pocket has dropped substantially since the 1960s, and they continued to drop through the 1990s: 48% in 1960, 20% in 1990, and 15% in 2000 (cited by Iglehart 2002a). Through much of the 1980s and 1990s, individual households on average spent roughly only 5% of their income on out-of-pocket health care costs (Strunk, Ginsberg and Gabel 2001). These data suggest that, on average, the level of risk protection for most is quite high and that health costs remain within a range of what most individuals can prudently budget for without undue hardship.

On the other hand, we know that the insured continue to be burdened by a great deal of unpaid medical bills. In one study from the late 1980s, almost half of the unpaid bills were attributed to patients with insurance (Light 1992, 2506). Similar trends continued throughout the 1990s with the burden of health care costs among the insured very unevenly distributed. One in eight families spend more than 10% of their income on health care. As the age of families rises, that percentage increases dramatically, with those older than sixty-five spending more than 50% of income on insurance premiums and out-of-pocket costs (Kuttner 1999b, 168). In addition, those with the largest health care expenditures in 1963 had a much lower ratio of expenses to income than is the case more recently, suggesting that, "while borrowing and saving could plausibly substitute for formal health insurance contracts in 1963, that was not a realistic option for most people in 1996" (Glied 2001). In short, while on average, it may be argued that many are faring well enough in terms of the level of economic protection afforded by insurance, there are still those for whom the underinsurance represents a significant economic burden.

By contrast, it is notable that others continue to argue that overinsurance characterizes the U.S. market. The heart of the overinsurance claim is that generous coverage for routine services encourages overutilization, understood as additional use that is stimulated by having insurance but does not yield additional medical benefit (Pauly 1971; Robinson 1999a). Judgments are clouded by a remarkable lack of health outcomes data by which to evaluate the conflicting claims of those who think we are overinsured and those who think we are underinsured. The degree of systematic knowledge about quality of health care in the United States is surprisingly small (Schuster, McGlynn, and Brook 1998). The one conclusion reached from a comprehensive literature review is that "there are large gaps between the care people should receive and the care they do receive. . . . This is true for all three types of care—preventive, acute, and chronic" (Schuster, McGlynn, and Brook 1998).

While many studies do show little adverse health effect from decreased medical care utilization, those same studies show that the negative impact on the poor is greater. Moreover, we know from patient surveys that large numbers postponed or failed to get needed care, felt increased stress, experienced a temporary disability with significant pain or suffering, and in some cases experienced long-term serious consequences or disability (Kaiser Commission on Medicaid and the Uninsured 2002). Of particular concern perhaps are the possible health consequences of underinsurance for children, for whom care is essential for their proper development, and middle-age enrollees (45–64), for whom the management of chronic illnesses is an increasingly important benefit of medical care. For these groups, we have substantial evidence of the adverse impact of uninsurance (Iglehart 2002a; Kuttner 1999b), and thus protection against underinsurance is of critical concern.

It is likely that both descriptions are true. Overinsurance may characterize some parts of the population, where more services at greater costs do not yield greater medical benefit, while in other parts of the population, underinsurance may be a problem, both in terms of unmet costs and unmet medical need. Indeed, this bimodal picture is precisely what some portray as the U.S. situation today. They argue that we both overspend and overtreat for some, while underspending and undertreating for others (Schuster, McGlynn and Brook 1998). This is what Alain Enthoven and Richard Kronick label the "paradox of excess and deprivation" (Enthoven and Kronick 1991).

Winners and Losers: Market Trends and Enduring Lessons

The experience of the United States over the last several decades is not indicative of any inevitable path that markets must take in response to the threats of market failures. Markets are dynamic. They respond to other market and nonmarket influences in different ways. What was once old is once again new. It would be no surprise, for example, if, after some passage of time, some will chronicle (or advocate) the return to the era of pure managed care on the grounds that demand-side strategies fail to curb moral hazard while health outcomes for some groups actually worsen. Both fashion and professional dissatisfaction with market responses to market failures are hard to predict. A survey of recent American history reveals that what endures are the harsh effects that each of the main strategies can have on some groups, especially those already disadvantaged in important ways.

One ongoing concern is that those with greater health risks also are at greater risk for exclusion from insurance markets or limitations on coverage that effectively exclude them from services they most need. Those with fewer resources will be hit harder than those for whom the benefits of health insurance for routine matters are but a modest supplement to an already substantial income. Those whose health outcomes depend heavily on access to timely care and continuous medical monitoring and whose resources are fewest are among the worst off by any definition. Exclusionary underwriting, supply-side controls, and demand-side cost-sharing arrangements may be competitively rational responses by insurers to the potential for market failures, but evidence has shown that they threaten to reduce the health of some of the most medically and economically vulnerable members of society. When market exclusion and underinsurance consume the already limited resources of these groups, the resultant economic difficulty in meeting health needs can also deprive individuals of the scarce resources they require for ensuring other dimensions of well-being.

Our worries about the potential adverse impact of the main strategies for responding to failures in health insurance markets would be blunted if certain claims made by some market theorists hold true. One familiar claim by proponents of markets is that there is a positive "portfolio effect" such that everyone has sufficient reasons to favor markets overall, even when they know that some specific markets tend toward systematically disadvantaging them (Reinhardt 2001). The reason for such a claim is the prediction that, while some may be losers in certain markets, where their individual bad fortunes are a by-product of efficiency, on average, all will be winners in enough other markets such as to offset losses in any particular market (Pauly 1995).

There are two problems with the portfolio argument. First, on our theory, if losses in the health insurance market cause individuals to fall below a level of sufficiency with regard to health, that loss cannot be offset by gains in other dimensions in well-being. Health is important in its own right and for its own sake, independent of its instrumental value in achieving opportunity or other valued goods and services. While individuals may trade off one dimension of well-being for another, the structure of social systems that makes trade offs on behalf of its citizens cannot justly reduce one essential dimension of well-being below the level of sufficiency.

Second, that everyone has an equal average probability of being a winner most of the time, and a loser only some of the time, is both irrelevant and implausible in our nonideal account of justice. It is irrelevant because, even if true, the fact that things all work out well enough on average is not what concerns a nonideal theory. It matters that some, as a consequence of social organization, actually fall below sufficiency levels in one or more essential dimensions of well-being. Average levels of well-being, and certainly not the antecedent probability of achieving average levels of well-being, are not what justice demands.

That everyone has an equal average probability of being a winner most of the time is implausible as well. Such claims, when made as part of arguments regarding what hypothetical deliberators would choose for themselves in advance of actual need are highly controversial (Powers 1995). Most significantly for our present argument, such arguments are implausible for the reason that, for some persons under some social and economic arrangements, a "negative portfolio effect" is as reasonable to expect as the positive portfolio effect the optimists hypothesize. We know that in real-world situations, inequalities beget other inequalities, and that inequalities can compound and reinforce one another, making inequalities of all sorts harder to escape. Whether disadvantages produced by any particular response to market failure are lessened or compounded depends on the social and economic structures in which they operate. Here we turn to an examination of how the health insurance market within the United States operates as a concrete example of the many ways in which a negative portfolio effect can be produced.

5.4 Making Matters Worse: Employer-Based Insurance in the United States

The employer-based system of health insurance in the United States is the subject of considerable criticism (Powers 1991). Even the American Medical

Association advocates the elimination of the employment-based system of health insurance (Bodenheimer 1999b). However, it should be noted at the outset that the United States is not unique in tying health insurance to employment, at least for some portion of the population. There are some crucial differences between the U.S. system and other alternative approaches to employment-based insurance (Flood 2000; Stone 2000; Amelung, Glied, and Topan 2003). Our claim is that it is not the employment nexus per se that most warrants moral criticism, but the larger social and economic institutional arrangements in which they figure that are more important morally. We consider the injustices to which those arrangements contribute for those who are employed but not insured, those who are employed and insured but who bear greater burdens, and those who receive no public subsidy for purchasing insurance while other more fortunate members of society are publicly subsidized.

Employed But Not Insured: The Unequal Burdens of Uninsurance

Under the U.S. arrangement, there are many who are employed but not insured. Especially in the pre-1990s era, those left out included employees who were redlined, or excluded, from the marketing plans of insurers either because of their greater health risks or the perception of greater risks. They included higher-risk employment categories such as gas stations, construction companies, and restaurant employees, as well as dancers, florists, and hairstylists who were excluded in the 1990s out of a fear of high prevalence of HIV infection among those professions (Consumers Union 1990). Some employed persons thus lacked access to health insurance because their employers were unable to obtain insurance coverage based upon risks thought to be associated with the nature of the work or based on characteristics attributed to a class of employees (Light 1992). The result of redlining is that some of those with significant occupational health risks also bore greater costs of obtaining insurance to meet their increased costs of medical care, while others whose health risks may not be greater bore additional health costs as a consequence of social stigma and prejudice. Either way, greater economic burdens landed upon those whose other burdens were already high.

How much redlining continues to account for differences in insurance status is unclear. Increasingly, the size of the employer is having an enormous impact on health insurance. All of the Fortune 500 companies offer insurance, compared to less than half of firms with approximately 200 or fewer employees, and only one-fifth of companies with fewer than 6 employees (Kuttner 1999a). Both economies of scale available to the larger employers, plus the fact that many employees of larger businesses have jobs that offer better wages and benefits, account for these differences. On average, those who are better off in other ways are made better off in terms of health insurance as well, and so, too, the disadvantages in the labor market reinforce disadvantage in access to care through insurance. Even if, for the sake of argument, workers in industries with higher health risks ought to pay more in premiums, it is difficult to argue that those who work for smaller employers (and who often have lower wages) should be left with no choice but to seek coverage on their own in the often cost-prohibitive private insurance market.

Costs of health insurance for the employed, near poor (those whose annual income ranges up to 200% of poverty level) can range from 26–40% of income, depending on the market in a geographic area (Gabel, Kurst, Hunt 1998, cited in Kuttner 1999a). Moreover, "individual insurance is expensive for what the buyer gets, and individual insurers try to tailor premiums and coverage to risk" (Pauly and Percy 2000, 24). Were some other mechanism, such as large-scale purchasing alliances, available as a complement or substitute for the employer-based system, then employees of larger firms would not have the more favorable premium and coverage options that are denied to employees of smaller firms.

Workers in seasonal and part-time employment such as migrant agriculture and unskilled construction jobs are also less likely to have employment-related health insurance benefits than other employees (Kaiser Commission on Medicaid and the Uninsured 2003). This is an important fact, in part because of the composition of that workforce. African American and Hispanic or Latino persons disproportionately occupy jobs that are more dangerous, less likely to be full time, more likely to be seasonal, and in smaller firms offering fewer benefits. They are for those reasons more likely to be uninsured than the general population.

Almost 25% of African Americans are uninsured, more than one and one-half times the rate of white Americans, and although eight in ten are employed only 53% have employer-sponsored insurance, compared to 73% for whites (Brown et al. 2000). Moreover, only half of the African American population below poverty level is eligible for Medicaid (Brown et al. 2000). The Hispanic and Latino populations also fare badly in an employment-based system. At the end of the 1980s, two-thirds of Hispanics living below poverty level were employed, but only 13% of their employers provided health insurance (Falcon 1990). In addition, more than two-thirds of Hispanics below the poverty level did not have private insurance and were not eligible for Medicaid (Congressional Research Service 1988; Falcon 1990). A decade later, little had changed. One-third of Latinos still had no health insurance, and of the 11.2 million uninsured Latinos, 9 million were in working families (Hellander 2001; Brown et al. 2000).

The upshot is that a system of health care financing that relies upon locus of employment as the primary vehicle for obtaining health insurance not only favors the economically well off who have better wages and benefits, but it also inherits and compounds the economic and social injustices resulting from historic patterns of employment discrimination. To ensure that the means chosen to make insurance available in the marketplace do not reinforce or reproduce systematic injustices to groups of persons already burdened by lower economic opportunities and patterns of discrimination, either of two solutions is necessary. Either all firms must be required to offer insurance to their employees at comparable prices and with comparable benefits, or else some other social entity would have to perform that task. Only then can the employer-based system stay in place without its contributing to the further disadvantage of already disadvantaged segments of society. In short, some sort of requirement of universal participation is necessary, whether or not the employer-based nexus is retained.

Employed and Insured, But with Greater Burdens

A second problem associated with the employer-based system in the United States is that there are some who are employed and insured, but who bear greater economic and health burdens as a direct consequence of the way the employer-based system is organized and regulated. Unlike other countries that also rely in some part on an employer-based health insurance component of the overall financing arrangement, the United States permits a high degree of variability in both premium and coverage.

Employees of businesses with lower health risks can command a lower group health care premium than is available to the community as a whole. The prevalence of experience rating in most parts of the United States means that employee premiums can vary substantially for the same level of coverage. Not only do occupational risk differences account for the variance in premium costs, so too do average age of the members of the pool, the number of members of the pool, their educational levels, and the random distribution of health status.

Moreover, for the same reasons that many who work for small firms are uninsured, many who are insured either have to pay more for group insurance coverage at comparable levels whether or not their health risks are higher, simply because they are not part of a larger pool, or they receive less coverage than those in larger pools. Large pools allow the insuring entity to spread the risk widely, thereby minimizing the risk of financial ruin. Larger self-insuring employers can negotiate more benefits from hospitals, physicians, and laboratory service providers. The ultimate consequence is that more services can be purchased for the same premium as per unit price drops. Also, the overhead costs of plan administration are dramatically different, with overhead amounting to approximately 5% for large firms compared to 20% for smaller firms (Hyman and Hall 2001). Hence, for a variety of reasons, not only does working for a smaller employer put employees at greater risk of not being insured, but it also places them at greater risk either of having to pay considerably more for insurance or get less for the same premium (GAO 1997; Jensen et al. 1997). For much of the 1990s, available evidence suggested that the more common practice was coverage reduction rather than the imposition of substantial premium differences over what larger firms experienced (Morrisey, Jensen, and Morlock 1994; Jensen et al. 1997).

Public Subsidies for the Better Off as Well

A third source of injustice within the employer-based system of health care finance in the United States is that it relies upon a system of public subsidies that is the inverse of that used in other countries. Most countries employ some form of premium subsidy for those who cannot afford the costs of health insurance. However, in the United States, those who are employed and insured through work are subsidized by tax breaks. Both employees and employers receive federal income tax deductions for employer-sponsored health insurance, while those who are not employed by eligible employers (the unemployed and the self-employed), and those who are employed but not insured through employment, do not. This form of premium subsidy is all the more striking from the perspective of justice because it benefits only those already relatively more fortunate members of the largely middle and upper class. By many estimates it is in the range of 124 to 141 billion dollars annually (Sheils and Hogan 1999; Silow-Carroll, Kutyla, Meyer 2001; Berman 2002), a figure greater than some estimates of the new expenditures (above the current 35 billion dollars for uncompensated care) that would be necessary to extend health insurance to everyone (Hadley and Holahan 2003).

Moreover, the employees in the highest tax brackets and having the most generous insurance plans get the largest share of the tax subsidy, while the lowest-paid workers enrolled in plans with the highest share of out-of-pocket costs receive the smallest public subsidy. In some estimates, 68.7% of the subsidy goes to the 36% of the population with family incomes above $50,000 (Sheils and Hogan 1999). The value of the tax break to a family making $100,000 per year was estimated in 1999 to be $2,357 while the value to those below $15,000 is $71 (Sheils and Hogan 1999). These who are both economically and medically better off, or at least well enough off to be employed, get a big helping hand from the government, while many of the working poor and others without employer-sponsored insurance get nothing.

Morally Relevant Differences

The foregoing suggests that there are three features of the U.S. system of employer-based insurance that make it different from other employer-based systems, and those differences largely explain why the U.S. system fails to meet the most minimal standards of justice in health insurance markets.

First, employers are not required to make health insurance available to their employees. Nor is any other entity legally charged with such responsibility, or even the responsibility to ensure market conditions such that these excluded employees can obtain suitable insurance otherwise. The absence of a strong governmental role in the regulation of the employer-dominated group insurance markets means that the employed but uninsured have no option but to purchase insurance in the vastly more expensive individual market, even when there is no substantial difference in health status. In many instances, existing disadvantage is compounded by excluding those persons who are discriminated against unjustly in the labor market on other grounds and those whose incomes are among the lowest.

Second, the lack of uniformity of premium costs and coverage benefits imposes greater economic and health burdens on some, typically those who are among the less financially able to bear the added burdens. The lack of community rating in most states and permissive federal regulation of coverage requirements leaves the market open to experience rating and coverage variations in the group insurance market and even greater coverage variations in the individual market. The consequence is that the economically less well off must pay more for equivalent coverage or get less coverage for equivalent premiums.

Third, tax subsidies for the premiums of the economically better off, especially when they subsidize the economically best off the most heavily, embody a principle that prioritizes access to health insurance in direct relation to ability to pay. Premium subsidies elsewhere, by contrast, reverse that principle, giving priority to the economically worst off (Faden and Powers 1999).

From our point of view, an employer-based system that lacks an employer mandate or other mechanism for ensuring universal participation, lacks community rating or other controls on premium variation, lacks uniformly applicable coverage levels, and provides premium support for the economically better off, gets matters precisely backward. Our account of justice requires, first, that the basic social arrangements ensure that everyone has a level of risk protection needed for a sufficiency of health and, second, that social and economic arrangements that systematically disadvantage some persons and groups, both in their health and in other dimensions of well-being, must be combated.

5.5 Private Markets and Public Safety Nets

The remedy for those who are excluded from the market, as well as those who are underinsured, as a consequence of responses to the threat of market failure, might take a number of forms. One possibility is the greater governmental regulation of the market along lines suggested by our account of the minimal requirements any market-based health insurance system must meet. Another is the suggestion by some proponents of vouchers for purchasing private insurance through a system of publicly funded, income-graduated premium support for low-income persons who would then purchase policies in the private market under legal constraints that they do not impose cost-sharing on the poor (Pauly 1971). Another option is the replacement of the private market altogether with a public single-payer program modeled along the lines of the Canadian system. Still another option is an expansion of public programs as a safety net for those excluded from the market or those whose available coverage is insufficient to guarantee adequate access to care without overly burdensome costs.

As Allen Buchanan correctly observes, no theory of justice is likely to "tell us what the appropriate division of labor is between private and public entities for securing equitable access to health care in a particular society at a particular point in its history" (Buchanan 1998). However, we do think that our theory can shed light on some ways in which the division of labor between public and private entities is unjust.

Programs for the Poor

Public safety net programs existing side by side with private markets, while far better than nothing, often stop short of what justice may require inasmuch as this kind of arrangement can contribute in new ways to the disadvantages the worst off members of society already experience. Those who must rely upon the public programs may suffer most heavily if the increase in support for delivering public-sector benefits does not keep pace with remuneration for services provided in the private-sector programs. This is precisely the case in the Medicaid program serving the poor in the United States (Gruber, Kim, Mayzlin 1999; Iglehart 1999a). Substantially lower reimbursement rates for services delivered to the Medicaid population than is paid by private insurers often means fewer physicians willing to treat the poor. While physician reimbursement rates in the more generous Medicare program for the elderly of all income levels vary geographically, they are consistently much greater than those of the Medicaid program (Colby 1994; Iglehart 2002b; Vladeck and Fishman 2002). Public programs exclusively serving the poor lack the broad political constituency of the Medicare program, and as a consequence many argue that they are "unequal by design" and deeply resistant to improvement (Vladeck and Fishman 2002). Medicaid never has been adequate to cover all of those below poverty levels; at its highest in the late 1960s, it covered only around two-thirds of the poor, but it has consistently covered less than half of the nonelderly poor and has been declining slowly over the course of many years (Iglehart 1993; Iglehart 1999a; Vladeck and Fishman 2002).

Age-Based Programs

The exclusion of the elderly that led to the creation of the Medicare program reflects an important but generally unacknowledged aspect of the split between public and private responsibilities. The system of age-based market segregation, where the bulk of the less risky, younger population continues to get its medical care coverage through the market and the older, more expensive members of society get theirs through publicly funded programs, undermines any efforts to achieve generational justice. Such a system does not encourage individuals or institutional decision makers, within either the private or public sector, to think seriously about health care priorities over a complete lifetime. Unlike the administrators of single-payer plans, who must operate under the expectation that they will have financial responsibility for the lifetime health outcomes of the population they serve, neither private- nor public-sector decision makers are in a position to make rational and fair decisions about which treatments get priority; whether prevention will be preferred over acute care; how much, if any, to spend for the clinical application of experimental therapies; whether the claims of the young or the old are most pressing; and so on.

With a public/private split based on age, private-sector companies are in the business of insuring people only during the healthiest and least costly years of life, leaving their more expensive, often unpredictable bills to be paid by the public sector once they become Medicare eligible. This arrangement creates an expectation of short-term responsibility that limits the incentives for plan managers to invest resources sufficient to maintain the long-term health of their enrollees. Matters are made even worse, however, by the fact that even managed care organizations—which do take on the job of planning for all of their enrollee's health needs—have no reason to expect those enrollees to be their responsibility for more than a few years. People move in and out of plans, often because employers shift to new plans for reasons of cost (Jensen et al. 1997). The result of age-based market segmentation, especially when combined with other market reasons for insurers not to expect to have responsibility for decisions over a longer planning horizon, is that neither individuals concerned about prudent use of resources over their own lifetimes, nor the social institutions charged with making collective social policy, are required to address questions of allocation among the generations. For a theory of justice such as ours, where the obligations to the young are especially urgent, and attention to the profound and pervasive effects of social determinants over a life course are of central importance, this lack of accountability undermines efforts to achieve justice.

Intermittent Coverage

The plurality of health care financing mechanisms, reliance upon employment-based insurance for a workforce of considerable mobility, and a variety of limitations on access through public safety net programs leaves a substantial proportion of the population who experience gaps in insurance coverage for substantial periods of time. The impact of these gaps in market-based coverage is compounded by the fact that the public programs fail miserably at meeting the problem of intermittent insurance. There are substantial delays, waiting periods, and burdensome eligibility requirements for most public programs, and many economically disadvantaged persons never receive benefits even when by law they are eligible because of administrative impediments and social stigma (Institute for Medicaid Management 1978; Bye and Niles 1989; Rowland, Salganicoff, Keenan 1999; Vladeck and Fishman 2002).

The number of uninsured at any given time understates the magnitude of the uninsurance problem and the gaps not met by Medicaid or any other public safety net. Over the course of twenty years, the number of persons who are uninsured for some portion of a year has exceeded the number who are uninsured at any moment in time by one-third to a half, and when measured over a two-year period, that percentage increased greatly (Swartz and McBride 1990; Bennefield 1998; Schoen and DesRoches 2000; Haley and Zuckerman 2003). The failure of public programs to fill the gap is powerfully illustrated by the fact that approximately 40% of uninsured children are eligible for Medicaid but do not receive it. Multiple factors are responsible for this outcome, including administrative burdens, eligibility and citizenship proofs, stigmatizing personal disclosures, and unwillingness on the part of state governments to take on new financial obligations to the poor, even after various expansions in the program increased the number of children who are eligible (Iglehart 1999a; Vladeck and Fishman 2002).

One reason for concern about gaps in insurance is their long-term effects on health. There are many individuals and groups—such as those in poor health, children in critical developmental stages, and those with chronic illnesses—for whom timely and regular access to medical interventions of the sort generally available only to those with continuous, comprehensive health coverage is terribly important. Those without continuous coverage are two to three times more likely to go without needed care and to have problems paying medical bills as those with continuous coverage (Shoen and DesRoches 2000). Without coverage, children are especially vulnerable. They receive fewer immunization, diagnostic, and screening services and are less likely to receive care for chronic conditions such as ear infections and asthma (Kuttner 1999b). The lapse of insurance may fall within a period of illness or disease, and the need for continuity of access to health care is frustrated. If the onset or exacerbation of a medical condition occurs prior to obtaining replacement insurance, the condition may go untreated in a timely fashion, increase preventable hospitalizations, and produce more disability and even shortened life spans. Moreover, the adverse consequences of interruption of access to care may be particularly great in the context of pre-natal or well-baby care, where lack of access may result in long-term developmental disabilities, and the efficacy of treatment depends upon regular and routine medical intervention.

The mobility of the workforce is another complicating factor in any system in which persons fall through the cracks between public and private programs. Studies suggest that high-turnover employees tend to be younger, less well-paid, less likely to have health insurance, and disproportionately concentrated among already disadvantaged minority populations (Schorr 1990; Bureau of the Census 1990 and 2003). In such cases, even relatively modest medical expenses may mean financial ruin as well as preventable illness and disability. Lack of access to medical care, therefore, matters additionally because it can be the gateway to many other disadvantages affecting multiple dimensions of a person's life prospects. Gaps in insurance and their attendant consequences do not occur in a highly integrated, single-payer system where all citizens are continuously enrolled. Indeed, as the German labor market has become more like that of the United States, there has been a substantial decoupling of insurance from the sickness funds sponsored by employers due to the inability of that system to maintain continuity of coverage within a workforce characterized by increased job mobility, more women in the workforce, higher divorce rates, and more complex child custody patterns (Amelung, Glied, and Topan 2003).

Yet another group that is adversely affected by the peculiar mix of public and private funding mechanisms are those who are chronically ill throughout their middle years, too young for Medicare and too ill for full-time employment through which insurance coverage might be obtained. Many have objected to proposals for raising the age of Medicare eligibility from sixty-five to sixty-seven on the grounds that persons whose poor health may be compromised by continued employment may be forced to choose between staying in the workforce in order to remain insured, and retiring and having to find affordable replacement insurance in a private market where higher medical risk will make securing such insurance difficult, if not impossible. While it may be true that, on average, relatively younger members of the senior community can expect to remain in the workforce longer and to have greater longevity and more years free of debilitating illnesses, such changes would mean that a substantial number of sixty-five- and sixty-six-year olds will be left uninsured (U.S. House of Representatives 1999). The problem affects more than just those in the sixty-five to sixty-seven age group. If it is morally unacceptable that persons in the sixty-five to sixty-seven age group should be caught in the dilemma just described, it is also morally unacceptable that younger persons should be similarly trapped. And yet many are. It is commonplace for workers age sixty-four and younger to tailor their employment decisions around the need for health care coverage. Even when these younger workers have medical problems and they would benefit from early retirement or part-time employment, their need for guaranteed health care compels them to keep on working.

People with chronic medical conditions are most likely to have their health negatively affected by the gaps in medical care coverage, especially when the periods of uninsurance are lengthy (Ayanian et al. 2000). Data also firmly support the claim that lack of insurance among those nearing retirement puts them at increased risk of a decline in health status (Baker et al. 2001). Securing optimal health outcomes for people with chronic illnesses requires regular, high-quality medical management of the sort generally not available to the uninsured.

How exactly to craft a policy that effectively targets those in poor health and with chronic illnesses is, however, difficult. Current policies guided, in part, by considerations of greatest perceived medical need reveal some familiar drawbacks. For example, criteria for establishing disability eligibility under Medicaid are problematic at best. Often a showing of "total disability" is required, and such a requirement can be overly burdensome for persons with chronic medical conditions, such as lupus and Crohn's disease, that produce intermittent disabilities. Persons with such conditions may be in particularly great need of continuous access to care for many years prior to a definitive medical conclusion that the patient is permanently unable to function in the workforce.

A critic might object that such problems can be addressed more efficiently by targeted public programs, such as disease-specific coverage for all children with asthma or all children with diabetes, modeled after the Ryan White CARE Act of 1996. This disease-specific approach could also be directed towards adults as, for example, was the case with the End Stage Renal Dialysis program (Newhouse 1994). A major problem with a disease-specific approach, however, is that chronic illnesses are often asymptomatic in their early stages, yet in some cases intervention during these early stages is necessary to maximize health outcomes. In one study of breast cancer, for example, uninsured women were more likely to be diagnosed with more advanced disease than women who had health insurance; four to seven years after their initial diagnosis, they were 49% more likely to have died (Ayanian et al. 1993). A policy that extended medical care coverage eligibility based on existing disease could not address such an inequality. Approaches that are narrowly tailored to meet the needs of those clearly identifiable as ill at a particular point in time risk missing those, who without continuous access to medical care in periods of lesser, or less obvious, medical need would fail to protect a sufficient level of health over the course of a lifetime.

More than Health Is at Stake

The assessment of whether the combined means for financing access to health care meets the requirements of justice depends on its impact on more than health alone. Our theory recognizes a variety of additional arguments relevant to what justice requires in the design of health care delivery systems. First, the provision of health care often contributes to the realization of a constellation of other dimensions of well-being that overlap with health, and, second, some ways of organizing the division of labor between the public and private spheres of health care delivery undermine other dimensions of well-being.

The first of these consideration reminds us that we should not ignore the added importance of improving dimensions of well-being that overlap health and the importance of selecting strategies that can improve multiple dimensions. Early medical interventions can detect and beneficially affect the developmental trajectory of childhood cognitive skills. Primary health care, if sufficiently attentive to health education needs, can advance cognitive development by aiding persons in understanding and taking charge of their own health, improving their capacities for decision making, and aiding in the formation of mature, imaginative, and compassionate life plans. Even health care directed toward persons at or near the end of life can offer patients information relevant to planning the remainder of their lives, and it can further their capabilities in dealing with their personal attachments, however much longer they have to live. In all of these examples, health and other dimensions of well-being overlap, and the case for expenditures of resources in this area is best made by pointing out the multiple aspects of well-being that are enhanced, rather than by claiming only that health occupies a special strategic place in the achievement of valuable life plans.

The second consideration points us in the direction of what a just health care system must avoid. When the uninsured do seek care, they may suffer indignities at least as troubling as any threat to their health. Presenting for medical care without an insurance card, like appearing at a border without a passport, marks a person as outside the community and puts her in a potentially demeaning, supplicant posture. Health care coverage is thus of significant value to each of us as individuals, even in the absence of any direct impact on our physical well-being. An individual's sense of dignity and self-respect is undermined when starkly confronted with the awareness of weakened or attenuated social bonds of empathy and compassion for her plight (Scheff, Retzinger, and Ryan 1989). Both charity and welfare can leave one a supplicant, humiliated in one's own eyes and ashamed in the presence of one's dependents. Even if someone gets the needed resources in the end, the injustice will not have been rectified. Some have to pay a price not exacted of others and it is often not an insubstantial one. The by-product of well-intentioned safety net programs is that people are treated in ways that are inconsistent with having respect shown for them or inconsistent with maintaining self-respect. (Wolff 1998, 107). Being treated in ways that are inconsistent with being respected can, of course, lead people to believe that they are not respected, and this belief can contribute to or reinforce a decline in their self-respect, also.

Inherent in such safety net programs is the need for some to account for oneself in ways others do not in similar circumstances (Wolff 1998, 108). They are required to demean themselves by having "to behave in a way or reveal things about themselves," for example, when we collect data needed for "conditional schemes of welfare" (Wolff 1998, 109, 110). We impose this burden on only one sector of society, namely, "that sector that is already among the most disadvantaged" (Wolff 1998, 111). A system of enforcement and surveillance aimed at keeping out the free riders or husbanding benefits for the sake of the deserving poor quickly takes on the feel of a mechanism of social control for those subject to its authority. The least well off not only risk losing out on what is required for preserving their health, but they also suffer from having to endure the harsh, negative judgments of others, which deprives them of a sense of personal security and control. Persons lacking access to goods that so powerfully influence individual life prospects experience an increased degree of vulnerability to harm, additional stress, and feelings of powerlessness and social disrespect, all of which have been shown to be associated with poorer health status (Wilkinson, Kawachi, and Kennedy 1998). Their awareness of their disadvantaged social status and their dependence on charity or welfare also undermines self-respect and their sense of themselves as the moral equals of the more fortunate members of society, and that awareness contributes to a sense of dependence and powerlessness that erodes self-determination (Wilkinson, Kawachi, and Kennedy 1998; Scheff, Retzinger, and Ryan 1989).

Such burdens are especially heavy when persons are unable to meet their obligations to care for and provide for their families. Indeed, the burden of such moral obligations to family and loved ones falls more heavily on those without material resources, including health insurance (O'Neill 1993, 303–304; Nickel 1987, 71–77). Those lacking health insurance have to live with the fear that if they or a loved one becomes ill or injured, they would not know how to secure or pay for the care that would be required. Without adequate access to medical care, individuals are not free to make decisions about whether to seek medical care based on concerns about their own or their children's health. They are forced to make such difficult choices burdened by the stress of having to balance their or their children's medical well-being against other basic needs, and they bear the added moral burden of knowing that they are unable to discharge the familial obligations which most members of society take to be among the most basic of all moral requirements.

Moreover, the development of self-respect, attachment and affiliation, and self-determination also depend crucially upon the timing of events within the overall life course. As Wilhemine Miller has argued, "if needy parents are not equipped with the resources to care adequately for their children, the development of persons with a diminished capacity for self-respect and moral maturation and development is virtually guaranteed" (Miller 1997, 31). Such children grow up with an awareness that they and their families lack access to basic social opportunities available to the majority of citizens. They grow up knowing that they are valued less than their more fortunate peers. They learn quite early that those who are there to protect and guide them are powerless and subject to public humiliation when they try to meet the needs of those dependents for whom they have special attachment and responsibility. Awareness of these things undermines these children's sense of self-worth and capacity for seeing themselves as persons able to exercise a substantial measure of control over their own lives through their own choices, of discharging their own obligations to loved ones, and as being worthy of consideration by others.

Because so many important dimensions of human well-being, arguably every bit as important to a plausible conception of justice as health, are negatively affected by lack of access to health care, the case for reduction in inequalities in access to care is not weakened by the empirical data showing limited contribution to improved aggregate health outcomes (Faden and Powers 1999). Health effects are important, to be sure, but so too are the effects on other dimensions of well-being, and any just division of labor between public and private entities in securing access to health care will be one that does not ignore the potential for enormous harm to those aspects of well-being. If the patterns of distribution leave many without care and the mechanisms for gaining access are burdensome, some will be too dispirited to discharge the duties of a good parent, too much subordinated to the will of others that they feel powerless and small by comparison, and too overwhelmed by fear or insecurity to assert their own interests against those who have power over a wide range of their daily lives. Such considerations often matter no less than the positive impact on health many defenders of universal access take into account on other grounds.

6

Setting Priorities

6.1 Introduction

The need for priority setting arises whenever there are "tragic choices." Tragic choices involve either decisions about whom to benefit when available resources are not sufficient to meet the needs of all claimants or decisions about what beneficial goods and services to produce when resources are not sufficient to produce everything of benefit. There is, of course, no need for devising priority-setting criteria or principles when such decisions are made by individuals in the market. However, when markets cannot or should not be relied upon, decision makers need some guidance for making just decisions about the production or distribution of limited resources.

Commentators disagree on whether any philosophical theory of justice can offer much practical guidance, especially in a vast middle range of cases involving, for example, the choice between two therapies or between two public health interventions. At one end of the spectrum, there are those who express considerable confidence that a determinate ranking order can be achieved by use of certain formal economic methods. Chief among those methods are cost-benefit analysis (CBA), cost-effectiveness analysis (CEA), and cost-utility analysis (CUA). The presumed justification of these formal economic methods lies in their capacity to approximate the economic efficiency of markets. Efficiency, in turn, is said to be of paramount moral value insofar as it is a reliable measure of utility maximization. Neoclassical economic theorists, for example, equate utility with the satisfaction of individual preferences. The moral case for markets, or some formal method as an alternative to reliance on markets, thus rests upon a judgment of which option best achieves the utility-maximizing aims of a utilitarian moral theory.

At the other end of the spectrum, however, are those who express considerable doubt that philosophical theories of justice can offer much practical guidance in resolving priority-setting problems. Leonard Fleck, for example, suggests that justice retains its moral regulatory role in assessing any priority-setting scheme, but from within those possible sets of institutional arrangements and policies many possible trade-off patterns will be "just enough" (Fleck 1994). In chapter 7, we discuss a variety of ways some theorists have proposed to supplement justice theories or to extend the reach of moral guidance either through some revisions in the formal methods themselves or the use of fair democratic procedures. Theorists at this end of the spectrum conclude that even if an overall system for social provision of public health or health care resources passes the test of justice, many distributive questions remain unresolved.

Because our theory is addressed to questions about the design of the basic social structure, the practical guidance our theory provides for the resolution of priority problems is frequently one step removed from the kinds of midlevel and micro-level decisions that public health officials, health plan managers, and clinicians make on a daily basis. Unlike some theorists, we do not aim to offer our own algorithm for allocation, nor do we defend a preferred, single distributive principle or criterion. We agree in principle with Fleck that after considerations of justice have been exhausted, many distributive questions will remain unanswered. However, our theory does apply to those institutions and institutional decision makers charged with the responsibility for setting resource priorities, be they public health agencies determining whether to make obesity, AIDS, or workplace safety the subject of the next national or international health campaign, or national health care plans determining whether to cover the latest life-extending technology. In this chapter, we discuss how our theory constrains decision making by setting limits to institutional arrangements and distributive principles that contribute to systematic disadvantage among groups of particular interest, including children. While an important part of our theory focuses on socially situated groups and the constellation of disadvantages and vulnerabilities that define their circumstances, our interest is not in the well-being of groups, per se. We are interested ultimately, of course, in the well-being of individuals, but in the real, historically situated world, how individuals fare is often a function of the status and standing of the groups of which they are a part. In addition, we explore the implications for priority setting of adopting a theory that incorporates considerations other than health that, as a matter of justice, should be taken into account.

Although our theory operates at the level of social design, we think that considerations of social justice can illuminate some problems that are largely neglected or dealt with differently within the traditional debates about priority setting. Primary among these problems are concerns with systematic disadvantage affecting socially situated groups, the developmental relevance of age, and to a lesser extent the issue of permissible trade-offs within health.

6.2 Mimicking Markets

The Origins and Practice of Cost-Benefit Analysis

The history and underlying assumptions behind formal economic methods for setting priorities provide a key to understanding both their initial attraction and their subsequent modification and refinement in response to external criticisms and misgivings by practitioners. According to many who first championed formal methods of economic appraisal, such methods are most appropriate when the impediments to the efficient operation of the market are so great that decision procedures meant to mimic market outcomes are preferable to the market itself. For example, interest in formal methods of resource allocation first arose in the context of concern about how decisions regarding large public works programs should be made. Such programs are outside of the usual market context in which the efficient use of resources is determined by purchasing decisions of individuals. For many economists, formal methods are grudgingly accepted as "second-best" solutions. Many tend to favor their use *only* when efforts to make markets work more efficiently are exhausted and there are good reasons to think that individual choices in the market place will not or cannot determine an efficient allocation.

Formal methods are thought particularly well suited to solving a kind of problem known as a *collective action problem*: even though everyone would benefit from an action, no one person has sufficient reason to act alone. David Hume long ago recognized the existence of such problems in his analysis of when governmental action is necessary. In Hume's example, any number of landowners will benefit from draining a swamp, but no individual landowner has sufficient motivation to bear the sole costs and burdens of doing what benefits everyone. If there is no entity such as the government to step in and take action on behalf of the collective good then everyone will be worse off individually. Because something of great public benefit will not be achieved, the overall effect is a loss of efficiency within a society.

Collective-action problems are thus a kind of market failure in which individual well-being cannot be secured through individual choice and action alone. The most familiar collective action problems that captured the attention of economists after Hume involve the distribution of goods that economists call "*public goods.*" Public goods represent an exception to the usual assumption that goods should be treated as commodities whose distribution is best left to the individual decisions of buyers and sellers in the market. Some goods such as clean air and water, some forms of disease prevention, and national defense are familiar examples of public goods (McLean 1987, 11–12). They are resistant to efficient market allocation because of the problem of "free riders." However much individuals may desire clean air or defense against foreign invasion, they cannot purchase either, for themselves or their families, without thereby providing the benefits to the "free riders" who make no contribution to their production. Sometimes nonmarket action by government is thus unavoidable in order to achieve social utility that cannot otherwise be obtained by self-interested individuals making individual purchasing decisions in the market.

Many economists nonetheless want these societal decisions to be based on criteria that ensure that they are as efficient as possible. Such decisions should thus *mimic markets*. Without some basis for determining whether a proposed policy or public investment offers a *net* utility gain, governmental decision makers may set public resource priorities in ways that do not achieve efficiency. Costs as well as benefits need to be taken into account simultaneously. Hence, cost-benefit analysis (CBA) emerged as a way to help decision makers determine whether government should undertake such activities as building dams to protect whole communities from flooding or constructing water and sewer treatment facilities to control the outbreak of communicable diseases (Mishan 1988; Warner and Luce 1982).

The theoretical objective of CBA is to determine whether a potential project produces a favorable ratio of benefits to costs. The assessment of both benefits and costs are made in monetary terms, and the goal is to determine whether a project produces a favorable ratio of aggregate economic benefits to economic costs. It is important to note that CBA, as originally envisioned by economists, should be distinguished from a less systematic approach that has gained common currency and has sometimes been used by both private firms and governmental agencies interested in calculating its own costs and benefits. For example, critics of the Ford Motor Company decision not to take steps to reduce the risk of fuel-tank explosions because it would increase the price of their popular Pinto automobile have described that decision as the product of a cost-benefit analysis. The claim is but a way of saying that the decision was based on a comparison of costs and benefits to the firm (or agency). Uses of CBA that take account only of the costs and benefits accruing to the institutional decision maker are sometimes referred to as the decision-maker approach (Johannesson 1995). Costs imposed on others and benefits enjoyed by others are deemed irrelevant in this sort of economic appraisal.

The CBA approach favored by economists for the evaluation of public programs, however, is an attempt to evaluate the desirability of a project based on an economic appraisal of *all of the costs and benefits that accrue to everyone* in society, not just those affecting the individual decision maker. The perspective of CBA, where the aim is to achieve overall efficiency, is thus a societal one, not the narrower perspective of an institutional decision maker concerned only with the institution's own costs and benefits. The proper aim of the CBA practitioner, therefore, is to develop a comprehensive list of costs and benefits without regard to the identities of the beneficiaries or the bearer of the costs.

An example offered by E. J. Mishan is illustrative of the CBA process (Mishan 1988). Suppose that the government is considering construction of a dam to create a reservoir. The decision maker first wants to catalogue the costs and benefits. There are, of course, the direct costs of construction. There are costs of land acquisition as well. If a hydroelectric plant is to be built, there are additional construction costs, as well as extra costs associated with building and maintaining access roads and parking lots. If the reservoir is open to the public for swimming and boating, there are costs of maintaining water level and monitoring water quality. There are costs to local citizens and the general public as well. If it is a free-flowing trout stream that is to be dammed, there will be costs attached to the loss of recreational opportunities for trout fishing enthusiasts, loss of the aesthetic value of the unspoiled hinterlands, environmental degradation from deforestation, potential loss of natural habitat for endangered species, air pollution from a coal-burning hydroelectric plant, and costs to the area residents who may be relocated, endure the disruption of years of construction, and put up with noisy tourists.

Construction of a dam will produce a variety of benefits as well. These might include flood protection, insect control that produces a reduction in disease, new and different recreational opportunities (boating instead of trout fishing), new economic development and thus more jobs and paying tourists, cheaper electrical power, and so on. The contents of the list are limited only by the imagination.

The next step is to assign an economic value to each cost and benefit. Some are relatively straightforward, especially the calculation of direct costs. Costs of construction can be estimated in the usual way that contractors who are submitting bids use to calculate the costs of labor and materials. However, items such as the value of trout fishing as compared to swimming and boating, the value of the aesthetic loss, and the nuisance to neighbors are not as easily estimated. The task of the CBA practitioner is to assign these items a monetary value, primarily by conducting what are called "willingness-to-pay" studies. If, for example, we want to assign a monetary value to the loss of aesthetic value, we would ask representative samples of persons affected by the dam how much they are willing to pay to avoid its construction, and then multiply that amount by the number of persons affected by the construction. In addition to the direct method of conducting willingness-to-pay studies, estimates of value can be assessed in indirect ways. We might rely on previous willingness-to-pay studies conducted in similar circumstances (if there are any), or we could look to examples of actual market behavior, say, for example, where nonprofit environmental groups have raised money to purchase, and thus protect, an area of land from development.

CBA has become a staple of economic assessment of public works projects, but it has garnered somewhat less influence in public health contexts. In one of the more controversial examples of how CBA might be used, some studies of the costs and benefits of governmental programs for discouraging smoking took into account the economic losses to the national treasury that would accompany success in smoking-cessation programs. While the unmistakable public health benefit of reduced smoking might be achieved, an important item in the "cost" side of the ledger is the added expenditures for retirement and medical care of those who, because of increased longevity, would live longer and cost more.

The implications of such analyses are troubling to some whose primary concern is the public's health. CBA as applied to disease prevention and control may lead to the endorsement of policies that, in purely public health terms, seem unethical. The underlying intuition of this line of criticism is that health is something that matters independently and ought not be freely traded off for the sake of economic efficiency. The heart of this objection is the view that public policy ought to be driven foremost by public health goals, such as saving lives and preventing illness and disability, independent of the purely efficiency-related objective embedded in a cost-benefit analysis. Our theory agrees with these critics on the grounds that the unrestricted aggregation of benefits and burdens can be unjust. It is unjust on our theory, not because we reject all aggregation as unacceptable, but because each of the essential dimensions of well-being sets limits to aggregation that CBA on its own does not. In the smoking-cessation example, one obvious source of injustice is that CBA, with its single-minded concern for net aggregate benefit, allows health to be traded off for economic efficiency (Hubin 1994). Suppose, for example, that an economic analysis of smoking-cessation programs took into account the benefits of increased sales of tobacco products, which lead to greater employment opportunities in manufacturing, marketing, and retail sales, together with greater tax revenue from the sale of cigarettes. The problem is that while such matters are relevant to any aggregate assessment of benefits and costs, these calculations are indifferent to the fact that the economic benefits are achieved at the likely price of some falling short of a sufficiency of health for a decent life.

Restricting CBA to Health

Some policy analysts propose a narrower use for CBA methods under circumstances in which some of the most obviously objectionable kinds of unrestricted trade-offs between health and other goods do not arise. Instead of using CBA to solve problems of how best to allocate public resources across the entire spectrum of potential public uses, CBA might be used to allocate public dollars that are dedicated to health and health alone. However, such proposals represent a significant departure from the theoretical foundations and practical aims proponents of CBA originally had in mind. By taking into account all contributions to utility (including the essential dimensions of well-being), and not just health, CBA is intended to mimic market allocation between goods of differing types. This is precisely what critics from within public health circles reject, however, and for those who advocate uses of CBA that do not make trade offs between health and other goods, the original justification for CBA as a method of obtaining allocative efficiency falls by the wayside.

Those who favor the use of CBA's application to public health do have one of the initial justifications for CBA to fall back upon. CBA can be used with the aim of achieving productive efficiency or getting the greatest "bang for the buck" with limited health resources. The aspect of CBA methods that is meant to achieve productive efficiency is its reliance on willingness-to-pay studies as a basis for assigning monetary value to various options for which there are benefits and costs. Consider the evaluation of dam projects. Willingness-to-pay studies provide analysts with tools of economic appraisal that allow them to measure preferences on matters for which there are no market data, such as the value persons place on recreational use of a lake created by a dam versus the value of a free-flowing trout stream. Similar techniques can be used to measure consumer health care priorities under conditions in which obtaining real market data about consumer preferences for the vast array of medical services they may one day need is unfeasible. Given the aim of making consumer behavior in the use of health care services more sensitive to costs otherwise borne by third-party payers, the idea of using a willingness-to-pay approach has much appeal for some, and they have suggested that this feature of CBA should be retained (Pauly 1995). The result is that the aim of productive efficiency—getting the greatest health benefits for limited resources dedicated to health—could still be achieved, even if hopes for achieving overall allocative efficiency are jettisoned by the absence of comparisons between health and other goods.

In the early 1990s, David Eddy offered just such a proposal for incorporating this limited form of CBA into health care coverage decisions. Eddy advocated what he calls "rationing by patient choice" (Eddy 1991). He asks us to imagine that a disease affects 1 out of 1000 people per year, and that after treatment there is still 10% mortality and considerable morbidity. The treatment does increase average survival rate, based on the three-year follow-up studies conducted thus far, but its long-term survival rate is unknown. Imagine further that this information was provided to insurance policy holders who must then decide if they want to purchase a rider that would cover the treatment for an additional $150 per year. Suppose virtually nobody chooses to buy the rider. He then notes that "[b]y declining the rider, those men have made the required connection between value and cost and have stated their personal judgment that the value of the treatment was not worth the cost" (Eddy 1991, 105). If we were to use CBA to make rationing and coverage decisions for public programs such as Medicare, we would likely rely on just this kind of preference information obtained from willingness-to-pay studies.

These more limited uses of CBA not only depart from its theoretical roots and initial purposes from within economic theory, but they also pose problems of justice within our nonideal theory. The justice of any proposed evaluation of the benefits of health care or public health policies through willingness-to-pay approaches is linked inherently to the differences in income and wealth within the surveyed population. The predicament is that substantial differences in ability to pay influence the way the preferences of the respondents are formed and tabulated. Compare the responses of a group of low-income persons ($10,000–20,000 per year) with higher income persons (over $40,000 annually) for a treatment that reduced side-effects of some medical tests (Gafni 1991). When asked whether they would pay $50 to reduce their risks, only 45% of the low-income group were willing to pay $50 or more, compared to 92% of the higher-income population. If the surveyed population is comprised of members of both income groups, the willingness to pay will be determined based on the population average.

Critics pose their moral objections to this sort of averaging in two different ways. One argument is that setting the value of a public health intervention tilts the scales in favor of the interests of higher-income persons who have more disposable income. If the outcome of a willingness-to-pay study is the public funding of that intervention, then public resources can go to support programs that offer a small marginal benefit for which those with more resources are willing to pay. On the one hand, in a program such as Medicare, the result might be a richer package of medical benefits for all. However, the critics' concern in each case is that low-income participants are forced to use limited resources to pay taxes or premiums when those resources might have benefited them more had they been used for goods other than health care or a different set of health-related goods. CBA's reliance on willingness-to-pay measures can therefore systematically direct more public resources to programs favoring the better-off members of society at the expense of the worst off. The claim is that low-income persons are compelled to pay for health care services or public health measures that the high-income population wants and can afford but which deprive low-income persons of the choice to dedicate scarce resources to the things that are more likely to benefit them. The tilt of public resources in the direction of the more affluent through willingness-to-pay data can be analogized to a kind of voting process in which decisions are dominated by members of constituencies that have been assigned more votes per member than the members of other constituencies: more money means more voting strength and policies chosen in this fashion give lesser weight to the preferences of those who could improve their health by some other set of spending priorities better reflecting their marginal utility. Increased inequality of health status therefore can be a direct consequence of inequality of voting rights.

Equally troubling is the contrary prospect that willingness-to-pay measures can understate the "true" value of an intervention. That a sampled population is unwilling to pay for some medical service or public health measure may reflect their limited ability to pay now for interventions that benefit them in the long term. The claim is that limited financial means can lead respondents to undervalue such things as car seat belts which, while viewed as expensive or not worth the money in the short run, may save lives, property loss, and injuries in the long run. The problem is not just short-term thinking, which is, of course, not specific to any income population, but also the difficulties of comparison between the value of expenditures meeting present needs and those affecting welfare in the distant future, difficulties which are exacerbated by the added pressures of in-adequate resources for meeting current needs.

The common denominator of both overvaluing and undervaluing public health programs or medical care options is the fact that willingness-to-pay approaches inherit all of the injustices of the social and economic structure in which they are used. Under conditions in which the distribution of in-come and wealth is not so great that preferences for goods that affect health are not skewed by differences in economic status, then willingness-to-pay approaches are morally less troubling. They are least problematic as a basis for setting priorities within health when the resources available for health are adequate for achieving a sufficiency of health for all and the preferences for some more trivial aspects of health are not allowed to trump provision of services and goods that are vital to those health objectives that figure more centrally in what plausibly counts as sufficiency in health.

6.3 Cost-Effectiveness and Cost-Utility Alternatives

Cost-Effectiveness

Various objections to CBA have led some health policy analysts towards an alternative formal method, cost-effectiveness analysis (CEA), which focuses on the evaluation of purely health-related outcomes and their ratio to costs. CEA utilizes outcomes that are sometimes referred to as "natural units" because they are expressed as medical or health endpoints. Examples of these natural-unit outcomes include number of lives saved, life-years saved, periods of disease-free survival (e.g., after treatment for cancer), reduction of infant mortality, or reduction of the cycle of acute illness. Once the relevant health outcome is identified, the aim of CEA is to define a ratio of aggregate costs of a health intervention to the aggregate change in health outcomes that result.

By comparison to CBA, CEA is relatively easy to perform and readily comprehensible to policy makers and the general public. CEA is also useful in providing advice to policy makers who must decide how to use limited resources to maximize health benefits. This is sometimes known as the problem of "allocation subject to a budget constraint." Instead of evaluating the full range of benefits and costs to society, as CBA was designed to do, many CEA studies start from the premise that policy makers have a fixed health budget and that they need advice on how best to achieve certain specific health-related objectives, such as reducing infant mortality, pre-venting workplace disability, or ensuring more years of disease-free sur-vival after treatment for some specific illness. To be consistent with a health budget approach, only costs and benefits directly related to health ex-penditures should be included. Costs borne by family members or other third parties are considered irrelevant (Johannesson 1995, 484). This re-striction fits well with many of the practical problems in health policy.

Frequently these problems arise in contexts in which the budgets are heavily dictated by political concerns and the sphere of influence on policy choices is largely a matter of advising decision makers on how best to get the most health-related benefits given the health-specific budget constraints under which they operate. Equally significant perhaps is the desire of some health policy analysts to focus on what they themselves identify as the relevant health objectives to be pursued and to act as advocates for programs they think most valuable, independent of the judgments of the general population who may lack the expertise or information.

The simplest and least controversial applications of cost-effectiveness analysis involves the comparison of two treatments, each yielding the same medical benefit for the same medical condition occurring within a discrete population of persons suffering from the disease. For example, CEA might be used to evaluate two treatment options for women with metastatic breast cancer. If both treatments yield the same five-year survival rate, but treatment A costs $15,000 per five-year survival and treatment B costs $10,000, then the latter treatment is clearly preferable. CEA in its simplest form then can be seen as a method for getting some desired health benefit for the least expenditure (Gramlich 1981, 7). Decision makers seeking guidance for how to allocate resources subject to a fixed budget constraint have a clear decision rule.

Cost-Utility Analysis

Many health policy decisions are not this constrained, however, and involve a need to chose between different kinds of health outcomes across different kinds of burdens on health. One of the major limitations of the traditional form of CEA is that it does not necessarily provide a basis for comparison of different kinds of public health or health care programs, nor does it offer a common basis for setting priorities. For example, one CEA study might compare two or more options for one kind of health objective, say, reduction of maternal mortality, while another CEA study bases its comparisons of options on their effectiveness in preventing diabetic retinopathy. Because traditional CEA studies focusing on one specific dimension of health have no way to integrate the different dimensions of health outcomes into a single health scale, comparisons of programs having widely different objectives are difficult.

Another problem for traditional CEA, at least from the perspective of someone who retains a commitment to the underlying principles of welfare economics, is the total lack of any role for patient or public preferences. The outcome measures are chosen by the analyst based on what he or she takes to be the most salient dimension of health in each context. In some instances, it may be improvement in infant outcomes, or in other contexts such things as lives saved may be plausible accounts of the objectives for a decision maker. The problem is not so much that the outcome measure is likely to be arbitrary, but that when the decision context is one in which the budget constraint affects funding for treatments and services of all kinds, the moral case for input of the public's values and preferences for outcomes of differing kinds arguably becomes stronger.

The obvious alternative is to seek a unified health measure that encompasses as many dimensions of health outcome as possible in a single scale and that reintroduces a substantial role for public preferences in the measurement process. Cost-effectiveness analyses using unified health measures are often known as cost-utility analysis (CUA) and are viewed by some influential policy analysts as a better tool when the aim is to set priorities for funding of programs and services of all kinds. Although CUA does not elicit information about the public's willingness to pay for each intervention or treatment, it moves closer to the original rationale underlying CBA, which gives considerable weight to what the public values most, rather than leaving the determination of the program objectives to the judgment and discretion of experts.

There are a number of ways of constructing the unified health measure for CUA, but all attempt to integrate various dimensions of quality of life with life expectancy. The most familiar approach involves the calculation of quality-adjusted life years (QALYs). Other measures include the Quality of Well-Being Index (QWB), Healthy Year Equivalents (HYEs), the EuroQual, and Disablity-Adjusted Life Year (DALY). There are, of course, disagreements among those who favor different unified health status measures, as well as disagreements about how the evaluations embedded in these measures are elicited. There are, for example, significant differences of moral relevance between QALYs and DALYs. We examine some of these differences below. For now, however, we concentrate on showing how some common approaches for eliciting preferences in QALY-like measures work.

A popular approach is known as the standard gamble method. Researchers ask study participants questions designed to elicit individual preferences for trade-offs between length and quality of life. Like many other methods, the value of a year of perfect health is set at 1.0 and death is set at 0. The standard gamble presents a choice between two alternatives: living in a health state A with certainty or taking a gamble on treatment for which the outcome is uncertain (Kaplan 1995). For example, for a specific medical condition, participants are asked to consider: What risk of death would you accept in return for being assured that if you survive, you will be entirely cured? If they would accept a 10% risk, QOL score is .9. Another popular method is known as the time trade-off method. Participants are asked: How much reduction in a life in good health would you prefer to a longer lifetime with a disability (e.g., on kidney dialysis)? If they would accept a 10% reduction in length of life, then the particular disease state is given a Quality of Life (QOL) score of .9.

All methods for QOL assessment invite objections. Individuals have been shown to reverse their original preferences in subsequent surveys. Responses to gambles involving a sure thing (e.g., survival in a health state in which your illness is cured) tend to reverse depending on whether the gamble is presented as a low probability of a high payoff or a high probability of a low payoff. In theory, such reversals should not occur. The problem is that the questions involving probability information make high cognitive demands on the study participants.

Three additional problems are worthy of brief mention at this stage. One worry is that the different approaches will yield divergent trade-off preferences. However, many defenders minimize this possibility, noting a remarkable degree of convergent validity among the various methods. A second worry is that the responses obtained using any one of the methods will diverge among populations surveyed, based on factors such as nationality, ethnicity, and socio-economic status, and that caution needs to be exercised in using the preferences of one group as a basis for allocation decisions affecting groups who may not safely be assumed to have the same preferences (Daniels 1991). A third worry is that the degree of variation in preferences may be substantial within a single survey population, suggesting that methods that aggregate preferences may not provide meaningful information. Many defenders of CUA dispute the degree of variation in preferences within populations and across groups, claiming that preferences elicited within samples and across a variety of groups show a remarkable degree of consistency (Kaplan 1995; Patrick et al. 1985). These are important methodological worries, to be sure, and if well founded, they pose significant moral worries as well. However, the moral significance of these methodological concerns is not the focus of this chapter. Instead, we consider what residual moral problems remain if such problems can be resolved satisfactorily. In chapter 7, we return to another set of arguably more problematic methodological worries from the perspective of social justice.

CUA and Welfare Economics

All formal methods have their conceptual foundations in welfare economic theory, the original aim of which is to introduce into policy analysis a societal perspective insofar as the recommended policy can be said to mimic the aggregate decisions of individuals in markets. CBA takes that task seriously but it is subject to a number of moral objections and is not as amenable to the practical tasks of health decision makers who have to make choices about how to allocate resources that are dedicated for health purposes. CEA is more flexible as a bureaucratic tool, but public preferences are abandoned. Because CUA reintroduces a substantial role for public preferences in the priority-setting process, it has a stronger claim to a societal perspective than CEA. Unlike CBA, however, the public preferences elicited in CUA are for health state trade-offs, not willingness to pay for different services. By contrast, CBA, with its emphasis on willingness-to-pay measures, seeks to mimic markets by finding out precisely what those economic preferences are. Without information about economic preferences, policy makers lack any basis for setting health priorities in a manner that preserves the link between cost and value (Pauly 1995).

CUA seeks to make up for the absence of cost information in the preferences elicited by combining information about the public's preferences for various health states with cost data assigned by analysts. The guiding assumption is that the resulting ranking would be one the public endorses. However, some defenders of CBA argue that there is no reason to suppose that the ranking generated by an approach that requires respondents to express their preferences for various health states in light of the costs associated with their realization will be the same as the ranking that is generated from preference data that omits cost data. As Mark Pauly observes, analysts in the end will have to make some judgment about what costs per QALY are acceptable and which are too high. If economic evaluation is inevitable anyway, we might as well do it right, not simply base allocation decisions on the kinds of cost effectiveness ratios we just happen to have settled upon without any real effort to gauge cost-conscious consumer preferences (Pauly 1995).

Some commentators suggest that league tables showing the range of cost-effectiveness ratios should guide decision making. In a league table, alternative public health and medical care interventions are ranked in a table in the order of their cost-effectiveness ratios using a common health measure like a QALY as the outcome of "effectiveness." It is not uncommon to find league tables in which some interventions cost over a million dollars per QALY while others cost only a few dollars. Some "cut-point" in the league tables can be chosen based on current practices, and funding could be restricted to those interventions and programs for which the cost-effectiveness ratio falls within the range of those found acceptable elsewhere within society. For example, an institutional decision maker in injury-prevention policy might choose to fund all interventions that have QALY ratios at least as efficient as seat belts, which can be inferred to have a socially acceptable QALY ratio, as they are already required by law. However, this too is problematic from the perspective of the aims of welfare economics. The risk of such a strategy is that the methods rely on an uncritical acceptance of the status quo, which itself has not been subjected to careful economic scrutiny. If the main problem in priority setting in health policy is the break in the link between cost and value, then what we most need from the health policy analysts is more information on the amount we are willing to spend, say, to save a life or obtain a QALY. Otherwise we keep setting spending priorities that are out of line with consumer preferences, and are, from the point of view of welfare economics, inefficient and inadequate as a representation of what members of society would choose for themselves were they able to do so in a market context.

CBA's claim to be a societal perspective on how to set priorities also rests on its aim of providing a comprehensive assessment of all benefits, whether health related or otherwise, and all costs imposed on any segment of society. CUA and other forms of CEA make a decisive break with CBA, not only in taking account of health-related benefits only, but also insofar as they count only health related costs, and in some instances, only those health related costs that are born by a health program's budget. As Johannesson notes, an approach to cost accounting consistent with the aim of CEA and CUA to set program priorities under a budget constraint would count only the health related costs borne by the program, not any of the costs born by the patients (Johannesson 1995, 484). Nonetheless Johannesson notes that most studies do in fact include at least some costs to patients, and some proponents of their inclusion argue that doing so strengthens CUA's claim to be a truly societal perspective (Weinstein et al. 1996). The authors of an influential U.S. consensus panel, whose aim was to standardize CEA (and in particular, CUA) studies, concluded that all nonhealth-related costs, including those born by patients, ought to be excluded (Weinstein et al. 1996; Garber et al. 1996).

The various recommendations for how best to conduct CEA (including CUA) studies reflect a kind of conceptual drift away from its underpinnings, in part to become more useful to program administrators, and in part to avoid ethical objections. If the aim is to rank programs and treatments on the basis of their true health benefits and costs to society as a whole, then in theory both the benefit and cost side of the equation should be as complete as possible, as CBA counsels. Objections to unrestricted trade-offs between health and other goods rightly, in our view, pull us in the direction of some form of CEA and away from the purely efficiency-driven rationale of CBA. However, the desire to make CEA fit the practical needs of those who want to make the most of a limited health budget too narrowly focuses attention on the costs the agency itself bears. We would not, for example, think it just to set priorities for prescribing postoperative antibiotics that are based on the drug that has the lowest costs for the funding agency but, from a larger social perspective, costs more in patient recovery time and absence from work (Dranove 1995). Such uses of CEA and CUA, on our theory, open the door to the possibility of injustice for the reason that failure to consider the costs borne by those who are served can adversely affect other essential dimensions of well-being or their social determinants. Modest costs imposed on patients or citizens, of course, do not rise to the level of injustice, but a blinkered bureaucratic focus on what the agency itself spends is not compatible with the aims of social justice.

The conceptual drift from original theoretical underpinnings is, of course, a problem for purists mainly among welfare economists. Less so for us, however. Our theory welcomes the drift from CBA to the focus on the importance of health in its own right, and even the more limited use of CBA's willingness-to-pay approach is rejected in circumstances of considerable economic inequality. CEA and CUA offer some improvements insofar as they do give more weight to the value of health in itself, but there is a moral loss as well. While CBA took into account all of the social costs and benefits of alternative policies in ways we rejected as embodying inappropriate forms of aggregation (if CBA alone is the basis for social decision), it at least had the merit of not ignoring much that is morally relevant. Leaving the nonhealth costs and nonhealth benefits completely out of consideration, however, is no step forward. The impact of social policies on other essential dimensions of well-being or upon the social determinants that profoundly and pervasively affect those other dimensions matters also in our view, and they must somehow enter into any decision that meets the requirement of justice.

6.4 Systematic Disadvantage

A major concern about the use of CEA and CUA, in our view, is the potential that its use in concrete social circumstances results in systematic disadvantage of the sort that our theory rejects as unjust. Others have expressed similar worries about the use of CEA and CUA, but the nature of such objections requires additional specification. The adoption of any criterion for setting health priorities will favor some and disfavor others. On any particular allocation of resources, some will die younger than they otherwise might, while others live longer, and some will live sicker lives than they might have, while others will fare better. In some instances, a criterion for setting priorities will result predictably in identifiable groups of persons getting fewer health-related resources than those who do not share characteristics of those groups. John Cubbon makes just this point. He notes that decision makers know quite well that any option for allocating health care resources will affect persons unequally, but "[a]lmost always there will be no option which leaves everyone under consideration better off than each of the alternatives" (Cubbon 1991, 183).

Indeed, CUA has drawn fire from many quarters based on claims that its use has predictably adverse implications for groups defined by age, disability, or having expensive medical needs. Such claims require a more careful look. Some of the standard objections, as we shall see, are only partially persuasive. For example, while the application of CUA tends to favor the young because on average they have more years to live, it does not do so in all instances. In a head-to-head choice between those whose baseline is very good and can be improved further and those with profound disabilities for whom an intervention produces little benefit, those with disabilities will get a lower priority. In other instances, however, when an intervention for a disability can produce a large incremental improvement in health, those with disabilities may fare better than those who are healthier. CUA is said to favor the cheap to treat. However, because CUA favors those whose ratio of health improvement to cost is highest, even very expensive interventions can be assigned high priority if they provide a more favorable ratio of benefits to cost than cheaper interventions that improve health far less. We consider some of these familiar objections and the appropriate qualifications in sections below. However, what is important to note at the outset is that those individuals sharing characteristics such as lower expected quality of life, lesser expected remaining life span, or lower ratio of benefit to cost, by design, receive a lower priority than those individuals having the capacity for greater QALY improvement for a given amount of available resources. The issue, then, is which, if any, of the trade-offs between persons and groups counseled by a commitment to QALY maximization are unjust.

Putting aside for the moment well-known controversies about the extent of CUA's potential impact on the elderly, those with disabilities, and the expensive to treat, we want first to concentrate on our theory's implications for how matters of justice in the use of QALYs in concrete social and economic contexts actually work. In our view, QALY-based distinctions such as low expected quality of life, decreased longevity, or low ratio of benefit to cost are not categorically unjust simply because some fare less well than others using that specific distributive algorithm. There is a great difference, for example, between the implications of QALYs in a society in which all persons and social groups fare at or above a level of health sufficiency and one in which some individuals and groups do not fare as well, and moreover might be made worse off by implementation of the QALY prioritization scheme. What matters additionally is that QALY-based allocation alone should not be used when doing so would compound existing inequalities of identifiable segments of the general population who, in virtue of other shared characteristics, already may experience inequalities of other sorts such that they fall below a level of sufficiency on one or more dimensions of well-being or would be made more likely to do so. On our theory, such outcomes are unjust.

Indeed, there are other equally important potential unjust consequences associated with the use of CUA and which must be monitored to ensure that CUA itself does not make existing health inequalities worse. As John Harris notes:

> Adoption of QALYs as the rationale for the distribution of health resources ... may well dictate very severe and systematic discrimination against groups identified primarily by race, gender or colour, in the allocation of resources, where it turns out that such groups are vulnerable to conditions that are not QALY-efficient. (Harris 1987, 119)

We can imagine a number of potential examples of the sort Harris gives. Many diseases, including those having some genetic basis, track racial or ethnic differences. To the extent that such differences already align with substantial economic or other social inequalities, a high cost of treatment or public health intervention or an expectation of poor health outcomes can mean that, in addition to all of the other disadvantages members of a group will experience, they will be given a low priority in eligibility in what they most urgently need to reach or maintain a level of sufficiency of well-being. In short, our theory counts as unjust the use of any priority-setting algorithm that adversely affects a sufficiency of health for some groups by creating, compounding, or perpetuating a range of disadvantages experienced by those segments of society such that the adverse effects are made harder to avoid or escape. CUA should not, therefore, be a vehicle for locking in the status quo. If some social groups experiencing multiple social disadvantages turn out to be ones for which health improvements are obtained only by interventions having a very low cost-effectiveness ratio, then we need to look behind those numbers. Justice, in its remedial aims, needs to know, for example, if the poor health and poor prospects for cost-effective health improvement is itself a consequence of prior injustice, either within health policy itself or more broadly. For example, it may be less efficient to address some health needs of the multiply disadvantaged because of injustices in access to timely and appropriate care or the failure to invest social resources in research into the causes, cures, and preventions of disease and disability that differentially affect disadvantaged groups. Alternatively, their health needs may be more expensive to address because of the long-term negative effects of inadequate education, social isolation, or increased exposure to environmental or occupational hazards.

These cautionary remarks regarding the use of CUA and other formal methods are not the whole story on our view, however. There are positive reasons for favoring the collection of more data by the measures that such methods employ. QALYs, DALYs, and the like, whatever their shortcomings and limitations, and nothwithstanding their potential contribution to injustice if used uncritically, are a source of essential moral data on our view. We need to know, for example, which social groups experience the greatest burden of disease, which social groups are least susceptible to incremental health improvement by existing interventions, and which groups are the most expensive to obtain health improvements for. We need to know these things so that we may have the informational base to recognize potential injustices and to know where to concentrate our efforts, even if, contrary to the recommendations of traditional CEA or CUA, we use that information to set priorities in ways that address these injustices rather than to strictly and uncritically maximize QALYs or other aggregate health benefits.

For us, the central problems of justice associated with the use of CUA and other formal economic methods for setting priorities arise when their use fails to redress or, worse, exacerbates larger patterns of inequality which it is the job of justice to police. In the next sections, we turn from this overarching moral problem for formal methods, which has not been much discussed, to the moral relevance of age in the setting of health priorities and then to some of the more specific, familiar moral worries about trade-offs within health that these methods generate.

6.5 The Relevance of Childhood, Old Age, and Human Development

Our theory emphasizes the importance of ensuring a sufficiency of well-being in all of its dimensions for children. We have argued in chapter 4 for this conclusion on two grounds. Our first argument is that the promotion of the essential dimensions of well-being for children is not something that children can achieve for themselves or for which they can be held responsible. Others must act on their behalf. Our second argument reflects a strategic reality. Some dimensions of well-being risk never being adequately developed if not cultivated and promoted early in life. Concern for children must begin at an early age in order to guard against the instantiation of social determinants that have a profound and pervasive negative impact on well-being not only during childhood but also in some cases across the life span. Were the second claim not true, then the emphasis we place on children would be lessened. Only those dimensions of well-being for which a good early start matters would be of central importance. In our view, however, the development of all of the essential dimensions requires attention across the entire life span, including the time of life in which the primary responsibility for ensuring well-being rests with others.

Our claims about the special importance of the needs of children also are directed at a particular context in which the duties of justice apply. In our view, the emphasis upon children comes into play in the design of the basic social structure, including social practices and political and economic institutions. Our emphasis on children therefore sets up the possibility of a conflict between the claims of the young and the claims of everyone else when the resources available for health or other societal programs are limited or scarce. However, when we consider the totality of social institutions and practices, our view admits of numerous ways in which the interests of children and the rest of us, but especially children and the elderly, can be reconciled around common commitments to promote bonds of attachment and affiliation and to advance self-determination.

In this section, however, our immediate focus is narrowed. We begin by examining how both a strict application of CUA and what we call pure age-based priority accounts handle the question of age. We then present the significant ways in which our theory differs from both these approaches with regard to the relevance of age.

QALYs and Fair Innings

A main difference among those who disagree about how age should matter in allocation arises among those theories that view age as directly relevant and those that view age as only indirectly relevant. Proponents of direct or pure age-based allocation criteria typically claim either that beyond some age threshold the weightiness of the moral claim for certain health resources lessens, or that it altogether disappears. One prominent version of a direct age-based approach to health care allocation is known as the "fair-innings" argument. It claims that health care resources ought to be distributed by giving priority to those who are younger. The rationale for such priority is the idea that older people are already better off by virtue of having lived longer and having had an opportunity for well-being that the younger person lacks. Hence, as the name "fair innings" suggests, the younger person is entitled to a similar opportunity. In the case of a choice between patients for a life-saving technology such as kidney dialysis, Michael Lockwood has claimed that "to treat the older person, letting the younger person die, would thus be inherently inequitable . . . the younger person would get no more years than the relatively few he has already had, whereas the older person, who has already had more than the younger person, will get several years more" (Lockwood 1988).

There are other variants of direct age-based priority-setting criteria as well. Some defend giving priority to those who are younger on the grounds that they are among the worst off. Kappel and Sandoe propose such a rationale (Kappel and Sandoe 1994, 86). Others offer variants of the argument that what justice demands is exhausted at the end of a natural life span in which most of life's central projects are completed (Daniels 1988; Callahan 1987). The key feature of each, however, is the claim that age itself should matter directly, and in most accounts, that at some age, justice-based claims weaken if not end.

CUA is different from direct age-based criteria for priority setting. Its application frequently advantages the young, but only contingently and only indirectly. This is because the QALY approach favors those who have more expected life-years ahead of them, and the old generally can expect fewer additional years than the young. However, the old do not automatically get lower priority. In fact, not all younger persons have more expected life years to be gained from a medical or public health intervention than the old. A treatment for younger people whose illness will not substantially improve as a consequence of medical intervention, and who thus will die soon anyway, will not have as high a priority as an intervention for healthier older people who will live longer and produce more QALYs. Differences in expected quality of life can also affect the general advantage that the young have in life expectancy. A simple example is illustrative. Suppose that we can provide an operation for either fifty-year-old or seventy-year-old patients. Suppose further that the cost of the operation is the same in both groups. If there is a sub-population of seventy-year-olds who are otherwise in good shape and can expect an additional ten years of longevity with a quality score of .9, then they have an expected QALY score of 9. A less healthy subpopulation of fifty-year-olds with complicating medical conditions may have a remaining life expectancy of twenty years, but with a poor quality score of .4, and thus they have an expected 8 QALYs to be gained by the operation. Accordingly, the older group is ranked higher by a QALY method in this case. Thus, the fact that quality also matters in the setting of priorities will ensure that age alone will not automatically result in a lower priority ranking for all older persons. For this reason, we say that methods such as QALYs that embody a time/quality trade-off approach take age into account only indirectly: QALYs technically favor those with greater remaining life expectancy. QALYs favor the young only contingently; when the costs of treating the old are low and the quality of life to be gained is substantial, the claims of older people move up in the rankings.

There can, of course, be intentional exceptions to the contingent relationship between CUA and age. For example, in the World Health Organization's

Burden of Disease project, a CUA measure called the Disability-Adjusted Life Year (DALY) was specifically constructed to place a greater weight on years lived in adulthood, as compared to years in childhood or old age. This controversial weighting, which was intended to capture the importance to all in society of those in the care taking decades of life, was an intentional manipulation of the internal logic of CUA and its contingent privileging of youth.

Both pure age-based accounts such as the fair-innings argument and CUA are subject to some powerful objections that we seek to avoid. A familiar objection to fair-innings (and related) accounts is that such views require us to give great weight to small differences in age. If Bill and Al are ages fifty and forty-eight respectively, the fair-innings approach requires us to give priority to Al, when most would argue that they should be given equal chances or that no morally relevant differences exist.

Depending on one's standpoint, a more plausible version of the fair-innings approach limits the force of this first objection somewhat by setting a threshold for its application. Below whatever threshold we count as a fair number of innings, differences in age would be treated as morally irrelevant for purposes of distribution (Harris 1994, 75). All who are below the age threshold have equal priority, in contrast to all who are above it (Kappel and Sandoe 1992, 309–11).

Similar objections can be made against CUA as well. With the use of CUA, if small differences in life expectancy (or cost or quality, for that matter) are allowed to determine a ranking, then it too would be subject to the same sort of objection. One solution is to count only *substantial* differences in years of life saved or quality of life in deciding how to rank order competing public health policies or medical care interventions. The result would be a wide latitude of acceptable variations in the quality-adjusted life years per unit of resources that would be treated equally in priority-setting schemes, and thus the arbitrariness of small differences would be lessened.

However, no such partial, technical fix is available for direct age-based approaches. Even a high threshold account of what counts as fair innings does not meet all of the objections. Cases in which there are large differences in age still raise deeply troubling issues. Suppose the threshold for fair innings is set at age 75. Suppose further that we have a shortage of vaccine for a new strain of flu. A policy decision has already been made to allocate the limited vaccine to those groups at highest risk of death should they contract the infection. We are now down to the last of the vaccine and must chose between two remaining "high-risk" groups—children who are currently in hospice care for terminal illnesses (these are children projected to have no more than six months left to live, although predictions can be wrong) and healthy people over 76 who have an average life expectancy of at least five years. While we do not have the same sort of problem exhibited in the choice between Bill and Al, the fair-innings approach still requires that we give the drug to the children on the grounds that those over seventy-five have already had their fair innings, while the QALY approach instructs us to give the drug to the older people on grounds of greater prospective benefit. The fair-innings approach thus treats a small reduction in inequality of life span between young and old as morally weightier than a substantial gain in longevity for the old. As a generalized account of health care allocation, this version of the fair-innings approach remains highly counterintuitive. It is troubling that the elderly have had a rich opportunity for a good life while these very ill children have had so little. But to give priority to terminally ill children, whose chances of having anything like a comparable life are negligible, gives too much weight to concerns about inequality. Justice does not always require reducing even very large differences in life span.

Youth, Life Expectancy, Old Age, and Justice

In sharp contrast to direct age-based accounts like the fair-innings argument, there is no place in our theory for age cut offs or even for age, per se. Instead, our focus is on childhood, not on whether one claimant is age six and another sixteen or sixty. We are concerned about childhood because of the particular claims and needs of that stage of life. For us, it is the special role that childhood plays in human development and human flourishing that makes childhood morally unique. Thus, unlike CUA, which only contingently favors the young, our theory explicitly privileges childhood in the design of social institutions and policies. However, we are not committed to a rigid, lexical ordering of priorities in which the interests of children always trump the interests of other social groups. A just society is concerned with nurturing the dimensions of well-being across the life span, and injustices that compromise well-being afflict adults and the elderly as well as children.

Indeed, there are at least two additional reasons for rejecting principles for priority setting that restrict allocations based on advanced age. First, theories of justice that tie entitlements to health resources to an age-based cut off yield counterintuitive implications in other dimensions of well-being. Dan Brock asks, for example, what reasoning prevents us from excluding other life-extending goods such as food from application of such a principle. If we are not to provide the very old with the medical technology of artificial systems for nutrition, why should we provide them with such social services as homebound meals or human assistance with feeding (Brock 1989, 312)? Although we believe Brock's challenge is less than telling, the principal point is correct. Approaches based on advanced age are morally blunt instruments. By contrast, on our view, age alone is never a sufficient basis for a lower priority for particular health goods and services or any other good that affects well-being in any of its essential dimensions.

Second, our view also rejects the categorical relevance of advanced age in priority setting for the reason that it is incompatible with ensuring other essential dimensions of well-being, most notably those of respect and attachment. The importance of these dimensions of well-being cuts across age differences. As we have argued earlier, at no point do requirements of justice based on the importance of the essential dimensions of well-being end simply because of advanced age.

Our theory thus differs from both CUA and the age-based approaches in the way that it addresses the bare fact of differences in length of life, either remaining (as CUA takes into account) or life span (as the fair-innings argument considers). It is the developmental significance of childhood and adolescence that matters to our account of justice, not differences in age, per se. Our theory places emphasis upon children for reasons having to do with the profound and pervasive effects on well-being that can only be addressed by others and which often can be addressed adequately only if done so from childhood forward. It does not privilege forty-eight-year olds over fifty-year olds, and it certainly does not offer guidance for a choice between Bill and Al. There are no morally relevant differences based on one group having lived slightly longer already or having slightly more years of life remaining than another group, nor does our theory count all large differences in health outcomes—including life span—as unjust, and hence in need of redress in all cases. It certainly does not require that a just health policy smooth out all differences in life span, for example, when inequality of life span is only marginally lessened and no other, morally relevant story is to be told about the origin of those disparities.

Our theory does require that the totality of social institutions be designed with an eye to sufficiency of health, and that aim of sufficiency includes a commitment to social policies that promote the reduction of unjust inequalities of life span. Substantial population variations in life span under our view certainly do trigger a demand for heightened scrutiny as they are indicative of lack of health sufficiency, as do longevity differences that track clusters of multiple disadvantage such as those that accompany group-based oppression. In order to judge the moral significance of differences in life span, we need more moral data of the sort we argued for at the end of chapter 4.

Moreover, the duties of social justice arising at the level of institutional design do not translate into moral instructions for how to treat individual claimants in clinical contexts. As we have emphasized throughout, our account of social justice is concerned with the well-being of socially situated groups. Life span or life expectancy differences among individuals do not trigger a requirement of justice to even out inequalities on a case-by-case basis, say, by comparing the relative weight of claims of those particular persons who just happen to be in the emergency room queue at any morally arbitrary moment in time. Indeed, the morality of interpersonal relations generally rules out such comparisons. By contrast, in conditions of scarcity what is not ruled out is the design of health policies that make it more likely that those who are currently toddlers will live to their late seventies than that those who are currently in their late seventies will reach their late eighties. In fact, these are just the sort of policies that justice demands on our view.

That said, however, justice also requires attending to the well-being of those in their seventies and eighties, and beyond. As it happens, there is increasing evidence that well-being in advanced age is as much if not more a function of social connection and respect than of access to medical technology. Also relevant to considerations of social justice is who the elderly are, as well as who cares for them. Poor elderly are disproportionately women, as are those on whom the burdens of care taking generally fall. In the decades to come, the sheer numbers of elderly throughout the world but especially in countries like China and India will increase dramatically, with potentially disastrous implications for the elderly and for the (largely) middle-aged women on whom they will hope to depend. There are many ways in which the design of social institutions can and should prevent or at least mitigate the injustices of abandonment, isolation, and unremitting care taking that this demographic shift portends for both the old and for women.

We turn next to a different kind of argument against how age, particularly advanced age, is treated in QALYs. This argument, also developed by Kappel and Sandoe (subsequent to their priority to the worse-off argument), derives from a utilitarian perspective. They question an assumption they take to be central to the QALY approach. It is the assumption that an improvement in the health quality of one's life has the same utility for all persons regardless of their age or stage in life. We ordinarily think, for example, that pain relief matters just as much at ninety as it does at twenty, or that ease from respiratory distress has value independent of age. Some recent empirical survey research lends support for this assumption. Domains of health such as pain and discomfort, and anxiety and depression, are widely viewed as equally important to alleviate at any age; they are not viewed simply as acceptable declines in health that are a normal part of aging (Brouwer, van Exel, Elly 2005).

However, Sandoe and Kappel argue that not all domains of health or quality of life are of this character. Increasing an individual's mobility and ability to walk without assistance is, they argue, often worth more to a person at age thirty than it is at age seventy-five (Kappel and Sandoe 1992, 298). The person who is seventy-five may find that sitting and reading is satisfaction enough, whereas that degree of sedentariness will not match well with the expectations and desires of the thirty-year old for an active life. They conclude that the aim of maximizing an individual's overall utility (and hence social utility ultimately) needs to take account of the stage in life in which he or she gets the medical benefit and, as a consequence, can derive more nonmedical utility. The implication of this utilitarian argument about the good is that QALY methods may not be ageist enough. If what we seek is the greatest gains in overall social utility or well-being, then we do better to provide more medical care and other health-affecting resources for the benefit of the young than even the QALY approach might provide.

While our view shares their willingness to count dimensions of well-being other than health benefits as relevant to health policy priority setting, as well as the general view that the achievement of well-being within the dimension of health itself may depend on the life stage in which positive social determinants of well-being are introduced, our pluralist account of the essential dimensions of well-being parts company with the unrestricted trade-offs that a pure utilitarian calculus licenses. We emphasize a different implication of their general claim that stage of life may affect how an intervention matters morally. The relevance of some domains of health functioning do not fade with age. Ensuring a sufficiency of health is not in our view simply a matter of ensuring comparable lifetime health prospects across the population. Any plausible account of sufficiency in health must be able to accommodate some distinction among those domains of health that matter equally at any age (e.g., pain and depression levels) and those that arguably are more urgent to address at younger ages in order to ensure sufficient lifetime health prospects.

Moreover, the relevance of essential dimensions of well-being other than health do not fade with age. Respect and the bonds of attachment are two notable examples, and they also explain in part our intuitive reluctance to overweight utilitarian concerns of the sort Kappel and Sandoe highlight. In our view, it is not the low utility of investment in old age that figures prominently in what justice requires. Instead, our emphasis lies elsewhere. Our focus on children's claims rests on the fact that without early intervention and assistance early in life, multiple disadvantages in health and in other dimensions of well-being may be inescapable and therefore unjust. That childhood is a morally crucial stage of life is compatible, however, with our claim that the needs and interests of even the very old also are matters of justice. Sufficiency in health is more than a lifetime of health prospects; the suffering of severe physical pain or profound depression has an equal call on us regardless of the age of the sufferer. Second, dimensions of well-being other than health, such as attachment and respect, also bear on what justice demands.

We shall have more to say in the next two sections about how and why the importance of nonhealth dimensions function as justice-based constraints on trade-offs within health. However, our rejection of pure age-based approaches in favor of a view that takes quality of life into account as well as considerations of life span invites comparison with another recent variant of the fair-innings view. Alan Williams argues that what matters morally is not simply that some live longer (have more innings) than others but that some have better prospects for health, overall, during their lifetimes (Williams 1997). For example, if one group lives longer but lives sicker, it is conceivable that its lifetime health prospects are comparable to another group who live shorter but healthier lives. The upshot is what might be called a quality-adjusted fair-innings view, with the outcome measure of interest Quality Adjusted Life Expectancy (QALE). How long one lives is no longer solely relevant, as it is in a pure age-based approach. Instead, what is relevant is how many healthy years of life a person lives or can be expected to live.

Eric Nord objects that the quality-adjusted fair-innings approach is committed to the counterintuitive claim that "QALYs beyond a certain age should count very little" and thus that present suffering in older people who have otherwise lived healthy lives would have to be discounted in priority-setting contexts (Nord 2005, 259). The problem, as Nord explains it, is that the quality-adjusted fair-innings view not only gives priority to the young in access to life-saving interventions, as defenders of the original fair-innings approach argue, but in addition it gives the young priority when it comes to functional improvements and symptom relief for nonfatal conditions" (Nord 2005, 261).

Williams's view constitutes a particular conception of sufficiency in health. If health sufficiency is viewed as nothing more than a person's aggregate lifetime health prospects, or QALE, then this categorical priority in favor of the young over the old with regard to *any* possible health improvement in any possible context would be unavoidable. However, this is not our view of what sufficiency in health consists in. Any plausible account of sufficiency in health must be concerned not only with actual or expected levels of health over a lifetime but also with the moral relevance of more fine-grained distinctions among the distinct domains of health that capture the levels of people's health at any point in time. Among those domains, for example, are mobility, fertility, sexual functioning, anxiety, depression, pain, memory, and many more. As we have already noted, some health needs such as significant pain or severe depression have strong claims in justice regardless of the age group experiencing them. We agree that any plausible account of sufficiency in health must take account of quality of life as well as life span. However, we part company with any view that is not able to accommodate the moral significance of three further distinctions. First, the priority we place on children rests in large part on the fact that some domains of health, as well as of other dimensions of well-being, are compromised *over a lifetime* by a failure to thrive in childhood and adolescence. Accordingly, stage of life matters greatly in our theory and often in ways that assigns higher priority to children in social allocation because of what a commitment to ensuring health sufficiency minimally demands. Second, sufficiency in health certainly has to do with how long one lives; all other things being equal, deaths in childhood and among young adults are of greater concern from the standpoint of justice than deaths later in life. Nevertheless, as we argued in chapter 6, whether or to what extent differences in life span matter morally depends critically not only on the magnitude of the difference in length of life (or, for that matter, health-related quality of life), but also on morally relevant features of the groups whose life spans are being compared and on the reasons that the difference exists. Third, as we have already argued, any plausible account of sufficiency in health must be able to accommodate the view that some domains of health matter equally at any stage of life. The survey research cited previously, as well as our own claims about the importance of pain and depression regardless of stage of life, are cases in point. A central problem with the quality-adjusted fair-innings approach is that, while incorporating health status as well as life span into judgments about what justice demands is intuitively plausible, doing so in a way that effaces reasonable distinctions among the domains of health which make up aggregate quality of life measures can be a morally blunt instrument no less than some other proposals we have discussed. A proper appreciation of the differences among domains of health can go a long way toward developing an account of sufficiency in health that reflects some important moral and medical differences relevant to priority-setting tasks.

6.6 Beyond Separate Spheres of Justice

In section 6.5, we considered how both a more nuanced elaboration of what sufficiency in health means and the moral relevance of non-health-related dimensions could guide allocation decisions in contexts in which age differences are a part of the moral equation. In this section we further explore how our theory can account for some deeper sources of moral anxiety about unrestricted trade-offs within health, generally. In some instances, at least, we think the most plausible grounds for thinking that some limits are appropriate on such trade-offs rests not with the presumed differences in health benefits subject to aggregation but with the failure to give appropriate weight to other, non-health-related considerations. After developing our view in more detail, we turn our attention in section 6.7 to how it bears on four specific types of conflict.

Our view stands in marked contrast with the "separate spheres" doctrine embraced in some form by theorists of many stripes. The term is from Michael Walzer's book *Spheres of Justice*. The doctrine holds that there are multiple spheres of justice, each with its own unique, single principle or singularly relevant set of considerations for determining what justice requires. When applied to public health and health policy, this doctrine contends that only health-related considerations such as health benefit or medical need are morally relevant in determining what is due to whom. Walzer, for example, argues that only health needs are relevant to determining distributive shares of health care resources. Frances Kamm similarly argues that there are numerous "irrelevant utilities" or possible benefits that should not count in deciding whom to save from death, whom to treat, or whom to otherwise aid with health-related resources.

The doctrine has considerable appeal because it precludes the use of certain kinds of irrelevant or inappropriate considerations in making moral trade offs. However, we do not agree that its blanket exclusionary approach offers the best account of the set of moral considerations relevant to justice in any particular sphere of social life. We consider a number of arguments made on behalf of the separate-spheres doctrine, as well as a number of ancillary arguments meant to delineate the proper scope of its application, in order to show that the doctrine should not be rigidly applied.

The first argument is addressed to the potential for injustice when considerations of social utility are allowed to count. Two persons who will both die without a transplantable organ are said to have equal health needs. Many will argue that nothing in their individual biographies—their capacity to derive greater personal utility from survival, the non-health-related benefits that might accrue to dependent family members, or the greater utility that might be produced for society overall—is relevant to the decision of who should get the organ. The separate-spheres doctrine thus ensures that morally suspect considerations that are not related to health do not count.

We agree that it is important to prevent morally inappropriate factors from being taken into account, but we do not agree that the exclusionary breadth of the separate-spheres doctrine is needed to rule out what is arguably irrelevant in such cases. By taking account of a plurality of essential dimensions of well-being, each having considerable independent moral weight, our theory does not license the sort of unrestricted moral calculus that some would find objectionable. For much the same reasons others oppose unconstrained aggregation techniques, we reject the use of similarly unconstrained CBA. More important, our worry throughout has been that a blanket exclusion of everything but health benefits also risks ruling out much that is arguably morally relevant.

Another line of reasoning adds to the plausibility of the separate-spheres doctrine in some contexts by narrowing the scope of its application. Frances Kamm argues that the doctrine should be applied to micro-allocational decision contexts, and not to macro-allocational decisions. Micro-allocation contexts involve decisions in the "here and now." In these, we have some limited supply of goods to distribute among identifiable claimants who stand before us. The emergency room physician with patients awaiting treatment is the standard kind of example. Macro-allocational contexts, by contrast, usually involve decisions about production and the impact is on future, statistical persons rather than contemporaneous, identifiable claimants in need. Legislators or government officials for example, must decide how many hospital beds to authorize, what kinds of vaccine programs to implement, what modes of research to pursue, what health education campaigns to launch, which medical interventions to cover in publicly funded or regulated insurance plans, and so on.

Kamm argues that the separate-spheres doctrine applies to the emergency room decisions but not to the legislator's decision. It means that legislators are allowed to freely trade off health and other goods without restriction, and benefits other than health are treated as potentially morally relevant. Not so with clinicians, however; the doctrine dictates that nonhealth concerns should never count.

The distinction between decisional contexts has some intuitive appeal inasmuch as many of us reasonably have misgivings about permitting, let alone requiring, clinicians to take on the moral task, on a case-by-case basis, of interpreting and implementing the requirements of social justice. It is a far cry from our claiming that the totality of social institutions and practices must achieve certain ends to concluding that particular people have either the right or the responsibility as they make individual decisions on a case-by-case basis to see to it that social justice in the aggregate is served. In the specific context of health, many arguments are put forward in support of this view, including the importance of preserving the fiduciary character of the clinician-patient relationship, as well as the general implausibility of relying on individual decisions to achieve societal ends. Far better, many argue, to have the tough allocational rules set at the macro level, by legislators or their institutional designees who are properly positioned to take account of the wider considerations of social justice.

Public health officials, who frequently operate at the macro level, have not generally embraced the full implications of this view, however.

Many in public health implicitly or explicitly endorse the separate-spheres doctrine in their own work. Our discussion in chapter 4 of how to structure HIV screening programs in the late 1980s is an example. While some urged that these programs be restricted to low-income women in order to maximize health-related benefits, we objected that the possibility of social stigma, reinforcement of offensive social stereotypes, ostracism by family and community, loss of child custody, and other non-health-related considerations ought to count as heavily as health-related ones. Targeted screening was thus rejected because we also rejected the claim that health benefits alone, let alone the maximization of health benefits, should be all that counts. This was, in effect, a rejection of a version of the separate-spheres thesis in a macro-level decision.

Whatever basis there might be for thinking micro-allocational contexts morally different, the case for the separate-spheres doctrine at the macro level that is our concern seems to us remarkably weak. This is not to say that we think that there is a bright line between macro- and micro-allocation decision contexts. Many decisions shade into one another, for example, when production decisions and distribution decisions are vested in a single institutional authority. At the level of public policy formation, however, our theory starts with the defeasible presumption that all six essential dimensions of well-being are morally relevant as a matter of justice.

An argument by Walzer on behalf of the separate-spheres doctrine, on closer inspection, actually favors our position. Walzer argues that allocating some goods on the basis of a single distributive principle, unique to that sphere of justice, can be instrumental in preventing unjust patterns of social domination. He observes that there is great danger in the contrary alternative, namely, allowing one distributive principle to govern in multiple spheres. For example, access to some goods such as money or market clout, if allowed to determine each person's share of goods in multiple spheres, creates a situation in which those who fare well in one sphere will fare well in others, and those who fare badly will fare badly in all others as well. Some persons or groups could dominate access to a range of the most important goods of human existence, and indeed, dominate other persons as well by virtue of their dominance in one sphere.

Walzer's hypothesis is a reasonable one in many instances, and we have made some arguments of that sort in this book. However, his ultimate concern is nondomination, and his concern extends to the protection of a plurality of human goods, including health. While not allowing other goods to count can be contingently instrumental to that end, a failure to acknowledge the moral relevance of consequences for well-being other than health can contribute to domination rather than alleviate it.

The HIV program just described is a case in point. Consider also our analysis in chapter 5 of health care policies. While some ways of organizing private health insurance markets, coupled with public safety net programs, can provide a country's citizens with access to health benefits, such policies can do so in ways that undermine the realization of other essential aspects of human well-being that are every bit as important to a just system of health care access as health care itself. The risk is that such social institutions and policies fail to foster social respect for members of certain disadvantaged groups, an appropriate degree of self-determination for those the policies are meant to assist, or an ability to maintain familial and other intimate relationships.

If we take seriously Walzer's insight that an important part of justice is the prevention of social domination and that domination can occur with respect to various aspects of human well-being, then we have some duty to ensure that the totality of social institutions, practices, and policies is designed with an eye toward lessening or preventing systematic inequalities affecting multiple dimensions of well-being. In the following section we consider how taking certain nonhealth considerations into account might help explain some instances of what often seems problematic when trading off differing sorts of health benefits.

6.7 Trade-Offs within Health

Many of the most familiar criticisms of CUA arise from the fact that CUA aggregates health benefits of diverse kinds into a common, unified health metric and then seeks the maximization of those benefits per unit of resources for society overall. The source of controversy is the fact that a common health metric used by CUA, or by any decision rule in which health benefits of different sorts are aggregated, tends to treat health losses of one kind to some persons as appropriate trade-offs against the health gains of another kind by yet other persons. Although CUA is the frequent target of such objections, the worries we examine are of more general significance for many attempts to set priorities. We consider four such objections. The upshot for the proponents of each objection is that the priority rankings CUA rules assign to some health states or outcomes must be amended or even reversed.

The first objection asserts the moral uniqueness of life saving. It claims that among health concerns there is something morally unique about the saving of a human life that makes this activity a priority. Moreover, the claim about moral uniqueness also maintains that the saving of human lives should not be aggregated or traded off readily, even in instances where there are substantial differences in numbers of lives that could be saved or in life expectancy or quality of life.

The second objection is the numerous-small-benefits problem: the claim is that there are instances in which smaller health benefits to many people ought not to outrank larger health benefits to fewer people even if the former alternative produces more QALYs (or other measure of aggregate health benefit) than the latter. The moral-uniqueness objection and the small-benefits objection are related but not identical concerns. This second and in some respects more comprehensive objection does not suppose that among the contested claims for a scarce resource, life saving is sui generis. Instead, the small-benefits objection is broader in that it resists the aggregation of any health states of vastly dissimilar magnitude.

The third objection, the rule of rescue, is—like the moral-uniqueness objection—only concerned with life saving, but it is narrower still. The rule of rescue's more specific claim is that there is a more stringent moral duty to respond to threats to life than to other health-related concerns when there are *identifiable* persons in immediate need of saving or "rescuing" from death.

The fourth objection holds that, contrary to CUA's preference for aiding first those who are the most cost-efficient to help (e.g., realizing the most QALYs), we should give at least some priority to the worst off, or people whose medical conditions make them among the worst off. This involves a potential reversal of priority if, as well may be the case, the medically worst off turn out to be those who, if aided, will derive the least health benefit from a given expenditure of resources.

The Moral Uniqueness of Life Saving

The moral-uniqueness objection starts from the premise that life saving imposes morally unique obligations that get lost in the aggregation process or in other assumptions of the QALY calculus. Consider first the moral costs of aggregation when lives are at stake. Suppose, for example, we have sufficient resources either to screen and treat a group of women for breast cancer and thereby save an expected one hundred lives, or screen and treat a different group of women for a rarer disease that is more expensive to address and save ten lives. Many traditional public health approaches would have no trouble deciding which program to fund: assuming that there are no other health-related differences among the claimants, the breast cancer program should be implemented because that option produces the greater aggregate benefit, that is, the most lives saved. Critics, however, complain that, at least when something as consequential as human life is at stake, choice in favor of the larger number of beneficiaries, merely because the larger number represents a greater aggregate benefit, is not a morally acceptable way of determining winners and losers (Taurek 1977). John Harris makes clear that the implications of such a view may extend beyond straightforward concerns about the propriety of aggregating human lives to more subtle concerns about whether life expectancy or quality of life should be allowed to matter in the life-saving context. He claims, "Each person's desire to stay alive should be regarded as of the same importance as that of anyone else, irrespective of the quality of their life or its expected duration" (Harris 1985, 101). While others may view only a very short amount of additional time, say weeks or even days, as being of little value, Harris argues that it is for the individual herself to decide whether this extra time is worth having (Harris 1985, 89; Harris 1987, 120–21; Harris 1988a, 265).

Other, somewhat more modest versions of the uniqueness objection agree that the subjective interests each has in continued survival deserves some weight additional to what might be granted in a simple QALY calculation, for example. However, the more modest views do not share the assumption that the subjective preferences of persons affected by such policies or decisions are morally determinative of what justice requires. Just how much weight the subjective point of view merits is the subject of considerable discussion (Brock 1988; Kamm 1988a). In our view, there are limits to the level of precision we can expect in such matters (Daniels 1993). However, we agree with something more fundamental in attempts by Frances Kamm and others to estimate the weight that should be accorded to an individual's subjective preferences. For Kamm, the deeper concern is about what respect for persons requires when such difficult trade-offs must be made. Indeed, respect figures centrally among the essential dimensions of well-being that are important as a matter of justice. In addition, our own intuitions are that other concerns, including the preservation of bonds of attachment, figure equally as much, especially in our anxieties about how decisions affecting life and death are made. If we are correct about what is really most fundamentally at stake, it is evidence that, contrary to the assumptions of the separate-spheres doctrine, much more than health itself is morally relevant in explicating the intuitions that lie behind worries about moral uniqueness of life saving.

The Numerous-Small-Benefits Problem

When is it justifiable to permit a smaller number of substantial health benefits to be outweighed by a larger number of smaller health benefits? Conversely, when is it justifiable to permit the preservation of a few limbs to take priority over the prevention of numerous common colds? Frances Kamm suggests we explicate such questions by focusing on what sacrifices it would be reasonable to reject for the sake of another's health. In such a view, even the sacrifice of a limb may not be required of someone to save the life of another person, but a few days with a cold seems harder to reject. Kamm thus requires that we take into account the subjective point of view of everyone involved in trade-offs of dissimilar health goods. She thinks that it is wrong to deprive a person of a chance for preserving a limb in order to bestow a much lesser health benefit on another person because to do so fails to take seriously how the sacrifice matters to the people affected. Trade-offs among nonequivalent interests are therefore restricted. This restriction on nonequivalent trade-offs holds even when the total amount of benefit is greatly increased by an increase in the number of people who would receive the lesser benefit (Kamm 1993, 148). Restrictions on such trade offs based on the importance of the purely subjective perspective, however, only apply in micro-allocation contexts such as those faced by physicians in an emergency room. Kamm thus rejects the perspective of a utilitarian form of deliberation in which unrestricted trade-offs are permitted in these decision making contexts. However, as we noted previously, Kamm widens the range of permissible considerations within macro-decision contexts. (Kamm 1993, 1998a). The precise contours of Kamm's attempt to map what she takes common sense moral intuitions to recommend is complex and intentionally incomplete, but she notes that even our macro-level decisions remain constrained somewhat by the exclusion of some benefits that would still count as irrelevant considerations under her theory. Our theory, by contrast, builds on the list of essential dimensions of well-being as an account of what is in fact morally relevant in macro-level decisions about institutional design. There are no easy answers, of course, simply because we have an enriched menu of morally relevant considerations. In fact, our theory adds a further layer of complexity to the already difficult numerous-small-benefits problem. The additional worry is that, at certain points, micro-level decisions shade into macro-level ones, and the distinction as a marker for a clear moral difference loses some of its intuitive plausibility.

The numerous-small-benefits problem is exhibited vividly in the decisions faced by policy makers who must decide what health care services to fund or what public health interventions to undertake. The most discussed example of a formal priority setting in American health policy (conspicuous also because such methods have so rarely been used in actual practice) is the legislation known as the Oregon Basic Health Services Act, passed in 1989. The goal was to expand Medicaid coverage to all Oregonians below the poverty level and, through the federal waiver process, pay for the expansion by reducing the covered services according to a priority list that would be publicly developed. An eleven-member Health Services Commission was charged with the task of developing the list and making recommendations to the legislature for funding. The Commission drew up a lengthy list of pairs of medical conditions and their treatments based upon the widely accepted International Classification of Disease (ICD-9) (Medical Management Institute 2006) and judgments of appropriate treatment taken from leading treatment manuals and consultations with practitioners from all major medical specialties. The Commission's medical committee made judgments about the medical effectiveness and costs of each treatment, again relying heavily on the assessments and experiences of relevant experts, and supplemented those judgments using telephone survey data designed to obtain the public's preferences for the different health states affected by these treatment-condition pairs.

The first prioritized list was released in 1990, but public criticism led to further rethinking of the fundamental guiding assumptions. Among the many criticisms of the process was that the rankings generated by the straightforward cost-utility approach were counterintuitive. Perhaps the most famous such counterintuitive ranking was the placing of the capping of teeth above the performance of appendectomies.

What implications do Kamm's arguments have for public policies like the Oregon Basic Health Services Act that constrain what doctors and nurses are allowed to do? Kamm's suggestion is that social decision makers (e.g., legislators) may aggregate significantly lesser losses and greater losses when the basis of their decision is a calculation of comparative costs rather than a judgment that the losses are equivalent (Kamm 1993, 181–4). For example, when a social decision maker decides not to fund a life-saving or limb-preserving treatment and instead funds a lesser benefit for a greater number, she need not be making judgments of equivalency; she may be merely judging that she does not want to pay the cost of aiding the people who will suffer the most (Kamm 1994, 32). The conclusion seems to be that, while aggregating interests based on an assumption that substantially dissimilar interests are equivalent would violate a principle of equal respect, aggregating on a scale of costs does not (Kamm 1993, 182–3; Kamm 1994, 32; Kamm 1987, 270).

Critics of the Oregon plan clearly find such trade-off decisions in macro-allocation contexts almost as troubling as ones made in the emergency rooms. The reason, we suspect, is that the way such decisions are experienced by those who make them and by those most immediately affected by them does not easily track the distinction between equivalent interests and equivalent costs. The phenomenology of decision is less likely to differ so sharply in actual policy contexts when decision makers are vividly aware that what physicians and nurses will be able to do and what people in need will experience depends in large part on what legislators have decided is the appropriate basis for setting priorities. To the extent that considerations of respect and personal attachment, as we claim, explain a great deal of the motivation for setting limits on such trade-offs in micro-allocation contexts, we think that the same considerations remain vividly in mind among macro-level decision makers. This *transparency* of morally relevant considerations between the two decisional contexts does not dictate an answer to how we deal with the numerous-small-benefits problems. However, we think that an implication of a theory of social justice, operating at the level of social design, is that such transparency is not only unavoidable but desirable. Social institutions, in order to be just, must be designed in ways that allow for the full range of development and expression of the capacities for attachment, respect, and affiliation by those who must implement and live by social policies. What precisely a proper concern for these non-health-related considerations ultimately recommend is an open question in our minds, but we think that they count, as a matter of justice.

Rule of Rescue

The "rule of rescue" is a term coined by Albert Jonsen to describe the priority many people place on rescuing *identifiable* persons at imminent risk of death with little or no regard to cost (Jonsen 1986, 172–74). One of the major political events affecting the development of the Oregon Medicaid program was the highly public plight of Coby Howard, a seven-year-old boy suffering from leukemia, who died while awaiting Medicaid funding for a transplant. As David Hadorn observed, "any plan to distribute health care services must take human nature into account.... [P]eople cannot stand idly by when an identified person's life is visibly threatened if rescue measures are available" (Hadorn 1991, 2219).

What, then, is it about identifiable persons at risk of death that makes their claims so compelling that they should undo the rankings of CUA? A number of answers have been suggested. Some have argued that the source of this felt obligation lies in the symbolic value of defying cold, calculating economic rationality in the face of human tragedy (Eddy 1994, 1795; MacLean 1986, p.87). Hadorn suggests that the special moral requirements for responding to immediate and identifiable need extends beyond instances of risk of death to other dread outcomes as well (Hadorn 1991, 2219).

Critics, by contrast, have suggested that this "felt duty" is not a genuine moral obligation but an expression of sympathy or compassion, and that there are good reasons to doubt whether it is morally correct or rational to sacrifice many "mere statistical lives" for the sake of a few identifiable lives (C. Fried 1969). Even utilitarians, however, who generally might be thought least likely to endorse the rule of rescue have argued for the rule on the grounds that even with fewer lives saved more of value might be accomplished. Others contend that it is a mistake to ignore the fact that there is "considerable social value in reinforcing acts driven by compassion and sympathy...[and] that people obtain benefit from the belief that they are living in a caring and humane society" (McKie and Richardson 2003).

While our account differs from the utilitarian one, we also view some non-health-benefits of this sort as relevant to allocation decisions in health policy because we hold the impact on the other essential dimensions of well-being to be relevant to justice. If there is a case based in justice—and not compassion alone or general considerations of utilitarian maximizing — for sometimes allowing the rule of rescue to undo the rankings of CUA, then in our view it is the importance of preserving the bonds of attachment. How much difference in any particular institutional context the value of attachment might have compared to the value of health is certainly an open question, but in our view it counts. In some cases it counts enough that failure to respond to identifiable need is not simply evidence of a lack of compassion but a lack of development of capacities of human sympathy and that lack constitutes an injustice. In our view, injustices of social abandonment can be as significant when they occur within the context of decisions of legislators and policy makers as those made at the bedside.

The injustices of social abandonment and the moral urgency associated with rescue are not restricted to worries about cost-utility trade-offs in health care policy. Indeed, their moral pull and relevance are equally if not more present in public health and social policies, more broadly. The devastating tsunami that rocked South Asia and the world in the closing days of 2004 produced an enormous immediate loss of life and left many more in need of rescue from imminent death and disease for lack of clean water, shelter, food, and medicine. Even if it were the case that the global public health responses to this extraordinary tragedy would have produced more QALYs had they been deployed elsewhere in the world, to have done so would have been profoundly unjust and not merely unseemly or lacking in compassion.

Our appeal to matters outside the health sphere as relevant to determining a just allocation of health resources is not, however, open-ended in the way the utilitarian calculus is. Our theory does not risk treating persons as mere means, for example, when we make priority decisions that reflect what is owed to people as ends in themselves, not only in terms of their health, but in terms of what is owed them with regard to respect and attachment.

Priority to the Worst Off

A final objection to unrestricted health trade-offs such as those CUA licenses is that it may not leave room for a reasonable degree of priority to the worst off. Because the positive aim of our theory is defined in terms of an aspiration to achieve a sufficiency in each of the essential dimensions of well-being, a further question that the proponent of some duty to aid the medically worst off groups might ask is this: How do we choose between groups who fall just below the level of sufficiency and can be raised to a level of health sufficiency if a scarce resource is dedicated to them, and those groups who are so badly off that they will remain well below the level of sufficiency even after being aided (Brock 2002)? While we do not think that there is any generally right answer to such a question, our theory does provide some important relevant guidance.

Our commitment to the pursuit of sufficiency in health or in any other essential dimension of well-being is limited by the requirements of the other essential dimensions. Our theory does not permit the abandonment of those whose health status can never be brought to the level of sufficiency, nor does it automatically grant a priority to those who can easily be brought to health sufficiency. To do so would violate our commitments to ensuring a level of sufficiency in those areas for which sufficiency is within the realm of possibility. In the case of persons with severe mental retardation, for example, we may not be able to achieve the same level of overall health, reasoning development, or self-determination as is generally possible for others. However, to deny health or social benefits to people with mental retardation merely because resources could be used instead to assist others for whom health sufficiency is in reach violates both our commitment to respect and our commitment to attachment. Our theory thus preempts the categorical trumping of the needs of the medically worst off by the needs of those slightly below sufficiency, who if aided would achieve the aim of health sufficiency. However, we do hold fast to the view that there is a stringent, but not absolute, priority to the worst off such that those at the bottom, no matter how this is defined, have an entitlement to scarce resources. Particularly when little can be done to improve the health of the worst off, or when what can be done would exhaust most if not all of the resources available (the so-called bottomless pit problem), then the needs of the worst off should yield to the needs of others, including those whose health can be brought closer to a level of sufficiency. This result, while some may think harsh, is tempered by what we think is a more plausible understanding of a family of duties to aid the worst off. Just because the medically worst off ought not be given comparable health priority when little can be done to improve health, that is not the end of the story. Priority to the worst off may be appropriate in other respects, for example, by way of compensation for dimensions of well-being that cannot be improved or priority for those dimensions in which improvement toward sufficiency is possible.

6.8 Conclusion

We have argued in this chapter that, although our theory operates at the level of the design of the basic social structure, it nonetheless has important implications for how priority decisions should be made at the macro level, and sometimes at the micro level as well. We have argued that the requirement to prevent or counteract patterns of systematic disadvantage implies, at minimum, the application of a kind of "moral sensitivity analysis" to the use of any of the formal methods. Moreover, we have argued for a special priority for children in health and other dimensions where the requirements of human development necessitate interventions and protections at critical junctures early in the life course. We have claimed that some issues involving trade-offs within health, especially when differences in age are thought to be of great moral relevance, should not be resolved by pure age-based approaches. Rather, it is our view that a well-developed view of sufficiency in health reveals domains of health that matter equally throughout all life stages. We have argued also that our claim that all of the essential dimensions of well-being are potentially morally relevant in all areas of public health and health policy constitutes a rejection of a blanket application of the separate-spheres doctrine. Moreover, while we do not assume that our account offers precise, determinate guidance in decisions regarding some of the most contested cases of trade offs within health, we do think that a case has been made for the proposition that what is often most centrally at stake in these controversies is, in fact, some other nonhealth dimension of well-being. Other strategies for more determinate guidance where the reach of justice theory runs out remain important as a supplement to justice. We take up in chapter 7 some of those strategies designed to extend the range of practical guidance for public policy decision makers, and we note especially those instances in which even then, the need for more work from within the confines of justice theory remains.

7

Justice, Democracy, and Social Values

An important line of recent argument emphasizes both the limitations of theories of justice to resolve priority-setting issues and the need to incorporate the public's values into such decisions. In the case of cost-utility analysis (CUA), the aim has been to temper its recommendations in order to make more room for considerations of justice in distribution. In other cases, the aspiration is to fill out the details where theory leaves off. We acknowledge the importance of both aspirations, but we argue that many of the proposals do less than promised without having to recur to theories of justice for help. We argue also that our theory constrains the permissible range of choices produced by the various democratic or procedural justice approaches.

7.1 Lost on the Oregon Trail

The Oregon Medicaid experiment was a crucial turning point in the way the public and policy makers came to see how priorities might be set. Indeed, the experiment garnered as much attention abroad as it did within the United States.

The original aim of the priority-setting process employed in the Oregon Medicaid program was to expand Medicaid coverage for "basic" medical services like prenatal care to more Oregonians by limiting provision of some expensive medical care. However, from the outset the drafters of the legislation recognized that it was not enough to rely strictly on cost-effectiveness rankings to generate funding priorities. The preferences of the public were thought essential to securing political legitimacy and broad public support. Public input was obtained from forty-seven town meetings and a telephone survey. These efforts resulted in numerous revisions, and over a period of years many of the lower-ranked treatments moved up higher on the list than a straightforward cost-effectiveness ratio would permit. Over time, the envisioned trade-offs prompting the original legislation withered in significance. The list of covered services remained fairly comprehensive. Even transplants for all children and adults (federal law only requires coverage of children) were funded, and treatments falling "below the line" were covered by Medicaid when deemed necessary by physicians who practice in one of the state-approved managed care organizations. Since nearly 90% of the Medicaid population was covered by an MCO (Management Care Organization), the exercise of drawing the line lost significance. Many commentators thus speculated that, when public opinion is elicited, policy makers are unlikely to remain committed to or even endorse the kinds of trade-offs that cost-effectiveness rankings produce (Jacobs, Marmor, and Oberlander 1999, 166).

What has remained important from the Oregon experiment, however, is a consensus that some role for community or social values is essential for political legitimacy. Political legitimacy connotes more than the obvious pragmatic need for political support that any viable legislative or regulatory action requires. It implicates the further moral value associated with a policy's being consistent with the values of the citizenry in a democratic society.

How exactly the demands of efficiency and justice in priority setting are to be squared with the broadly democratic aims of taking adequate account of the public's values is rather complicated. We need to know what role or weight the public's values ought to have in determining priorities, and we need also to settle on some process for determining just what those values are and how they should be deployed.

One approach maintains that decisions about the setting of health priorities should be left to the workings of the democratic process through elected representatives, referenda, and the like. The appeal of this suggestion is obvious. Democratic accountability demands that those affected by the decisions ought to have a say. However, there are two major problems with such a suggestion. First, democratic processes are plausible vehicles for ascertaining the public's values in quite general terms. The particulars of policies as complex and detailed as those needed to set priorities for the allocation of limited resources among alternative public health programs or health care services are, however, beyond what most consider the reasonable realm of institutional competence of traditional political processes in a modern democratic society. Even the details of any reasonably complex legislative enactment require delegation to administrative authorities for much of its implementation.

The second, and theoretically more significant, challenge lies in the fact that the proper balance between the expressed preferences of the majority and the potentially conflicting demands of justice remains a highly contested moral and political question. One theoretical option is that of treating the judgments of democratic majorities as morally sufficient for decisions about priority setting. Such a view would be most easily reconcilable with a view of justice in which none of the potential recipients had a justice-based

claim on the resources to be allocated. On the assumption that the democratic procedures themselves were fair then whatever distribution emerged
would also be just.

However, there are two primary objections to the plausibility of such a
conclusion. The first objection questions the degree of moral legitimacy be-
stowed by democratic processes that do not conform to some additional moral
constraints on deliberation and decision making. We will return to worries of
this sort in the next section. The second worry is perhaps more fundamental.
Some who are attracted by a democratic procedural solution are reluctant to
endorse whatever outcomes arise from simple majoritarian democratic processes. It is, after all, a commonplace observation that the majority's raw
preferences themselves may be unjust. Such preferences can run afoul of
important distributive claims of minorities (ethnic, medical, or otherwise
defined). Critics of the simple majoritarian account of democracy include
those who subscribe to a theory of basic human rights. Human rights theories
serve as the basis for demarcating those decisions properly left to collective
judgment through democratic procedures for ascertaining community values
and those that implicate the basic human rights, the violation of which is
unjust regardless of collective judgments. If, as we suggested in chapter 2, our
account of the essential dimensions of well-being is a basis for a theory of
human rights, then to the extent that it is claimed that the outcomes of fair
democratic procedures are morally sufficient for establishing priorities such a
claim must be rejected. Political legitimacy, then, is seen as morally necessary
but not sufficient grounds for priority setting decisions.

A further question is whether and how much a theory of justice actually
guides or constrains allocation decisions. One prominent view is that theories of justice provide woefully inadequate guidance for how to make such
decisions in actual, practical contexts. Even if an overall system for social
provision of health resources passes the test of justice, many specific distributive questions remain unanswered. Where justice theory cannot offer
sufficient guidance on specific distributive matters, many hope that mechanisms of political legitimacy may extend the range of reasons for making
tough choices (Fleck 1994; Buchanan 1998). Justice, therefore, requires
supplementation. Just what sort of supplementary role is called for is open
to interpretation. Fleck, for example, seeks some procedures by which
possible trade-off patterns will be "just enough" (Fleck 1994), even if the
extended advice we might expect from procedural strategies will be modest.
For some choices, such as some of the more perplexing questions involving
trade offs between small benefits to many people against large benefits for
fewer people, a good case can be made for a number of policy choices
"within the domain of just democratic decision making" (Fleck 1994).
Moreover, for other such questions, "what is needed is not only a theory of
justice but also a political choice among the feasible alternatives for implementing it" (Buchanan 1998, 630).

A somewhat different rationale for seeking democratic legitimacy
through greater consistency with the public's values explicitly endorses a

morally important role for social preferences in filling in where theory leaves off. One suggestion behind this view is that, because agreement on theories of justice itself is lacking, satisfaction of the demands of political legitimacy becomes the crucial moral desideratum. Mary Ann Baily, for example, emphasizes the essential lack of agreement at the level of philosophical discourse as a key reason for putting greater weight on procedural devices for securing political agreement. In her characterization of Norman Daniels's view of political legitimacy, she sees an implicit two-stage process. We first subject all proposals to a kind of pass/fail test, and if moral reasoning renders no judgment that commands consensus among the differing accounts of justice, then we seek guidance from the public's values (Baily 1994). The task of supplementation in her view would be a kind of "second best" solution appropriate for setting priorities in those instances in which philosophical theory commands no widespread agreement on what priorities are required as a matter of justice.

Indeed, in some places Daniels's view seems very much like Baily's characterization. For example, he and his coauthor James Sabin sometimes claim that there are many questions of justice about which reasonable people disagree. Some of these disagreements are not about the concrete specifications of larger, shared philosophical principles but about comprehensive moral views that assign widely differing weights to various values such as life saving, the relevance of quality-of-life considerations, urgency, or need. In these cases, no higher principles are available for resolution, and we therefore need some procedures by which decisions can be viewed by all as legitimate (Daniels and Sabin 1998, 32–33). In other passages, however, it is not the pervasiveness of intractable moral disagreement at the level of overarching philosophical principle that is the stated motivating force behind the felt need for political legitimacy. Rather, it is the claim that "we need a fair process to supplement whatever agreement we have on principles, or legitimacy will fail" (Daniels and Sabin 1998; see also Daniels and Sabin 2002).

Whatever the argument supporting a need to supplement our justification for the priorities we endorse, where the guidance from philosophical theory runs out, appeal to fair procedures is of additional importance. However, our account of justice contends that even from within a theory of justice, significant constraints on priority setting arise, and the consequence is that what Fleck calls the "domain of just democratic decision making" is less expansive than some might acknowledge. In our view, philosophical guidance of considerable moral weight does not run out quite as readily as some seem to suggest. While we agree wholeheartedly with Fleck's overall assessment that, in many cases divergent decisions are "just enough," we argue that justice sets significant, less widely appreciated constraints on deference to fair procedures and community values. We have argued, for example, that the potential for systematic disadvantage matters crucially, that considerations of respect and maintaining the bonds of attachment limit choices that would otherwise result in the abandonment of those for whom it appears little can be done, and that these same considerations also constrain the use of advanced age as an exclusionary criterion. We have argued also that, whatever the force of the rule of rescue, its justification lies not simply in compassion or sympathy that falls short of genuine moral duty, but that the best argument for its application lies in its connection with essential dimensions of well-being not reducible to concerns about health alone. Moreover, we have argued that a part of what motivates the desire for limits on trade offs, even among dissimilar aspects of health, is best seen as resting on other, nonhealth considerations that fall within the purview of what justice requires in public health and health policy decision contexts.

7.2 From Substantive Justice to Democratic Procedures

As we noted already, democratic legitimacy, traditionally construed, comes from the actual expression of the will of the citizenry through democratic processes. However, two sorts of objections have emerged to reliance on that traditional notion. One objection is lodged against its feasibility. We shall take that up below. However, a second objection is more fundamental. It argues that genuine political legitimacy is attained, not simply by ordinary means of counting votes, independent of the deliberative processes by which those votes got cast, but only when democratic processes conform to some further moral requirements. This objection invites an alternative account of democratic legitimacy, one in which the acceptability of decisions is conditioned on additional procedural and substantive constraints designed to ensure fair deliberative processes (Gutmann and Thompson 1996).

Sometimes the proposed constraints fall largely within the procedural side of the procedural/substantive continuum. First developed in the context of priority setting within managed care but since expanded to priority setting in public health more globally, Daniels and Sabin's program of "accountability for reasonableness" is a prime example. They argue that accountability for reasonableness requires publicly accessible decisions and rationales; mechanisms for challenge, review, and dispute resolution; and regulatory structures that ensure that the other conditions of their program are satisfied. In a move that arguably nudges Daniels and Sabin's proposal a bit towards the substantive side, they also require that only those rationales or reasons that all "fair-minded people who are disposed to finding mutually justifiable terms of cooperation" accept as relevant to the decision be allowed to count (Daniels and Sabin 2002, 45).

The modesty of Daniels and Sabin's program is evident. The ability of the relevance condition to ensure the rightness of the rationales put forward is limited, and the program as a whole cannot provide any assurance of substantively just outcomes. As a general matter, there are multiple problems with even the most ambitious deliberative democracy approaches. Three are illustrative. Consider the following.

First, it is not clear how to determine whether any proposed set of deliberative processes is sufficiently fair or otherwise appropriate to do the moral work intended for it. Daniels argues that his and Sabin's accountability for reasonableness is a practical tool, the conditions of which should be acceptable to most people, and we tend to agree. At the same time, however, social scientists are beginning to pursue people's preferences for alternative procedures intended to ensure fairness and deliberation in priority setting and, not surprisingly, they are discovering that people disagree about the relative importance of different procedural options. For example, Wailoo and Anand (2005) conducted a survey in the UK intended to assess the relevance members of the public attach to six characteristics of procedures commonly associated with claims about fairness in priority setting: participation in decision making by affected parties, or voice; conistency; the absence of vested interests; transparency, reversibility, and accuracy of information. Although many respondents agreed with statements favoring the use of the six procedures, sizable numbers disagreed that consistency, reversibility, or avoiding vested interests were important procedures in specified priority setting contexts. No doubt, some believe that landing on the right set of procedures for deliberation in priority setting is merely a technical problem resolvable by further empirical research. We return to assumptions about the role of empirical research in resolving moral challenges in justice shortly.

Second, whatever deliberative procedures are ultimately adopted, there is a great risk that no solution will emerge because the depth of moral disagreement is so great. Some deliberative democrats acknowledge that possibility, but offer no assessment of how extensive the domain of indeterminacy is likely to be in a pluralist society. Even if all reasonable parties to the deliberation agree on the relevance of some reasons, there remain ample grounds for suspicion about how much agreement can be expected on their weight, and thus ample grounds for doubt about whether the proposed constraints on reasons can solve the priority-setting challenge.

Third, the kind of reason that any individual party to the deliberation might reasonably accept is heavily theory-laden, or embedded in particular conceptions of justice. The objection is not merely the simple worry that deliberators will work from within competing single-principle conceptions of justice, such as libertarianism, utilitarianism, or some version of egalitarianism. This simple worry is worry enough. However, a further concern is that those who think that a variety of competing principles of justice may be relevant may disagree about which one is most applicable in a particular distributive context.

This is not to say that there is no independent moral value in deliberative democracy, or even to suggest (as some deliberative democrats argue) that progress in refining our conceptions of justice permanently eludes us. Nor are our observations meant to give aid and comfort to those who are skeptical about the capacity of philosophical argument to offer guidance of any sort. The problem is that, when all is said and done, the requirement that deliberators offer public reasons for their decisions provides no better handle on what counts as a good reason than that provided by moral philosophy. Our doubts are focused on what these new morally fortified conceptions of democracy can hope to deliver without coming back to the hard work to be done by substantive views of justice in determining which inequalities matter most in any given context. We think that, in the end, arguments about the best theory of justice are unavoidable, and in particular, we think it is important to continue the search for better theories of justice that can have practical significance in actual, nonideal circumstances.

As a practical matter, approaches like Daniels and Sabin's cannot be expected to produce solutions in the sense of priorities that everyone will agree are just. Rather, institutional decision makers are still in the end required to make hard decisions, informed if not constrained by the outcomes of the deliberative or, in their case, accountability for reasonableness, process. At minimum, the process confers a greater likelihood of public acceptance of decisions institutional policy makers ultimately make. At best, such processes help narrow the range of morally permissible options available to policy makers. As such, accountability for reasonableness and other procedural, deliberative processes can be valuable practical aids in helping institutional decision makers to specify the morally acceptable options in particular priority-setting contexts. Perhaps most importantly, however, the outcomes of such processes, as well as the decisions ultimately made by institutional policy makers, must be constrained by substantive considerations of justice as embodied by universal human rights and the moral theories, such as ours, that underlie them.

7.3 Mimicking Majorities: Moralizing Preferences and Empiricizing Equity

Appeal to some procedural method for deliberation is but one of the main strategies for enhancing the political legitimacy of actual decisions. Instead of improving the quality of public deliberation in the political arena, some proposals suggest a technical fix for the defects of QALYs. The main thrust of these proposals is that in a democracy the preferences of the public matter. However, we need not rely on CUA's traditional way of ascertaining preferences. Instead of mimicking the efficiency of markets (as CUA intends), we might amend our empirical methods to mimic the judgments of democratic majorities. One such proposal is to temper the efficiency-driven recommendations of CUA by relying on intuitive moral rankings, such as those generated by public discussion of the Oregon Medicaid program, to adjust for the method's inegalitarian thrust. Another suggestion offered by some pioneers of CUA is that CUA be used only as an aid to the deliberations of policy makers (Russell et al. 1996), who are then expected to modify the results of CUA through a case-by-case consideration of the trade-offs that may offend. Thus, instead of basing decisions on a strict CE (cost effectiveness)–ratio ranking, what is often referred to as a "QALY league table," the suggestion is that policymakers adjust these rankings to reflect egalitarian or other moral concerns.

Other contributors (Nord 1999; Ubel 2000) are working on strategies to "empiricize" equity concerns and embed them in mathematical CUA models. Bolstered by empirical data that suggest that many of these moral objections are consonant with the public's preferences for how health care should be distributed, some writers go so far as to contend that the implications for public policy of CUA and QALYs are downright misleading (Nord 1999; Menzel 1999). Their solution to this problem is to explicitly introduce into CUA more fully moralized preferences, preferences that capture the societal values that appear to guide allocation decisions. In other words, their solution to the moral challenges to CUA is to empiricize concerns about justice by turning these concerns into data about the public's distributive preferences.

Cost-Value Analysis and the Person Trade-Off

Nord advocates that CUA be entirely replaced by a new variant of cost-effectiveness analysis (CEA), which he labels cost-value analysis (CVA). In cost-value analysis, the value or benefit part of the equation is no longer to be conceptualized in terms of units of health, as measured by QALYs. Instead, benefit or effectiveness is now to be conceptualized in units of social value that directly reflect the public's preferences for interpersonal trade-offs.

Nord's claim is that CUA asks the wrong question. Like all proponents of formal methods, Nord and his colleagues assume that health care priorities should be set so as to satisfy public preferences. But public preferences for what? CUA elicits preferences of individuals for trade-offs between time and quality in their own lives, aggregates those preferences, and then uses the results as a basis for interpersonal trade-offs. Although the techniques used in CUA, such as the "standard gamble" and the "time trade-off," give an idea of what individuals would want for themselves, they do not reveal what people would prefer as a principle for allocation. Thus, these techniques leave unanswered, and indeed unasked, what is seen by Nord, Menzel, and others as the relevant question for establishing health care priorities—the question of what the public's preferences are for interpersonal trade-offs.

According to this view, it is because CUA has asked the wrong question that the results of some CUA analyses have been so morally counterintuitive. Nord and his colleagues cite studies that suggest that, when respondents are asked directly about interpersonal comparisons using a technique called the "person trade-off," their preferences are markedly different from those elicited in traditional CUA surveys. For example, many respondents reject the pure health maximizing model embedded in CUA in favor of some weighted priority for the severely ill, even if—and this is crucial—the severely ill have reduced capacity to benefit from treatment and even if they cost more to treat.

It is in this sense that Nord claims that CUA is misleading. If decision makers are presented with quantitative empirical information about intrapersonal preferences, equity concerns regarding the limits of permissible interpersonal trade-offs will be overwhelmed by the seemingly precise, quantitative results of CUA. If, however, CVA is based on distributive preferences rather than preferences for health states, these justice considerations will be quantified and embedded in the CVA results, and thereby protected in the public policy process.

Conceptual and Methodological Problems

The empirical techniques for assessing distributive preferences are still in their infancy, as is commentary on what role, if any, such preferences should play in the formulation of public policy. There are many unanswered questions. What would it mean to assess the validity of preferences so obtained, to be able to say that the numerical representations of societal preferences are in some sense accurate? By what criterion can one establish that the preferences as measured and summarized constitute a predominant or even a majority preference in a given society? How valid are the preferences, even as measures of individual values? Person trade-off judgments, like all social psychological measures, are sensitive to how questions are framed. Framing effects are conventionally viewed as measurement problems that admit of methodological solutions. But this is only partly correct. If respondents are systematically more likely to express utilitarian preferences in one frame than in another, which preference is the accurate one? If respondents are confronted with this finding and asked to reconcile the apparent inconsistency in their judgments, is the resulting answer more accurate? If so, is this because their answers now represent more settled, more reflective judgments? But how can one know when a judgment is sufficiently reflective or sufficiently informed?

Even if the foregoing conceptual and methodological problems can be successfully addressed, some potentially powerful moral objections remain. Aggregate statistics can mask deep moral and political divisions. Consider a study conducted by Nord (1993) in which Norwegian politicians were asked to give their preferences for resource allocation in five different contexts. In each case, the respondents had to choose between two different groups of patients that varied by either the magnitude of benefit each group would receive, how sick the two groups were, or the ages of the two groups of patients. In each context, choosing one group could be interpreted as the QALY-maximizing or utilitarian preference. The utilitarian option was rejected by a sizable majority of politicians in every case, causing Nord to title the article in which these data are reported, "Health politicians do not wish to maximize health benefits" (Nord 1993). However, an interesting, but not altogether surprising, finding emerged when the responses were analyzed by whether the politicians were conservatives or social democrats. Conservatives were systematically more likely than social democrats to express a utilitarian preference. Indeed, in two of the contexts, as much as half of the conservatives made the utilitarian choice. Nord's response to this finding is to call for the assessment of preferences in samples large enough to avoid "political biases." For him, moral and political differences are seemingly methodological problems to be ironed out as the person trade-off technique for measuring societal preferences matures. Arguably, however, what Nord dismisses as bias is in fact a moral and political disagreement that needs to be featured in public debate, rather than buried in large samples and summary statistics. Thus, these data encounter, in effect, the same philosophical impasse that moral theorists, and perhaps deliberative democrats, have reached.

Ahistorical Trade-Offs

Yet another problem with attempts to empiricize equity concerns through the person trade-off method is that in the person trade-off context the respondent is working with hypothetical potential people who have no particular history or life circumstances apart from a specified medical condition or risk factor. This sort of abstraction involves a significant loss of moral information. The information loss is a double-edged sword, however.

The positive side is that it facilitates an impartial assessment. It protects against biases that work against the interests of marginalized groups. The negative side is that it masks from public consideration features of a situation that may be morally relevant in making just allocation decisions. What moral difference would it make, for example, if the burden of disease is considerably greater for some ethnic or other historically disadvantaged groups? Or for some persons with biographies that differ in their occupational or environmental risk exposures or face substantial risks that most others do not? We think such considerations should figure in a fuller account of justice in health priority setting. Thus, there is a risk that the attempts to empiricize equity concerns through person trade-offs may themselves mislead with respect to considerations of justice because of the attendant loss of morally relevant information.

Perhaps such matters could be addressed by eliciting other, more contextualized preferences, ones designed to get at these added concerns about remedying aspects of the social structure that contribute to unjust health status differentials. However, such concerns point to a family of cases in which those most vulnerable to bias may come out on the short end of the moral stick. If so, once again, there appears to be an impasse no more resolvable than those that plague moral philosophers.

7.4 Theory, After All?

As with procedural strategies for allocational problems, the stated ambitions of CVA vary. For example, where reliance on actual democratic procedures to inform policy making is unfeasible, using statistically representative samples in CVA surveys can be a vehicle for obtaining social values (Menzel 1999; Menzel et al. 1999; Ubel 2000). The findings of such research could be treated as advisory or ancillary to philosophical and political reflection in the same way all relevant empirical data ought to inform serious reflection on the demands of social justice. However, as Rebecca Walker and Andrew Siegel point out, this is not the stated aim of many of CVA's proponents. Menzel, for example, links the exercise to requirements of political legitimacy and the inability to elicit useful information about such preferences by traditional voting techniques (Menzel 1999). Ubel also suggests that such surveys have an added moral value when philosophical reflection is at an end and recourse to public values is called for (Ubel 2000). Walker and Siegel object that such survey methods confer no genuine democratic legitimacy at all. Even if the data obtained are representative—and that assumption is open to debate as well—the findings in no way constitute a democratically authorized representation of the public's will (Walker and Siegel 2002, 269–71). Much as critics of CUA claim that the standard gamble technique is not a real market transaction, the use of survey techniques to test the public's attitudes toward trade-offs is no substitute for real democratic choice. Such surveys, however well done, are not exercises that confer political legitimacy any more than are the exit polls on election day, however accurate either may be in gauging public opinion.

Walker and Siegel also note that CVA proponents argue for taking account of only filtered preferences, that is, those empirically derived preferences that pass certain moral tests (Menzel 1999). Depending on the robustness of these moral tests, however, eliciting people's distributional preferences may appear superfluous. Insofar as the moral tests tell us what preferences *should* be allowed to count, it is unclear what additionally is gained by assessing descriptively what people's preferences are (Walker and Siegel 2002, 266).

7.5 DALYs, Deliberation, and Empirical Ethics

Christopher Murray and colleagues, the developers of a variant of QALYs called Disability Adjusted Life Years (DALYs), suggest that at least some of these issues could be finessed by moving away from methods that aggregate the distributive preferences of individuals toward methods that involve some deliberative group process for establishing societal preferences (Murray and Acharya 1997). Murray attempts to provide a moral rationale for the choices incorporated in DALYs through what he calls the principle of "filtered consensus." This principle privileges values that are widely shared by many people after deliberation and discussion. If the reasons behind these widely shared, robust values are not in conflict with "ideal-regarding principles" of morality, they can be incorporated into the construction of DALYs.

Elements of Murray's principle of filtered consensus are evident in the protocol used to create disability weights. The protocol requires respondents to compare different health states using two variants of the person trade-off method. Respondents are confronted with any differences in comparisons that may result from these variations, as well as with the implications of their choices for social policy. Respondents also share their rankings with fellow participants, as well as their reasons for choosing as they did, in group discussion. Person trade-off assessments are thus continuously revised through a process of private reflection and group deliberation that can last from eight to ten hours. The ultimate goal is to achieve a consensus among the convened panels of experts who take part in the deliberative exercise.

The developers of DALYs have embarked on a project that aims, in effect, to integrate two of the three current responses to moral objections to CUA by deliberative democracy theory and the empiricizing of equity concerns. Both Murray and Nord suggest that it is a methodological matter which method for eliciting distributive preferences—the individual or the group—provides more empirically valid data. This response seems to us to miss the central point. Although we view the group deliberative process as having more methodological and moral appeal, it is unlikely that either method will satisfactorily address all the relevant moral concerns. The most crucial limitation is that it is deliberative without being democratic in any sense of the term. The deliberations are those of expert panels. If the aim is that of informed efforts to further specify the content of justice, then that may be an extremely useful exercise, but it will not confer some added measure of democratic legitimacy on decisions, which the armchair arguments of philosophers lack. Even if we were to rely on some representative sample of the public as a whole, at best we merely mimic the decisions of majorities in much the same way as some proponents of CEA and CUA claim that they are mimicking the outcomes of markets if markets functioned perfectly.

Jeff Richardson has proposed an alternative analytical framework for approaching questions of justice in priority setting that is very similar to the paths pursued by Murray and Nord and that does focus on representative samples (Richardson 2002; Richardson and McKie 2005). He maintains that defensible principles for setting priorities in health policy should be derived through an iterative process in which social science research establishes the public's values by eliciting the views of representative samples, these values are then subjected to ethical analysis, representative samples are then informed of the results of the ethical analysis and their values are reassessed, and so on. The process is repeated until a stable and ethically defensible set of principles is identified. Although Richardson refers to this process as "empirical ethics" it is worth noting what a central role ethical analysis and thus moral theory plays in his proposal. Moreover, Richardson maintains that the outcome of the process is only "our best hypothesis about what the community *thinks* is right, after deliberation, clarification and careful reflection" (Richardson and McKie 2005, 273, italics original) and that substantive disagreements about whether what the community thinks is right is in fact just could remain. Here, Richardson follows Daniels in saying that if the process used to incorporate the public's values is, for example, transparent and inclusive, then there are grounds for believing the resultant policies are legitimate.

Richardson and McKie see strong parallels between "empirical ethics" and deliberative democracy, and we would agree. The more modest aims of both, to expose the range of relevant views and to compel policy makers and citizens alike to articulate and defend their positions, can only serve to advance the public process of policy making. Although the extent to which these proposals actually confer some deep sense of political legitimacy is questionable, we recognize and endorse their utility in helping policy makers to narrow and specify the range of publicly acceptable alternatives and in fostering and expressing the social conditions necessary for respect for others. As Richardson and McKie point out, however, it is critical that empirical strategies especially, but also procedural ones as well, not mask genuine moral disagreements about how priorities should be set but rather surface them in ways that allow institutional policy makers to better understand how and why their public is divided. Moreover, regardless of how thoughtfully the public's preferences are identified and characterized, in the end, there is no substitute for substantive critique of public preferences to ensure that these preferences, if followed, do not result in unjust policies. Preferences and processes must be "laundered" (Goodin 1995) or "filtered" by theories of social justice and human rights in order to ensure, at minimum, that policies that set priorities for public health and health care services do not reinforce or compound those inequalities that are already among the most unjust.

8

Facts and Theory

A principal conclusion of chapter 7 is that empirical data about public preferences, no matter how sophisticated or thoughtful the methodology, cannot by themselves tell us how to construct just health policies. Neither, however, can theories of justice. If we have reached one insight in the writing of this book it is that the practical pursuit of justice in health policy requires the effective integration of the contributions of moral and political theory with the findings of social and biomedical science. This insight has guided the construction of our theory of justice, which starts with an understanding of the world as it is and then continuously invites and requires empirical inquiry in order to continuously revise what that understanding is. Our theory identifies and highlights the kinds of empirical questions that need to be asked and answered in the search for what health policies are just. It provides guidance to empirical researchers and policy makers about the kinds of data that are needed if considerations of justice are to be taken into account in the design of new policies and programs and in the evaluation of existing policies and practices.

This book thus lies at the intersection of two distinct but overlapping theoretical paths. One path recognizes the centrality to questions of justice of complex facts about the social world. The other path recognizes that justice is concerned with more than how valuable human goods are distributed. Unlike other theories that focus on the primary goods that all persons are presumed to want, whatever else they might want, we focus on the morally salient human ends that each of us want, regardless of whatever else we might want. For us, these ends include the respect of others, personal security, health, the development of reasoning capacities and of capacities for attachment to others, and the ability to determine for oneself some important aspects of one's own destiny. These are each distinct human ends, all of which matter to justice generally as well as to justice in the specific context of public health and health policy.

Our claim is not only that there are multiple dimensions of well-being that a theory of justice should take into account, but also that among these ends are those that are not readily explicable in ordinary distributive terms. Having the respect of others as social equals, having personal attachments, and having the capacity for leading self-determining lives are essential elements of human well-being but they are not securable simply by ensuring a just distribution of resources such as wealth and income. Rather, they require attention to the structure of a wide range of social institutions and practices that govern far more than how desirable goods such as income or wealth are distributed.

Our account of the essential dimensions of well-being is not meant as an alternative to some more traditional philosophical attempts to spell out the essential elements for a good life for an individual. Nor is it meant as a criterion of what constitutes a distinctively human life. In this respect, our project bears faint resemblance to the philosophical tasks of the ancients who asked how best to live. Our list of essential dimensions of well-being is offered as an account of those things *characteristically* present within a decent life, whatever a person's particular life plans and personal commitments. The more moderate claim we make when we label some dimension of well-being as essential is that it is important enough to be an independent concern of justice. The job of justice, positively stated, is the task of securing a sufficient level of each dimension for each individual, insofar as possible. What we can do and be, whatever else we might want to do and be, are what matters essentially in our theory of justice.

Amartya Sen's groundbreaking work on human capabilities, as well as Martha Nussbaum's subtle refinements of crucial points, have been profoundly significant in shaping our own pluralist account of the dimensions of well-being that matter from the perspective of justice. In the end, we chose not to adopt the capabilities language for our own theory. In part, we preferred the more traditional language of well-being that is common both within some philosophical traditions and in many of the social sciences. In addition, our theory parts company with both Sen and Nussbaum insofar as we do not endorse the political or moral primacy of protecting and promoting functional capabilities over the aim of achieving actual functioning. We do not assume that the most basic aim of justice is captured fully by the emphasis on the capabilities of adults who are then free to develop or exercise those capabilities as they see fit. In many instances, and in the case of children especially, the best account of the positive aim of justice is more directly concerned with outcomes than with available choices. Often what someone can be is determined as much or more by factors that are external to what that individual can do for herself at a given moment.

Two additional features of our account of justice deserve additional mention. Much of what troubles us about earlier discussions of justice in health and health care is the extent to which dimensions of well-being other than health are seen as competing considerations external to justice and the extent to which questions of justice as they affect morally relevant groups are ignored. The HIV screening programs for poor women of color that were proposed in the 1980s were, in our view, not simply unwise, insensitive, or uncaring, but unjust in the adverse impact they would likely have on the social respect and capacity for self-determination of people who already were members of a multiply disadvantaged group. Two important implications of our view are, first, that it is a mistake to think of justice in separate spheres, each with its own uniquely relevant concern such as health, and, second, while justice ultimately may be a matter of how individuals fare with respect to each affected dimension of well-being, an important moral datum often is missed if we ignore the fact of membership in socially situated groups or the importance of patterns of systematic disadvantage.

The second intersecting path leading into our theoretical approach is the aforementioned importance of the empirical contributions of social and biomedical science. Much of what the data show about the causal bases of inequalities amplifies and confirms our philosophically driven intuitions that justice must be as concerned about groups as individuals and that the carving up of theories of justice into separate spheres is misguided. Theories of justice without data regarding the way inequalities interact cannot result in just health or other social policies. Any plausible theory of justice needs not only the data provided by empirical researchers who seek to gauge public attitudes about fairness, but also the data provided by social and biomedical researchers who seek to understand how complex social and economic relationships affect health and the other essential dimensions of well-being. Such information is crucial for a theory such as ours in which the central question is, Which inequalities matter most? The answer we propose is that inequalities that contribute to systematic patterns of disadvantage are the ones that matter most. It is these inequalities, as well as those that represent a lack of sufficiency in one or more dimension of well-being, that are the primary object for our remedial account of justice.

Empirical research therefore can tell us many things crucial to our inquiries that an exercise of philosophical reflection alone cannot. Some who fare worse than others, often in multiple respects, are members of groups who are socially situated within densely woven patterns of disadvantage. Poor health, while a central concern for any theory of justice, is not the only measure by which we should judge whether social and institutional arrangements, including those specific to public health and health policy, are just. Some people have a limited array of valuable life options from which to choose, exercise little power and authority within political and economic arenas, and in numerous other possible ways can be counted as less fortunate than others. Inequalities of one kind beget inequalities of another, and over the course of a lifetime (or at least long stretches of time) the compounding of disadvantages makes avoidance or escape difficult without heroic effort or unexpected good luck.

Empirical research sheds light on the contingent social circumstances that affect the life prospects of socially situated groups, including the familiar disadvantaged groups defined by gender, race or ethnicity, poverty, or religion. In addition, patterns of systematic disadvantage are revealed in the work of epidemiologists, developmental neuroscientists, and other researchers whose observations on the causal determinants of health and other measures of well-being over a life course highlight the importance of securing adequate well-being during childhood if the prospect of a decent life as adults is to be preserved. One of the distinguishing features of our account of social justice is thus that we view inequalities that undermine the well-being of children to also be paradigmatic of the kinds of inequalities that are among the most urgent to address. Our theory privileges children not merely because of their dependency on others but also because unless we achieve a sufficient level of many of the dimensions of well-being at developmentally critical periods in childhood, the likelihood that we will have the capacity to pursue a decent life as adults is severely curtailed.

Social scientists, economists, epidemiologists, and others engaged in understanding the complex causal pathways that account for health status and health disparities, as well as accounting for a host of other adverse consequences for well-being, provide the raw materials for our theory of justice. Equally, however, it is our aim that our theory, in turn, provides the raw material for further empirical inquiry by stimulating the discussion of what new kinds of empirical questions ought to be asked. For example, we hope that our theory provides insights of the sort that will encourage research that cuts across the separate spheres. We want to know what impact methods of health care delivery and finance have on dimensions other than health, just as we want to know what impact the structure of income safety net programs and educational policies may have on health.

Many of the kinds of empirical questions our theory relies upon and invites are under way in various arenas. The plurality of social determinants of health, other than health care access, continues to be a topic of great interest, as is the quest to better understand the causal influence of poverty on health, on the one hand, and of health on poverty, on the other hand. Moreover, our theory invites a more fine-grained analysis of the specific causal mechanisms that connect differential income and wealth with health disparities. Our theory does not start with a fixed hypothesis regarding which of the various means or vectors is causally most responsible for health outcomes. As a consequence, what will matter most will become, in part, an empirical question. What will matter most on our theory will depend on what the data show, and in particular, on what the data show with regard to how inequalities in health and other dimensions of well-being causally interact.

Data alone, however, cannot provide the full story. We need also some theoretical framework within which to assess the moral significance of what empirical research reveals. A number of approaches from within public health, epidemiology, health psychology, and elsewhere provide insights into the causal pathways by which the life prospects of some are adversely affected. Most philosophical theories of justice start with a set of distributive principles meant to govern a well-ordered society. Empirical data, if deemed relevant, are used to demonstrate how well certain widely perceived injustices, such as health disparities, are a consequence of the failure to implement those distributive principles. We start, instead, with the messy reality of a poorly ordered world, in which common place injustices trap some socially situated groups in extraordinarily disadvantaged circumstances. We ask what a commitment to social justice requires in the world as it currently is. An important task of social justice is to work vigilantly to ameliorate, and where possible prevent, the conditions by which some groups fall below a level of sufficiency in one or more dimensions of well-being, and in the most urgent of cases, the conditions that create those densely woven patterns of systematic disadvantage from which escape is enormously difficult.

Empirical research and theory can tell us how best to do this important work of social justice. Empirical research, and the public health statistics that surveillance and research generate, can tell us what groups are falling the most behind, and in what ways. These data are morally crucial. They tell us how public health programs and health policies are affecting the different dimensions of well-being, and whether these interventions are affecting differentially groups that, from the standpoint of social justice, are of most interest. Empirical research and theory also provide insights into the complex causal pathways that affect well-being, insights that can help shape new policies and programs intended to reduce unjust inequalities. Together empirical research and theory inform how to translate the demands of social justice into social policy.

Our hope is that progress in social justice, public health, and health policy can be made by integrating a number of strands of philosophical reflection, political theory, social science theory, and social and biomedical research in ways that piggy-back on the accomplishments of a variety of contributors from multiple disciplines and intellectual traditions. We were inspired to build our theory in this way in large part because in our own careers we have been fortunate to traverse a path in which public health, health policy, biomedicine, social science, law, and philosophy have continuously intersected, and we have seen firsthand the richness of insights that such an interdisciplinary community produces. Our further hope is that our theory will stimulate and help shape new empirical research that will provide the basis for increasingly better practical guidance in answering questions about which inequalities matter most.

REFERENCES

Acs, G., S. Long, M. Marquis, and P. Short. 1996. Self-insured employer health plans: Prevalence, profile, provision, and premiums. *Health Affairs* 15:67–78.

Addington, W., C. K. Cassel, O. Fein, A. Haines, R. S. Lawrence, and M. McCally. 1998. Poverty and ill health: Physicians can, and should, make a difference. *Annals of Internal Medicine* 29:726–33.

Agency for Healthcare Research and Quality. 1997. Theory and reality of value-based purchasing:Lessons from the pioneers (AHRQ Publication No. 98–0004). Rockville, Md.: AHRQ.

Alaimo, K., C. M. Olson, E. and A. Frongillo Jr. 2001. Low family income and food insufficiency in relation to overweight U.S. children:Is there a paradox? *Archives of Pediatric and Adolescent Medicine* 155:1161–67.

Alexander, G. R., M. D. Kogan, and S. Nabukera. 2002. Racial differences in prenatal care use in the United States: Are disparities decreasing? *American Journal of Public Health* 92 (12):1970–75.

Aligne, C. A., P. Auinger, R. S. Byrd, M. Weitzman. 2000. Risk factors for pediatric asthma contributions of poverty, race, and urban residence. *American Journal of Respiratory and Critical Care Medicine* 162 (3 part 1):873–77.

Altman D., D. M. Cutler, R. Zeckhauser. 1998. Adverse selection and adverse retention. *American Economic Review* 88:122–26.

Amelung, V., S. Glied, and A. Topan. 2003. Health care and the labor market: Learning from the German experience. *Journal of Health Politics, Policy and Law* 28:693–714.

American Academy of Pediatrics Committee on Community Health Services and American Academy of Pediatrics Committee on Practice and Ambulatory Medicine. 2003. Increasing immunization coverage. *Pediatrics* 112:993–96.

American Public Health Association. 1950. *Rehabilitation of the crippled* (Policy statement No. 5002). Washington, D.C.: APHA.

———. 1983. *Decade of disabled persons* (Policy statement No. 8320). Washington, D.C.: APHA.

————. 1988. *Discrimination against the disabled in the health care field* (Policy statement No. 8811). Washington, D.C.: APHA.

————. 1993. *People with disabilities in national health care reform* (Policy statement No. 9307). Washington, D.C.: APHA.

Anand, S., F. Peter, and A. Sen, eds. 2005. *Public health, ethics, and equity.* New York: Oxford University Press.

Arias, E. 2002. United States Life Tables, 2000. *National Vital Statistical Reports* 51 (3). Atlanta: Centers for Disease Control and Prevention.

Anderson, E. 1999. What is the point of equality? *Ethics* 109:287–337.

Andersson, H. W., S. J. Gotlieb, K. G. Nelson. 1997. Home environment and cognitive abilities in infants born small-for-gestational-age. *Acta Obstetrica et Gynecologica Scandinavica* (Suppl.) 165:82–86.

Annan, K. A. 2001. *We the children: Meeting the promises of the world summit for children.* New York: United Nations Children's Fund.

Aristotle. 1946. *Politics.* Translated and edited by E. Barker. Oxford: Oxford University Press.

Arneson, R. 1989. Equality and equal opportunity for welfare. *Philosophical Studies* 56:73–93.

Arrow, K. 1963. Uncertainty and the economics of medical care. *American Economic Review* 53:941–73.

————. 1973. Some ordinalist-utilitarian notes on Rawls' theory. *Journal of Philosophy* 70:245–63.

Ayanian, J. Z., B. A. Kohler, T. Abe, and A. M. Epstein. 1993. The relation between health insurance coverage and clinical outcomes among women with breast cancer. *New England Journal of Medicine* 329:326–31.

Ayanian, J. Z., J. S. Weissman, E. C. Schneider, J. A. Ginsburg, and A. M. Zaslavsky. 2000. Unmet health needs of uninsured adults in the United States. *Journal of the American Medical Association* 284:2061–69.

Baier, A. 1985. Doing without moral theory. In *Postures of the mind.* Minneapolis: University of Minnesota Press.

————. 1994. The need for more than justice. In *Moral prejudices.* Cambridge: Cambridge University Press.

Baily, M. A. 1994. The democracy problem. *Hastings Center Report* 24:39–42.

Baker, D. W., J. J. Sudano, J. Albert, E. Borawski, A. Dor. 2001. Lack of insurance and decline in overall health in late middle age. *New England Journal of Medicine* 345:1106–12.

Bankowski, Z., J. H. Bryant, and J. Gallagher. 1997. *Ethics equity and health for all.* Geneva, Switzerland: World Health Organization.

Beauchamp, T. 2004. Does ethical theory have a future in bioethics? *Journal of Law, Medicine, and Ethics* 32:209–17.

Bennefield, R. 1998. *The dynamics of economic well-being: Health insurance, 1993–95: Who loses coverage and for how long.* Current Population Reports P-70–64. Washington, D.C.: U.S. Bureau of the Census.

Ben-Shlomo, Y., and D. A. Kuth. 2002. A life course approach to chronic disease epidemiology: Conceptual models, empirical challenges, and interdisciplinary perspectives. *International Journal of Epidemiology* 31:285–93.

Berlin, I. 1969. *Four essays on liberty.* Oxford: Oxford University Press.

Berman, L. E. 2002. *Tax incentives for health insurance.* Tax policy discussion paper. Washington, D.C.: Urban Institute.

Bindman, A. B., K. Grumbach, D. Jaffe, D. Osmond, and K. Vranizan. 1998. Primary care physicians' experience of financial incentives in managed care systems. *New England Journal of Medicine* 339:1516–21.

Blackwell, D. L., M. D. Hayward, and E. M. Cirmmins. 2001. Does childhood health affect chronic morbidity in later life? *Social Science and Medicine* 52 (8):1269–84.

Bloche, M. G. 1999. Clinical loyalties and the social purposes of medicine. *Journal of the American Medical Association* 281:268–74.

Boardman, J. D., B. K. Finch, C. G. Ellison, D. R. Williams, and J. S. Jackson. 2001. Neighborhood disadvantage, stress, and drug use among adults. *Journal of Health and Social Behavior* 42 (2):151–65.

Bodenheimer, T. 1999a. The American health care system—The movement for improved quality in health care. *New England Journal of Medicine* 340:488–92.

———. 1999b. The American health care system—Physicians and the changing medical marketplace. *New England Journal of Medicine* 340:584–88.

Bok, H., K. E. Schill, and R. R. Faden. 2004. Justice, ethnicity, and stem-cell banks. *The Lancet* 364:118–21

Borzi, P., D. M. Frankford, B. Moore, and S. Rosenbaum. 1999. Who should determine when health care is medically necessary? *New England Journal of Medicine* 340:229–32.

Brennan, T. A. 1998. Moral imperatives versus market solutions: Is health care a right? *University of Chicago Law Review* 65:345–64.

Britton, A., and J. Kahn. 2003. Government share of health care expenditures. *Journal of the American Medical Association* 289:1165.

Brock, D. 1988. Ethical issues in recipient selection for organ transplant. In *Organ substitution technology: Ethical, legal and public policy issues.* Boulder, Colo.: Westview Press.

———. 1989. Justice, health care, and the elderly. *Philosophy and Public Affairs* 18:297–312.

———. 1998. Aggregating costs and benefits. *Philosophy and Phenomenological Research* 58:963–68.

———. 2002. Priority to the worst off in health-care resource prioritization. In *Medicine and social justice.* Edited by R. Rhodes, M. Battin, and A. Silvers. New York: Oxford University Press.

Brouwer, W., N. B. A. van Exel, and E. Stolk. 2005. Acceptability of less than perfect health states. *Science and Medicine* 60:237–46.

Brown, E. R., V. D. Ojeda, R. Wyn, and R. Levan. 2000. *Racial and ethnic disparities in access to health insurance and health care.* Washington, D.C.: The Henry J. Kaiser Family Foundation.

Brown, L. D. 1998. Health reform in America: The mystery of the missing moral momentum. *Cambridge Quarterly of Healthcare Ethics* 7:239–46.

Buchanan, A. 1984. The right to a decent minimum of health care. *Philosophy and Public Affairs* 13:55–78.

———. 1995. Privatization and just health care. *Bioethics* 9:220–39.

———. 1998. Managed care: Rationing without justice, but not unjustly. *Journal of Health Politics, Policy, and Law* 23:617–34.

———. 2002. Social moral epistemology. *Social Philosophy and Policy* 19:126–52.

———. D. Brock, N. Daniels, and D. Wikler. 2000. *From chance to choice.* New York: Cambridge University Press.

Bureau of the Census. 1990. Health insurance coverage, 1986–1988. *Current Population Reports,* Series P-70, no 17. Washington, D.C.: U.S. Government Printing Office.

———. 2003. Health insurance coverage in the United States, 2002. *Current Population Reports,* Series P-60–223. Washington, D.C.: U.S. Government Printing Office.

Buseh, A. G., L. K. Glass, and B. J. McElmurry. 2002. Cultural and gender issues related to HIV/AIDS prevention in rural Swaziland: A focus group analysis. *Health Care for Women International* 23 (2):173–84.

Butler, S., and D. Kendal. 1999. Expanding access and choice for health care consumers through tax reform. *Health Affairs* 18:45–57.

Bye, B.V., and G. Riley. 1989. Eliminating the medicare waiting period for social security disabled-worker beneficiaries. *Social Security Bulletin* 52:2–15.

Calabresi, G., and P. Bobbitt *Tragic choices.* 1978. New York: Norton.

Callahan, D. 1987. *Setting limits: Medical goals in an aging society.* New York: Simon and Shuster.

CDC Diabetes Cost Effectiveness Study Group. 1998. The cost-effectiveness of screening for type-2 diabetes. *Journal of the American Medical Association* 280:1757–63.

Chassin, M. R., and R. W. Galvin 1998. National roundtable on health care quality. The urgent need to improve health care quality. *Journal of the American Medical Association* 280:1000–05.

Childress, J. F., R. R. Faden, R. D. Gaare, L. O. Gostin, J. Kahn, R. J. Bonnie, N. E. Kass, A. C. Mastroianni, J. D. Moreno, and P. Nieburg. 2002. Public health ethics: Mapping the terrain. *Journal of Law Medicine and Ethics* 30 (2):170–78.

Christman, J. 1991. Liberalism and individuals positive freedom. *Ethics* 101:343–59.

Clifford, K., and Iuculano R. 1987. AIDS and Insurance: The rationale for AIDS-related testing. *Harvard Law Review* 100:1806–24.

Cohen, G. A. 1989. On the currency of egalitarian justice. *Ethics* 99:906–44.

———. 1993. Equality of what? On welfare, goods, and capabilities. In *The quality of life.* Edited by M. Nussbaum and A. Sen. Oxford: Clarendon Press.

———. 1997. Where the action is:on the site of distributive justice. *Philosophy and Public Affairs* 26:3–30.

Cohen, J. 1989. Democratic equality. *Ethics* 99:727–51.

Colby, D. C. 1994. Medicaid physician fees, 1993. *Health Affairs* 13:255–63.

Commission on Children at Risk. 2003. *Hardwired to connect.* New York: Institute for American Values.

Committee on Understanding and Eliminating Racial and Ethnic Disparities in Health Care, Board on Health Sciences Policy, Institute of Medicine. 2003. *Unequal treatment: Confronting racial and ethnic disparities in health care.* Edited by B. D. Smedley, A. Y. Stith, and A. R. Nelson. Washington, D.C.: National Academies Press.

Congressional Research Service. 1988. *Medicaid source book: Background data and analysis*. Washington, D.C.: Congressional Research Service.

Consumers Union of the United States. 1990. The crisis in health insurance. *Consumer Reports*, 21–18.

Cook, R. J. 1994. *Women's health and human rights*. Geneva, Switzerland: World Health Organization.

Copp, D. 1992. The right to an adequate standard of living: justice autonomy, and the basic needs. *Social Philosophy and Policy* 9:231–61.

Coren, S. and D. Halpern. 1991. Left-handedness: a marker for decreased survival fitness. *Psychological Bulletin* 190:90–106.

Cubbon, J. 1991. The principle of QALY maximization as the basis for allocating health care resources. *Journal of Medical Ethics* 17:181–84.

Cudd, A. 1994. Oppression by choice. *Journal of Social Philosophy* 25: 22–44.

Cutler, D. M., and S. J. Reber. 1998. Paying for health insurance: The tradeoff between competition and adverse selection. *Quarterly Journal of Economics* 113:433–66.

Cystic Fibrosis Foundation. 2003. Patient registry 2002 annual report. Bethesda, MD: Cystic Fibrosis Foundation.

Daniels, N. 1985. *Just health care*. New York: Cambridge University Press.

———. 1988. *Am I my parents' keeper?* New York: Oxford University Press.

———. 1990. Equality of what: Welfare, resources, or capabilities? *Philosophy and Phenomenological Research* 50:273–96.

———. 1991. Is the Oregon rationing plan fair? *Journal of the American Medical Association* 265:2232–35.

———. 1993. Rationing fairly: Programmatic considerations. *Bioethics* 7:224–33.

———. 1998. Distributive justice and summary measures of population health services. In *Summarizing population health: Directions for the development and application of population metrics*. Edited by the Institute of Medicine Committee on Summary Measures of Population Health, Washington, D.C.: National Academies Press.

Daniels, N., B. Kennedy, and I. Kawachi. 2000. *Is inequality bad for our health?* Boston: Beacon Press.

Daniels, N., and J. E. Sabin. 1998. Last chance therapies and managed care: Pluralism, fair procedures, and legitimacy. *Hastings Center Report* 28 (2):27–41.

———. 2002. *Setting limits fairly*. New York: Oxford University Press.

Darwall, S. 1992. Two kinds of respect. In *Ethics and moral personality*. Edited by J. Deigh. Chicago: University of Chicago Press.

Davey Smith, G. 2001. Reflections on the limitations of epidemiology. *Journal of Clinical Epidemiology* 54:325–31.

Diamond, P. 1992. Organizing the health insurance market. *Econometrica*. 60:1233–54.

Dranove, D. 1995. Measuring costs. In *Valuing health care*. Edited by F. Sloan. Cambridge: Cambridge University Press.

Draper, D.A., R. Harley, C. Lesser, B. Strunk. 2002. The changing face of managed care. *Health Affairs* 11–23.

Dworkin, R. 1977. *Taking rights seriously*. Cambridge, MA: Harvard University Press.

———. 1981a. What is equality? Part 1: Equality of welfare. *Philosophy and Public Affairs* 10:185–246.

———. 1981b. What is equality? Part 2: Equality of resources. *Philosophy and Public Affairs* 10:283–345.

———. 1985. *A matter of principle.* Cambridge, MA: Harvard University Press.

———. 1990. Foundations of liberal equality. In *Tanner lectures on human values,* vol. 11. Edited by G. Peterson. Salt Lake City: University of Utah Press.

Eddy, D. 1991. Rationing by patient choice. *Journal of the American Medical Association* 265:105–08.

———. 1992. Cost-effectiveness analysis: A conversation with my father. *Journal of the American Medical Association* 267:1669–75.

———. 1994. Principles for making difficult decisions in difficult times. *Journal of the American Medical Association* 271:1792–98.

Ellwood, P. M., and G. D. Lundber. 1996. Managed care: A work in progress. *Journal of the American Medical Association* 276:1083–86.

Elster, J. 1982. Sour grapes: utilitarianism and the genesis of wants. In *Utilitarianism and beyond.* Edited by A. Sen and B. Williams. ✓ Cambridge: Cambridge University Press.

———. 1992. *Local justice.* New York: Russell Sage Foundation.

Emory, E., Z. Ansari, R. Pattillo, E. Archibold, and J. Chevalier. 2003. Maternal blood lead effects on infant intelligence at age 7 months. *American Journal of Obstetrics and Gynecology* 188(4):S26–32.

Engelhardt, H. T. Jr. 1996. *The foundations of bioethics.* 2nd ed. New York: Oxford University Press.

Enthoven, A. 1993. The history and principles of managed competition. *Health Affairs* 12:24–48.

Enthoven, A., and R. Kronick 1989. A consumer-choice plan for the 1990s. *The New England Journal of Medicine* 320:29–37, 94–101.

Enthoven, A., and R. Kronick. 1991. Universal health insurance through incentives reform. *Journal of the American Medical Association* 265:2532–36.

Epstein, A. 1995. Performance reports on quality—Prototypes, problems, and prospects. *New England Journal of Medicine* 333:57–61.

Estlund, D. 1998. Liberalism, equality, and fraternity in Cohen's critique of Rawls. *Journal of Political Philosophy.* 6:99–112.

Etheredge, L., S. Jones, and L. Lewin. 1996. What is driving health system change? *Health Affairs* 4:93–103.

Faden, R., and M. Powers. 1999. *Incrementalism: Ethical implications of policy choices.* Washington, D.C.: Henry J. Kaiser Family Foundation.

Faden, R., and N. Kass. 1998. HIV research, ethics, and the developing world. *American Journal of Public Health* 88 (4): 548–50.

Faden, R., G. Geller, and M. Powers, eds. 1991. *AIDS, women, and the next generation.* New York: Oxford University Press.

Faden, R., and N. Kass, eds. 1996. *HIV, AIDS and childbearing: Public policy, private lives.* New York: Oxford University Press.

Faden, R., H. A. Taylor, and N. K. Seiler. 2003. Consent and compensation: A social compact for smallpox vaccine policy in the event of an attack. *Clinical Infectious Diseases* 36 (12):1547–51.

Faden, R., L. Dawson, A. S. Bateman-House, D. M. Agnew, H. Bok, D. W. Brock, A. Chakravarti, X.-J. Gao, M. Greene, J. A. Hansen, P. A. King, S. J. O' Brien, D. H. Sachs, K. E. Schill, A. Siegel, D. Solter, S. M. Suter, C. M. Verfaillie, L. B. Walters, and J. D. Gearhart. 2003. Public stem cell banks: Considerations of justice in stem cell research and therapy. *Hastings Center Report* 33 (6):13–27.

Faden, R., N. Kass, and D. McGraw.1996. Women as vessels and vectors: Lessons from the HIV epidemic. In *Feminism and bioethics: Beyond reproduction*. Edited by S. Wolf. New York: Oxford University Press.

Faden, R., N. Kass, and M. Powers. 1991. Warrants for screening programs: Public health, legal, and ethical frameworks. In *AIDS, women, and the next generation*. Edited by R. Faden, G. Geller, and M. Powers. New York: Oxford University Press.

Falcon, A. P. 1990. *National coalition of Hispanic health and human services organizations report*. Washington, D.C.: National Coalition of Hispanic Health and Human Services Organizations.

Families USA Foundation. 1999. *Losing health insurance: The unintended consequences of welfare reform*. Washington, D.C.

Farley, P. J. 1985. Who are the uninsured? *Milbank Memorial Fund Quarterly/Health and Society* 63 (3):476–503.

Feldstein, M. 1973. The welfare loss of excess health insurance. *Journal of Political Economics* 81:251–80.

Finkelstein, Y., M. E. Markowitz, and J. F. Rosen 1998. Low-level lead-induced neurotoxicity in children: An update on central nervous system effects. *Brain Research: Brain Research Reviews* 27 (2): 168–76.

Finnis, J. 1980. *Natural law and natural rights*. Oxford: Clarendon Press. ✳ *15*

Fleck, L. 1994. Just caring: Oregon, health care rationing, and informed democratic deliberation. *Journal of Medicine and Philosophy* 19: 367–88.

Flood, C. 2000. *International health care reform*. London: Routledge.

Fox, D., and P. Fronstein. 2000. Public spending for health care approaches sixty percent. *Health Affairs* 19:271–73.

Frankfurt, H. 1971. Freedom of the will and the concept of a person. *Journal of Philosophy* 68:5–20.

———. 1987. Equality as a moral ideal. *Ethics* 98:21–43. ✓

Freeman, E. M. 1989. Adolescent fathers in urban communities: Exploring their needs and role in preventing pregnancy. *Journal of Social Work and Human Sexuality* 8 (1):113–31.

Fried, C. 1969. The value of life. *Harvard Law Review* 82:1415–37.

———. 1978. *Right and wrong*. Cambridge, MA: Harvard University Press.

Fried, P. A., B. Watkinson, and R. Gray. 2003. Differential effects on cognitive functioning in 13- to 16-year-olds prenatally exposed to cigarettes and marihuana. *Neurotoxicology and Teratology* 25 (4): 427–36.

Fuchs, V. 2002. What's ahead for health insurance in the United States? *New England Journal of Medicine* 346:1822–24.

Gabel, J., K. Kurst, K. Hunt. 1998. Health benefits for the terminally ill: reality and perception. *Health Affairs* 17:120–27.

Gafni, A. 1991. Willingness to pay as a measure of benefits: Relevant questions in the context of public decision making health care programs. *Medical Care* 29:1246–52.

Gale, C. R., F. J. O'Callaghan, K. M. Godfrey, C. M. Law, and C. N. Martyn. 2003. Critical periods of brain growth and cognitive function in children. *Brain* 127 (2):321–29.

Galea, S., and D. Vlahov. 2002. Social determinants and the health of drug users: Socioeconomic status, homelessness, and incarceration. *Public Health Reports* 117 (Suppl 1): S135–45.

Galvin, R., and A. Milstein. 2002. Large employers' new strategies in health care. *New England Journal of Medicine* 347 (12):939–42.

Garber, A. M., M. C. Weinstein, G. W. Torrence, and M. S. Kamlet. 1996. Theoretical foundations of cost-effectiveness analysis. In *Cost-effectiveness in health and medicine.* Edited by M. R. Gold, J. E. Siegel, L. B. Russell, and M. C. Weinstein. New York: Oxford University Press.

General Accounting Office (GAO). 1997. *Employment-based health insurance cost increase and family decreases.* GAO/HEHS-97–35. Washington, D.C.: U.S. Government Printing Office.

Gillespie, D., M. Claeson, H. Mshinda, H. Troedsson, and the Bellagio Study Group on Child Survival. 2003. Knowledge into action for child survival. *The Lancet* 362:323–27.

Ginzberg, E. 1999. The uncertain future of managed care. *The New England Journal of Medicine.* 340:144–6.

Glied, S. 1993. Employment and health benefits: A connection at risk. In *Employment and health benefits.* Edited by M. J. Field and H. T. Shapiro. Washington, D.C.: National Academies Press.

———. 2001. Health insurance and market failure since Arrow. *Journal of Health Politics, Policy, and Law* 26:597–65.

Gold, R., B. Kennedy, F. Connell, and I. Kawachi. 2002. Teen births, income inequality, and social capital: Developing an understanding of the causal pathway. *Health and Place* 8 (2):77–83.

Goldenberg, R. L., M. B. DuBard, S. P. Cliver, K. G. Nelson, K. Blankson, S. L. Ramey, and A. Herman. 1996. Pregnancy outcome and intelligence at age five years. *American Journal of Obstetrics and Gynecology* 175 (6):1511–15.

Goldman, N. 2001. Social inequalities in health: Disentangling the underlying mechanisms. *Annals of the New York Academy of Sciences* 954:118–39.

Gollub, E. L. 1999. Human rights is a U.S. problem, too: The case of women and HIV. *American Journal of Public Health* 89:1479–82.

Goodin, R. 1995. *Utilitarianism as a public philosophy.* Cambridge: Cambridge University Press.

Goodman, J., and G. Musgrave. 1992. *Patient power: Solving America's health care crisis.* Washington, D.C.: The Cato Institute.

Goold, S. D. 1996. Allocating health care: Cost-utility analysis, informed democratic decision making, or the veil of ignorance? *Journal of Health Politics, Policy, and Law* 21, 69–98.

Gornick, M. E., P. Eggers, T. Reilly, R. Mentnech, L. Fitterman, L. Kucken, B. Vladeck. 1996. Effects of race and income on mortality and use of services among Medicare beneficiaries. *The New England Journal of Medicine* 335:791–99.

Gramlich, E. 1981. *Benefit-cost analysis of government programs.* Englewood Cliffs, NJ: Prentice-Hall.

Grantham-McGregor S. 1995. A review of studies of the effect of severe malnutrition on mental development. *Journal of Nutrition* 125 (8 Suppl): 2233S-38S.

Gray. J. 1996. *Mill on liberty: A defense.* 2nd ed. London and New York: Rutledge.

Greaney, T. L. 1998. How many libertarians does it take to fix the health care system? *Michigan Law Review* 96:1825–51.

Green, R. 1976. Health care and justice in contract theory perspective. In *Ethics and health policy.* Edited by R. Veatch and R. Branson. Cambridge, MA: Ballinger.

Griffin, J. 1986. *Well-being.* Oxford: Oxford University Press.

———. The distinction between criterion and decision procedure: A reply to Madison Powers. *Utilitas* 6:177–82.

Gruber, J., J. Kim, and D. Mayzlin. 1999. Physician fees and procedure intensity. *Journal of Health Economics* 18:473–90.

Gunatilleke, G., and A. E. B. Hammad, eds. 1997. *Health: The courage to care.* Geneva, Switzerland: World Health Organization.

Gutmann, A. 1981. For and against equal access to health care. *Milbank Memorial Fund Quarterly* 59:542–60.

Gutmann, A., and D. Thompson. 1996. *Democracy and disagreement.* Cambridge, MA: Belknap Press.

Hadley, J., and J. Holahan. 2003. Covering the uninsured: How much would it cost? *Health Affairs Web Exclusives* http://www.healthaffairs.org/cgi/context/full/hlthaff.w3.250v1/dc1 (accessed Sept. 13, 2005).

Hadorn, D. 1991. Setting health care priorities in Oregon: Cost-effectiveness meets the rule of rescue. *Journal of the American Medical Association* 265:2218–25.

Haley, J., and S. Zuckerman. 2003. *Is lack of coverage a short- or long-term condition?* Washington, D.C.: Henry J. Kaiser Family Foundation.

Halfon, N., and M. Hochstein. 2002. Life course health development: An integrated framework for developing health, policy, and research. *Milbank Quarterly* 80:433–79.

Hargraves, J. L., and S. Trude. 2002. Obstacles to employers' pursuit of health care quality. *Health Affairs* 21:194–200.

Harris, J. R. 1985. *The value of life.* London: Routledge and Kegan Paul.

———. 1987. QALYfying the value of life. *Journal of Medical Ethics* 13:117–23.

———. 1988a. Life: Quality, value, and justice. *Health Policy* 10:259–66.

———. 1988b. More and better justice. In M. Bell and S. Mendus, eds. *Philosophy and medical welfare.* Cambridge: Cambridge University Press.

———. 1994. Does justice require that we be ageist? *Bioethics* 8:74–83.

———. 1995. Double jeopardy and the veil of ignorance—A reply. *Journal of Medical Ethics* 21:151–57.

Hart. H. L. A. 1961. *The concept of law.* New York: Oxford University Press.

———.1982. *Essays on Bentham.* Oxford: Clarendon Press.

Havighurst, C. C. 1997. Making health plans accountable for the quality of care. *Georgia Law Review* 31:587–647.

Hellander, I. 2001. A review of data on the health sector of the United States. *International Journal of Health Services* 31:35–53.

Hellinger, F. J. 1998. The effect of managed care on quality: A review of recent evidence. *Archives of Internal Medicine* 158:833–41.

Hillemeier, M. M., J. Lynch, S. Harper, T. Raghunathan, and G. A. Kaplan 2003. Relative or absolute standards for child poverty: A state-level analysis of infant and child mortality. *American Journal of Public Health* 93 (4):652–57.

Himmelstein, D., and, S. Woolhandler 2003. National health insurance or incremental reform: Aim high or at our feet? *American Journal of Public Health.* 93:102–05.

Hofer, T. P., Hawood, R. A., R. Haywood, S. Greenfield, E. Wagner, S. Kaplan, W. Manning. 1999. The unreliability of individual physician report cards for assessing the costs and quality of care of a chronic disease. *JAMA* 281:2098–2105.

Hubin, D. 1994. The moral justification of benefit/cost analysis. *Economics and Philosophy* 10:169–94.

Hume, D. [1777] 1983. *An enquiry concerning the principles of morals.* Edited by J. Schneewind. Indianapolis: Hackett Publishing Company.

Hyman, D. and, M. Hall. 2001. Two cheers for employment-based health insurance. *Yale Journal of Health Policy, Law, and Ethics* 2:23–57.

Iglehart, J. K. 1992a. Health policy report: The American health care system. *New England Journal of Medicine* 327:742–47.

———. 1992b. Health policy report: The American health care system—Medicare. *New England Journal of Medicine* 327:1467–72.

———. 1993. Health policy report: Managed competition. *New England Journal of Medicine* 328:1208–12.

———. 1994. Health policy report: Physicians and the growth of managed care. *New England Journal of Medicine* 331:1167–71.

———. 1996. The National Committee for Quality Assurance. *New England Journal of Medicine* 335:995–99.

———. 1998. Health spending, the uninsured, and the information revolution. *Health Affairs* 17:7–8.

———. 1999a. The American health care system: Expenditures. *New England Journal of Medicine* 340:70–76.

———. 1999b. The American health care system: Medicaid. *New England Journal of Medicine* 340:403–8.

———. 1999c. The American health care system: Medicare. *New England Journal of Medicine.* 340:327–32.

———. 2002a. Changing health insurance trends. *New England Journal of Medicine* 347:956–62.

———. 2002b. Medicare's declining payments to physicians. *New England Journal of Medicine* 346:1924–30.

Ijsselmuiden, C. B., and, R. Faden. 1992. Research and informed consent in Africa: Another look. *New England Journal of Medicine* 326 (12): 830–34.

Institute for Medicaid Management. 1978. *Data on medicaid program: Eligibility, services, expenditures, fiscal years, 1966–78.* Washington, D.C.: Institute for Medical Management.

Jacobs, J. L. 1994. Gender, race, class, and the trend toward early motherhood. A feminist analysis of teen mothers in contemporary society. *Journal of Contemporary Ethnography* 22 (4):442–62.

Jacobs, L. R., T. Marmor, and J. Oberlander. 1999. The Oregon health plan and the political paradox of rationing: What advocates and critics have claimed and what Oregon did. *Journal of Health Politics, Policy and Law* 24: 161–80.

Jensen, G. A., M. Morrisey, S. Gaffney, D. Liston. 1997. The new dominance of managed care:Insurance trends in the 1990s. *Health Affairs* 16: 125–36.

Jha, P., A. Mills, K. Hanson, L. Kumaranayake, L. Conteh, C. Kurowski, S. N. Nguyen, V. O. Cruz, K. Ranson, L. M. Vaz, S. Yu, O. Morton, and J. D. Sachs. 2002. Improving the health of the global poor. *Science* 295: 2036–39.

Johannesson, M. 1995. The relation between cost-effectiveness analysis and cost-benefit analysis. *Social Science and Medicine.* 41:483–89.

Jones, G., R. W. Steketee, R. E. Black, Z. A. Bhutta, S. S. Morris, and the Bellagio Child Survival Study Group. 2003. How many child deaths can we prevent this year? *The Lancet* 362:65–71.

Jonsen, A. 1986. Bentham in a box: Technology assessment and health care allocation. *Law, Medicine, and Health Care* 14:172–74.

Kaiser Commission on Medicaid and the Uninsured. 2002 underinsured in America: Is health insurance adequate? Washington, D.C.: The Henry J. Kaiser Family Foundation.

———. 2003. The uninsured in America and the access to health care. Washington, D.C.: The Henry J. Kaiser Family Foundation.

Kamm, F. M. 1987. The choice between people: 'Common sense,' morality, and doctors. *Bioethics* 1:255–71.

———. 1993. *Morality, mortality: Death and whom to save from it.* New York: Oxford University Press.

———. 1994. To whom? *Hastings Center Report* 24:29–32.

———. 1998a. Precis of "Morality, Mortality: Death and whom to save from it." *Philosophy and Phenomenological Research* 58:939–45.

———. 1998b. Replies. *Philosophy and Phenomenological Research.* 58:969–75.

Kaplan, R. 1995. Utility assessment for estimating quality-adjusted life years. In *Valuing Health Care.* Edited by F. Sloan. Cambridge: Cambridge University Press.

Kappel, K., and, P. Sandoe. 1992. QALYs, age, and fairness. *Bioethics* 6:297–316.

———. 1994. Saving the young before the old—A reply to John Harris. *Bioethics* 8:85–92.

Kass, N. E. 2001. An ethics framework for public health. *American Journal of Public Health.* 91:1776–82.

Kawachi, I., B. Kennedy, and, R. Wilkinson. 1999. *The society and population reader: Income inequality and health.* New York: The New Press.

Kogan, M. D., G. R. Alexander, B. W. Jack, and M. C. Allen. 1998. The association between adequacy of prenatal care utilization and subsequent pediatric care utilization in the United States. *Pediatrics* 102 (Part 1): 25–30.

Korsgaard, C. 1996. *The sources of normativity*. Cambridge: Cambridge University Press.

Kronick, R., D. Goodman, J. Wennberg, and E. Wagner. 1993. The marketplace in health care reform: The demographic limitations of managed competition. *New England Journal of Medicine* 328:148–52.

Krumholz, H. M., S. S. Rathore, J. Chen, Y. Wang, M. Radford. 2002. Evaluation of a consumer-oriented Internet health care report card: The risk of quality ratings based on mortality data. *Journal of the American Medical Association* 287:1277–87.

Kuttner R. 1999a. The American health care system: Employer sponsored health coverage. *New England Journal of Medicine*. 340:248–52.

———. 1999b. The American health care system: Health insurance coverage. *New England Journal of Medicine* 340:163–67.

Kymlicka, W. 1990. *Contemporary political philosophy: An introduction*. Oxford: Oxford University Press.

LaFraniere, S. 2003. Millions of AIDS orphans strain southern Africa. *The New York Times*. 24 December.

Larmore, C. 1987. *Patterns of moral complexity*. New York: Cambridge University Press.

Leon, D. A. 1998. Fetal growth and adult disease. *European Journal of Clinical Medicine* 52 (S1):S72–S82.

———. 2000. Common threads: Underlying components of inequalities in mortality between and within countries. In *Poverty, inequality, and health: An international perspective*. Edited by D. A. Leon and G. Walt. Oxford: Oxford University Press.

Light, D. W. 1992. The practice and ethics of risk-related health insurance. *Journal of the American Medical Association* 267:2503–08.

Locke, J. [1699] 1965. *Two treatises of government*. Edited by P. Laslett. New York: Mentor.

Lockwood, M. 1988. Quality of life and resource allocation. In *Philosophy and medical welfare*. Edited by J. Bell and S. Mendus. Cambridge: Cambridge University Press.

Loewy, E. H. 1998. Justice and health care systems: What would an ideal health care system look like? *Health Care Analysis* 6:185–92.

Lomasky, L. 1981. Medical progress and national health care. *Philosophy and Public Affairs* 10:65–88.

———. 1987. *Persons, rights, and the moral community*. New York: Oxford University Press.

Lopez. A. D., J. Saloman, O. Ahmad, C. J. L. Murray, D. Mufat. 1999. Life tables for 191 countries:Data, methods and results. *GPE Discussion Papers Series*, no. 9. Geneve, Switzerland: World Health Organization.

LoSasso, A. T., L. Perloff, J. Schield, J. Murphy, J. Mortimer, P. Budetti. 1991. Beyond cost: responsible purchasing of managed care by employers. *Health Affairs* 18:212–23.

Loury, G. 2002. *The anatomy of racial inequality*. Cambridge, MA: Harvard University Press.

———. 2003. Racial stigma: Toward a new paradigm for discrimination theory. *American Economic Review* 93:337.

Lucas, J. R. 1965. Against equality. *Philosophy* 40:296–307.

———. 1977. Against equality again. *Philosophy* 52:255–80.

MacLean, D. 1986. Social values and the distribution of risk. In *Values at risk*. Edited by D. Maclean. New Jersey: Rowman and Allanheld.

Mann, J. M. 1995. Human rights and the new public health. *Health and Human Rights* 1(3):229–33.

———. 1997. Medicine and public health, ethics and human rights. *The Hastings Center Report* 27 (3):6–13.

———. 1998. Dignity and health:The UDHR's revolutionary first article. *Health and Human Rights* 3 (2):30–38.

Manning, W. G., and M. S. Marquis. 1996. Health insurance: the tradeoff between risk pooling and moral hazard. *Journal of Health Economics.* 15:609–39.

Marchand, S., D. Wikler, and B. Landesman. 1998. Class, health, and justice. *Milbank Quarterly* 76:449–67.

Marquis, S., and S. Long. 1999. Trends in managed care and managed competition, 1993–97. *Health Affairs* 18:75–88.

———. 2001. Prevalence of selected health insurance purchasing strategies in 1997. *Health Affairs* 20:220–30.

Mastroianni, A. C., R. R. Faden, and D. Federman, eds. 1994. *Women and health research: Ethical and legal issues of including women in clinical studies,* vol. 1, Washington, D.C.: National Academy Press.

Maxwell, J. 1998. Managed competition in practice: Value purchasing by fourteen employers. *Health Affairs* 221–26.

Maxwell, J. and P. Temin. 2002. Managed competition vs. industrial purchasing of healthcare among the Fortune 500. *Journal of Health Politics, Policy and Law* 27:5–30.

Medical Management Institute 2006. ICD-9-CM. Alpharetta, Ga.: Medical Management Institute.

May, T. 1994. The concept of autonomy. *American Philosophical Quarterly* 31:133–44.

McKie, J., and J. Richardson. 2003. The rule of rescue. *Social Science and Medicine* 56:2407–19.

McLean, I. 1987. *Public choice.* Oxford: Basil Blackwell.

Melhado, E. M. 1998. Economists, public provision, and the market: Changing values in policy debate. *Journal of Health Politics, Policy, and Law.* 23:215–63.

———. 2000. Economic theory, economists, and the formulation of public policy. *Journal of Health Politics, Policy, and Law* 25:233–56.

Menzel, P. 1992. Equality, autonomy, and efficiency: What health care system should we have? *Journal of Medicine and Philosophy,* 17:33–57.

———. 1999. How should what economists call "social values" be measured? *Journal of Ethics* 3:249–73.

Menzel, P., M. Gold, E. Nord, J. Pinto-Prades, J. Richardson, P. Ubel. 1999. Toward a broader view of values in cost-effectiveness analysis of health. *Hastings Center Report* 29:7–15.

Mill, J. S. [1859] 1991. *On liberty and other essays.* Edited with an introduction by John Gray. Oxford: Oxford University Press.

————. [1861] 1986. *The subjection of women.* Amherst, NY: Prometheus Books.

Miller, R. H., and H. S. Luft. 1994a. Managed care plan performance since 1980: A literature analysis. *Journal of American Medical Association* 271:1512–18.

————. 1994b. Managed care plans: Characteristics, growth, and premium performance. *Annual Review of Public Health* 15:437–59.

Miller, D. 1992. Distributive justice: What people think. *Ethics* 102:555–93.

Miller, W. 1997. *Egalitarianism and self-respect.* Doctoral dissertation. Georgetown University.

Minino A. M., E. Arias, K. D. Kochanek, S. L. Murphy, and B. L. Smith. 2002. Deaths: final data for 2000. *National Vital Statistics Report* 50 (15):1–119.

Mishan, E. J. 1988. *Cost-benefit analysis.* 4th ed. London: Unwin Hyman.

Morrisey, M. A., G. A. Jensen, and R. J. Morlock. 1994. Small employers and the health insurance market. *Health Affairs* 13:149–61.

Murphy, L. 1999. Institutions and the demands of justice. *Philosophy and Public Affairs* 27:251–91.

Murray, C., and A. Acharya. 1997. Understanding DALYs. *Journal of Health Economics* 16:703–30.

Musgrove, P. 1999. Public spending on health care: How are different criteria related? *Health Policy* 47:207–23.

Mustard, C. A., P. Kaufert, A. Kozysjys, T. Mayer. 1998. Sex differences in the use of health care services. *New England Journal of Medicine* 338:1678–83.

Nagel, T. 1979a. Equality. Reprinted in *Mortal questions.* Cambridge: Cambridge University Press.

————. 1979b. The fragmentation of value. Reprinted in *Mortal questions.* Cambridge: Cambridge University Press.

————. 1991. *Equality and partiality.* New York: Oxford University Press.

National Academy of Social Insurance. 1999. *Medicare and the American social contract.* Final report of the study panel on Medicare's larger social role. Washington, D.C.: National Academy of Social Insurance.

Newachek, P. W., J. J. Stoddard, D. C. Hughes, and M. Pearl. 1998. Health insurance and access to primary care for children. *New England Journal of Medicine* 338:513–19.

Newhouse, J. P. 1993. An iconoclastic view of health cost containment. *Health Affairs* 1:152–71.

Newhouse, J. P. 1994. *Free for all? Lessons from the Rand health insurance experiment.* Cambridge, MA: Harvard University Press.

————. 1996. Reimbursing health plans and health providers: Efficiency in production versus selection. *Journal of Economic Literature* 34: 1236–63.

Nickel, J. 1987. *Making sense of human rights.* Berkeley: University of California Press.

Nord, E. 1993. Health politicians do not wish to maximize health benefits. *Journal of the Norwegian Medical Association* 113:1171–73.

————. 1999. *Cost-value analysis in health care.* Cambridge: Cambridge University Press.

———. 2005. Concerns for the worse off: Fair innings versus severity. *Social Science and Medicine* 60:257–63.

Nord, E., J. Pinto, J. Richardson, P. Menzel, P. Ubel. 1999. Incorporating societal concerns for fairness in numerical valuations of health programs. *Health Economics* 8:25–39.

Nozick, R. 1974. *Anarchy, state, and utopia.* New York: Basic Books. &

Nussbaum, M. 1988. Nature, function, and capability: Aristotle on political distribution. In *Oxford studies in ancient philosophy, supplementary volume.* Edited by J. Annas and R. Grimm. Oxford: Clarendon Press.

———. 1990. Aristotlean social democracy. In *Liberalism and the good.* Edited by B. Douglas, G. Mara, and H. Richardson. New York: Routledge.

———. 2000. *Women and human development.* Cambridge: Cambridge University Press.

Nussbaum, M., and A. Sen, eds. 1993. *The quality of life.* Oxford: Clarendon β Press.

O'Neill. O. 1993. Justice, gender and international boundaries. In *The equality of life.* Edited by M. Nussbaum and A. Sen. Oxford: Clarendon Press.

Pan American Health Organization. 2003. *Violence against women: The health sector responds.* Washington, D.C.: Pan American Health Organization.

Pande R. P., and A. S. Yazbeck. 2003. What's in a country average? Wealth, gender, and regional inequalities in immunization in India. *Social Science and Medicine* 57:2075–88.

Parfit, D. 1991. Equality or priority? (Lindley Lecture, University of Kansas). Lawrence: Philosophy Department, University of Kansas.

———. 1998. Equality and priority. In *Ideals of equality.* Edited by A. Mason.

Patrick, D., Y. Sittampalam, S. Somerville, W. Carter, M. Berger. 1985. Cross-cultural comparison of health status values. *American Journal of Public Health* 75 (part 2):1402–07.

Pauly, M. 1968. The economics of moral hazard. *American Economic Review* 58:531–37.

———. 1971. *Medical care at public expense.* New York: Praeger.

———. 1974. Overinsurance and the public provision of insurance: The roles of moral hazard and adverse selection. *Quarterly Journal of Economics* 88:44–62.

———. 1978. Is medical care different? In *Competition in the health sector: past, present, and future.* Edited by Warren Greenberg. Germantown, MD: Aspen Systems.

———. 1980. Overinsurance: Conceptual issues. In *National health insurance: What now, what later, what never?* Edited by Mark Pauly. Washington, D.C.: American Enterprise Institute.

———. 1995. Valuing health care benefits in money terms. In *Valuing health care.* Edited by F. Sloan. Cambridge: Cambridge University Press.

———. 1998. Managed care, market power, and monopsony. *Health Services Research* 33:1537–1562.

Pauly, M., and A. M. Percy. 2000. Cost and performance: A comparison of the individual and group health insurance markets. *Journal of Health Politics, Policy and Law* 25:9–26.

Peterson, M. A. 1998. Managed care: Ethics, trust, and accountability. *Journal of Health Politics, Policy and Law.* 23:611–15.

Pettit, P. 1996. Freedom as antipower. *Ethics* 106:576–604.

————. 1997. *Republicanism :A theory of freedom and government.* Oxford: Oxford University Press.

Pincus, T., R. Esther, D. A. DeWalt, and L. F. Callahan. 1998. Social conditions and self-management are more powerful determinants of health than access to care. *Annals of Internal Medicine* 129:406–11.

Pogge, T. 1998. A global resources dividend. In *Ethics of consumption: The good life, justice and global stewardship.* Edited by D. A. Crocker and T. Linden. Lanham, MD: Rowman and Littlefield.

————. 2000. On the site of distributive justice: Reflections on Cohen and Murphy. *Philosophy and Public Affairs* 29:137–69.

————. 2002. Responsibilities for poverty-related ill health. *Ethics and International Affairs* 16 (2) :71–9.

————. 2004. Relational conceptions of justice: Responsibilities for health outcomes. In *Public health, ethics, and equity.* Edited by S. Anand, F. Peter, and A. Sen. Oxford: Clarendon Press.

Powers, M. 1991. Justice and the market for health insurance. *Kennedy Institute of Ethics Journal* 1:307–23.

————. 1992. Efficiency, autonomy, and communal values in health care. *Yale Law and Policy Review* 10:316–61.

————. 1994. Repugnant desires and the two-tier conception of utility. *Utilitas* 6:171–6.

————. 1995. Hypothetical choice approaches to health care allocation. In *Allocating health resources.* Edited by J. M. Humber and R. F. Almeder. Clifton, NJ: Humana Press.

————. 1997a. Justice and Genetics: Privacy protection and the moral basis of public policy. In *Genetics secrets: Privacy, confidentiality and new genetic technology.* Edited by M. Rothstein. New Haven, CT: Yale University Press.

————. 1997b. Managed competition: How incentives reforms went wrong. *Kennedy Institute of Ethics Journal* 7:353–60.

————. 1998. Theories of justice in the context of human subjects research. In *Beyond consent: Seeking justice in research.* Edited by J. Kahn, A. Mastroianni, and J. Sugarman. New York: Oxford University Press.

————. 2000. Genetic information, ethics policy and confidentiality: overview. *In Encyclopedia of biotechnology: Ethical, legal, and policy issues.* New York: John Wiley and Sons.

————. 2002. Privacy and genetics. In *Companion to genethics.* Edited by J. Burley and J. Harris. Oxford: Blackwell Publishers.

Powers, M., and R. Faden. 2000. Inequalities in health, inequalities in health care: Four generations of discussion about justice and cost-effectiveness analysis. *Kennedy Institute of Ethics Journal,* 10:109–27.

————. 2002. Racial and ethnic disparities in health care: An ethical analysis of when and how they matter. In *Unequal treatment:Confronting racial and ethnic disparities in health care.* Edited by B. D. Smedley, A. Y. Stith, and A. R. Nelson. Committee on Understanding and Eliminating Racial and Ethnic Disparities in Health Care, Board on Health Sciences Policy. Washington, D.C.: National Academy of Sciences, Institute of Medicine.

President's Commission for the Study of Ethical Problems in Medicine and Biomedical and Behavioral Research. 1983. *Securing access to health care*, vol. 1. Washington, D.C.: U. S. Government Printing Office.

Public Health Leadership Society. 2002. Principles of the ethical practice of public health. Version 2.2. New Orleans: Public Health Leadership Society.

Rabito, F. A., C. Shorter, and L. White. 2003. Lead levels among children who live in public housing. *Epidemiology* 14(3):263–268.

Rakowski, E. 1991. *Equal JUSTICE*. Oxford: Oxford University Press.

Rasekh, Z., H. M. Bauer, M. M. Manos, and V. Iacopino. 1998. Women's health and human rights in Afghanistan. *Journal of the American Medical Association* 280:449–55.

Rawls, J. 1971. *A theory of justice*. Cambridge, MA: Harvard University Press.

———. 1982. Social unity and primary goods. *Utilitarianism and beyond*. Edited by A. Sen and B. Williams. Cambridge: Cambridge University Press.

———. 2001. *Justice as fairness: A restatement*. Cambridge, MA: Harvard University Press.

Raz, J. 1986. *The morality of freedom*. Oxford: Clarendon Press.

Redelmeir, A. D., S. Singh. 2001. Survival in academy-award winning actors and actresses. *Annals of Internal Medicine* 134:955–62.

Reinhardt, U. E. 1996. Health system change: Skirmish or revolution? *Health Affairs* 15:114–15.

———. 2001. Can efficiency in health care be left to the market? *Journal of Health Politics, Policy, and Law* 26:967–992.

Richardson, H. Autonomy's many normative presuppositions. *American Philosophical Quarterly* 38:287–303.

Richardson, J. 2002. The poverty of ethical analysis in economics and the unwarranted disregard of evidence. Edited by C. J. L. Murray, J. Salmon, C. Matthews, A. D. Lopez. *Summary measures of population health: Concepts, ethics, measurement, and application*. Geneva: World Health Organization

Richardson, J., and J. McKie. 2005. Empiricism, ethics and orthodox economic theory: What is the appropriate basis for decision making in the health sector? *Social Science and Medicine* 60:265–75.

Robinson, J. 1999. The future of managed care organization. *Health Affairs* 18:7–24.

———. 2001a. The end of asymmetric information. *Journal of Health Politics, Policy, and Law* 26:1045–53.

———. 2001b. The end of managed care. *Journal of the American Medical Association* 285:2622–28.

Rodriguez-Garcia R., and M. N. Akhter. 2000. Human rights: the foundation of public health practice. *American Journal of Public Health* 90:693–94.

Rorty, R. 1991. *Objectivity, relativism, and truth*. Cambridge: Cambridge University Press.

Rosenbaum, S. 1992. Rationing without justice: Children and the American health system. *University of Pennsylvania Law Review* 140:1859–80.

Rosenberg, A. 1995. Equality, sufficiency, and opportunity in the just society. *Social Philosophy and Policy* 12:54–71.

Rothschild, M., and J. Stiglitz. 1976. Equilibrium in competitive insurance markets: An essay on the economics of imperfect information. *Quarterly Journal of Economics* 90:629–649.

Roubideaux, Y. 2002. Perspectives on American Indian health. *American Journal of Public Health* 92(9):1401–03.

Rousseau, J.-J. [1755] 1984. *A Discourse on inequality.* Translated by Maurice Cranston. London: Penguin Books.

Rowland, D., J. Feder, and P. S. Keenan. 1998. Uninsured in America: The causes and consequences. In *The future U.S. healthcare system: Who will care for the poor and uninsured?* Edited by S.H. Altman, U. E. Reinhardt, and A. E. Shields. Chicago: Health Administration Press.

Rowland, D., A. Salganicoff, and P. Keenan. 1999. The key to the door: Medicaid's role in improving health care for women and children. *Annual Review of Public Health* 20:403–26.

Russell, L., M. Gold, J. Siegel, N. Daniels, M. C. Weinstein. 1996. The role of cost-effectiveness analysis in health and medicine. *Journal of the American Medical Association* 276:1172–77.

Ruttenberg, J. E. 1993. Revisiting the employment-insurance link. *Journal of Health Politics* 18:75–81.

Sanders-Phillips, K. 2002. Factors influencing HIV/AIDS in women of color. *Public Health Reports* 117 (Suppl. 1):S151–6.

Sanders-Phillips, K., and S. Davis. 1998. Improving prenatal care services for low-income African-American women and infants. *Journal of Health Care for the Poor and Underserved* 9 (1):14–29.

Scanlon, T. M. 1986. The diversity of objections to inequality. The Lindley Lecture, University of Kansas. Lawrence: Philosophy Department, University of Kansas.

Schantz, S. L., J. J. Widholm, D. C. Rice. 2003. Effects of PCB exposure on neuropsychological function in children. *Environmental Health Perspectives* 111(3):357–576.

Scheff, T. J., S. M. Retzinger, and M. T. Ryan. 1989. Crime, violence, and self-esteem: Review and proposals. In *The social importance of self-esteem.* Edited by A. M. Mecca, N. J. Smelser, and Vasconellos J. Berkeley: University of California Press.

Schoen, C., and DesRoches, C. 2000. Uninsured and unstably insured: The importance of continuous health insurance coverage. *Health Services Research*: 35:187–206.

Schorr, A. 1990. Job turnover—A problem with employer-based health care. *New England Journal of Medicine* 323:543–45.

Schuster, M., E. McGlynn, R. Brock. 1998. How good is he quality of health care in the United States? *The Milbank Quarterly* 76:51–63.

Sen, A. 1979. Equality of what? In *Liberty, equality, and law: Selected Tanner lectures on moral philosophy.* Edited by S. M. McMurrin. Cambridge: Cambridge University Press.

———. 1982. *Choice, welfare, and measurement.* Oxford: Blackwell.

———. 1983. Poor relatively speaking. *Oxford Economic Papers* 35:153–69.

———. 1985. Well-being, agency, and freedom: The Dewey Lectures, 1984. *Journal of Philosophy* 82:169–221.

———. 1992. *Inequality reexamined.* Cambridge, MA: Harvard University Press.

———. 1993. Capability and well-being. In *The quality of life.* Edited by M. Nussbaum, and A. Sen. Oxford: Clarendon Press.

———. 2000. Forward. In *Is Inequality bad for our health?* Edited by N. Daniels, B. Kennedy, and I. Kawachi. Boston: Beacon Press.

Shapiro, D. 1998. Why even egalitarians should favor market health insurance. *Social Philosophy and Policy* 15:84–132.

Sheils, J. and, P. Hogan. 1999. Cost of tax-exempt health benefits in 1998. *Health Affairs* 18:176–81.

Shi, L. 1992. The relation between primary care and life chances. *Journal of the Poor and Underserved.* 3:321–35.

Silow-Carroll, S., T. Kutyla, and J. A. Meyer 2001. The state of employment-based health coverage and business attitudes about its future. Washington, D.C.: Economic and Social Research Institute.

Sloan, F. A. 1993. Does the market choose the right incentives to get to the desired outcomes? Market failure revisited. In *Competitive approaches to health care reform.* Edited by, R. Arnould, R. Rich, and W. White. Washington, D.C.: Urban Institute.

———. 2001. Arrow's concept of the health care consumer: A forty-year retrospective. *Journal of Health Politics, Policy, and Law* 26: 899–911.

Small, R. 2002. The ethics of life expectancy. *Bioethics* 16:307–334. *L Expecty*

Sox, C. M., K. Swartz, H. R. Burstin, and T. A. Brennan 1998. Insurance or a regular physician: Which is the most powerful predictor of health care? *American Journal of Public Health* 88:364–70.

Starr, P. 1982. *The transformation of American medicine.* New York: Basic Books.

Stone, D. 1993. The struggle for the soul of health insurance. *Journal of Health Politics, Policy, and Law* 18:287–317.

———. 2000. United States. *Journal of Health Politics, Policy and Law* 25:953–958.

Strunk, B. C., P. B. Ginsburg, J. R Gabel. 2001. Tracking health care costs: Hospital care surpasses drugs as the key cost driver. *Health Affairs.* Web exclusives: W39–W50

Sullivan, K. 2000. On the "efficiency" of managed care plans. *Health Affairs* 19:139–148.

Sullivan, M. L. 1993. Culture and class as determinants of out-of wedlock childbearing and poverty during late adolescence. *Journal of Research on Adolescence* 3(3):295–316.

Sumner, W. 1987. *The moral foundation of rights.* Oxford: Clarendon Press.

Swartz, K. and T. McBride 1990. Spells without insurance: Distributions of durations and their link to post-in-time estimates of the uninsured. *Inquiry* 27:281–288.

Taurek, J. 1977. Should the numbers count? *Philosophy and Public Affairs* 6:293–316.

Taylor, C. 1979. What's wrong with negative liberty? *The idea of freedom.* Edited by A. Ryan.

————. 1982. The diversity of goods. In *Utilitarianism and beyond*. Edited by A. Sen and B. Williams. Cambridge: Cambridge Univesity Press.

————. 1985. The nature and scope of distributive justice. Reprinted in *Philosophy and the Human Sciences, Philosophical Papers, 2*. Cambridge: Cambridge University Press.

Temkin, L. 1993. *Inequality*. Oxford: Oxford University Press.

————. 1995. Justice and equality: Some questions about scope. *Social Philosophy and Policy*. 12:72–104.

Tsuchiya, A., and A. Williams. 2005. A "fair innings" between the sexes:Are men being treated inequitably? *Social Science and Medicine* 60: 277–286.

Ubel, P. 2000. *Pricing life*. Cambridge, MA: MIT Press.

United Nations Children's Fund. 1990. *Plan of action for implementing the world declaration on the survival, protection, and development of children in the 1990s*. New York: United Nations Children's Fund.

————. 2003. *Africa's orphaned generations*. New York: United Nations Children's Fund.

United Nations General Assembly. 1948. Universal Declaration of Human Rights. Resolution 217a (III). Geneva: United Nations.

U.S. House of Representatives. 1999. Committee on Ways and Means. *Medicare and health care chartbook*. Washington, D.C.: U.S. Government Printing Office. UMCP 106–104.

Veatch, R. 1986. *The foundations of justice: Why the retarded and the rest of us have claims to equality*. New York: Oxford University Press.

————.1989. Justice, the basic social contract, and health care. Reprinted in *Contemporary Issues in Bioethics*, 3rd ed. Edited by T. Beauchamp and L. Walters. Belmont, CA: Wadsworth.

Victora, C.G., A. Wagstaff, J. A. Schellenberg, D. Gwatkin, M. Claeson, and J. P. Habicht. 2003. Applying an equity lens to child health and mortality: more of the same is not enough. *The Lancet* 362:233–41.

Vladeck, B., and, E. Fishman. 2002. Unequal by design: Health care, distributive justice and the American political process. In *Medicine and social justice*. Edited by R. Rhodes, M. Battin, and, A. Silvers. New York: Oxford University Press.

Wadsworth, M. E. J. 1999. Early life. In *Social determinants of health*. Edited by M. Marmot and R. G. Wilkinson. New York: Oxford University Press.

Wadsworth, M. E., and D. J. Kuh. 1997. Childhood influences on adult health: A review of recent work from the British 1946 national birth cohort study, the MRC National Survey of Health and Development. *Paediatric and Perinatal Epidemiology* 11(1):2–20.

Wailoo, A., and P. Anand. 2005. The nature of procedural preferences for health care rationing decisions. *Social Science and Medicine* 60: 223–236.

Walker, R. L., and A. W. Siegel. 2002. Morality and the limits of societal values in health care allocation. *Health Economics* 11:265–273.

Walzer, M. 1983. *Spheres of justice*. New York: Basic Books.

Warner, K., and B. Luce. 1982. Cost-benefit and cost-effectiveness analysis in health care. Ann Arbor, MI: Health Administration Press.

Wasserman, D. 2002. Aggregation and the moral relevance of context in health-care decision making. In *Medicine and social justice*. Edited by R. Rhodes, M. Battin, and A. Silvers. New York: Oxford University Press.

Weinick, R. M., Weigers, M. E., Cohen, J. W. 1998. Children's health insurance, access to care, and health status. *Health Affairs*. 17:127–136.

Weinstein, M. 1995. From cost-effectiveness ratios to resource allocation: Where to draw the line. In *Valuing healthcare*. Edited by F. Sloan. Cambridge: Cambridge University Press.

———. 1999. High-priced technology can be good value for money. *Annals of Internal Medicine* 130:857–858.

Weinstein, M. C., J. E. Siegel, M. R. Gold, M. S. Kamlet, and L. B. Russell. 1996. Recommendations of the panel on cost-effectiveness in health and medicine. *Journal of the American Medical Association* 276: 1253–58.

Weller, C. D. 1996. Secret life of the dominant form of managed care: Self-insured ERISA networks. *Health Matrix* 6:305–48.

Wennberg, D. 1998. Variation in the delivery of health care: The stakes are high. *Annals of Internal Medicine* 128:866–68.

Whitehouse, P., E. Juengst, M. Mehlman, and T. Murray. 1997. Enhancing cognition in the intellectually intact. *Hastings Center Report* 27:14–22.

Wiggins, D. 1980. Deliberation and practical reason. Reprinted in *Essays on Aristotle's ethics*. Edited by A. Rorty. Berkeley: University of California Press.

Wilkinson, R. G. 1997. Comment: Income, inequality and social cohesion. *American Journal of Public Health* 87:1504–06.

Wilkinson, R. G., I. Kawachi, and B. P. Kennedy. 1998. Mortality, the social environment, crime, and violence. *Sociology of Health and Illness* 20:578–97.

Williams, A. 1997. Intergenerational equity: an explanation of the fair innings argument. *Health Economics* 6:117–32.

Williams, B. 1962. The idea of equality. In *Philosophy, politics and society* (second series). Edited by P. Laslett and W. G. Runciman. Oxford: Basil Blackwell.

———. 1985. *Ethics and the limits of philosophy*. London: Fontana Press.

Wiseman, V., and G. Mooney. 1998. Burden of illness estimates for priority settings: A debate revisited. *Health Policy* 43:243–42.

Wiseman, V., and S. Jan. 2000. Resource allocation within Australian indigenous communities: A program for implementing vertical equity. *Health Care Analysis* 8(3):217–33.

Wittgenstein, L. 1958. *Philosophical Investigations*. New York: Macmillan.

Wolff, J. 1998. Fairness, respect, and egalitarian ethos. *Philosophy and Public Affairs* 27:97–122.

Wong, M., R. Anderson, C. Sherbourne, R. Hays, M. Shapiro. 2001. Effects of cost sharing on care seeking and health status: Results from the Medical Outcomes study. *American Journal of Public Health* 91:1889–94.

Woolf, S., R. Johnson, G. Frye Jr., G. Rust, D. Sutcher. 2004. The health impact of resolving racial disparities: An analysis of U.S. mortality data. *American Journal of Public Health* 94 (12):2078–81.

Woolhandler, S., and D. Himmelstein. 1991. The deteriorating administrative efficiency of the U.S. health care system. *New England Journal of Medicine* 324:1253–58.

Woolhandler, S., and D. Himmelstein. 2002. Paying for national health insurance and not getting it. *Health Affairs* 21:88–98.

World Bank. 1999. *World development indicators*. Washington, D.C.: World Bank.

World Health Organization. 1946. Preamble to the constitution of the World Health Organization as adopted by the International Health Conference. New York: Official Records of the World Health Organization, no. 2, p. 100.

———. 2003a. Future trends and challenges in rehabilitation. Geneva, Switzerland: World Health Organization.

———. 2003b. *Investing in the health of the poor: A strategy for sustainable health development and poverty reduction in the Eastern Mediterranean Region*. Geneva, Switzerland: World Health Organization.

———. 2003c. *Right to water*. Health and Human Rights Publication Series, No. 3. Geneva, Switzerland: World Health Organization.

Wyohannes, M. 1996. Where, and why, women are at risk. Country focus: Ethiopia. *AIDS Analysis Africa* 6 (5):9, 15.

Xu, K., and D. Evans, K. Kawabata, R. Zeramdini, J. Klauus, C. J. Murray. 2003. Household catastrophic health expenditure: A multi-country analysis. *The Lancet* 362:111–117.

Young, I. 1990. *Justice and the politics of difference*. Princeton, NJ: Princeton University Press.

AUTHOR INDEX

SUBJECT INDEX

Made in the USA
Middletown, DE
05 January 2017